Technology, Defense, and External Relations in China, 1975-1978

Other Titles in This Series

The Medieval Chinese Oligarchy, David G. Johnson

Women in Changing Japan, edited by Joyce Lebra, Joy Paulson, and Elizabeth Powers

The Chinese Military System: An Organizational Study of the People's Liberation Army, Harvey Nelsen

Cadres, Commanders, and Commissars: The Training of the Chinese Communist Leadership, 1920-45, Jane L. Price

Mineral Resources and Basic Industries in the People's Republic of China, K. P. Wang

Mineral Economics and Basic Industries in Asia, K. P. Wang and E. Chin

Huadong: The Story of a Chinese People's Commune, Gordon Bennett

China's Oil Future: A Case of Modest Expectations, Randall W. Hardy

A Theory of Japanese Democracy, Nobutaka Ike

Perspectives on a Changing China: Essays in Honor of Professor C. Martin Wilbur on the Occasion of His Retirement, edited by Joshua Fogel and William Rowe

Encounter at Shimoda: Search for a New Pacific Partnership, edited by Herbert Passin and Akira Iriye

The Problems and Prospects of American–East Asian Relations, edited by John Chay

The Politics of Medicine in China: The Policy Process, 1949-1977, David M. Lampton

Intra-Asian International Relations, edited by George T. Yu

Chinese Foreign Policy after the Cultural Revolution, 1966-1977, Robert G. Sutter

Westview Special Studies on China and East Asia

Technology, Defense, and External Relations in China, 1975-1978
Harry G. Gelber

This volume surveys efforts by China's post-Mao leadership to adopt modern technology in China's industrial and economic sectors while focusing new attention on an increasingly obsolescent defense structure. The author presents these efforts against the background of the external political and military environment to which the PRC must react. He outlines the foreign policy and strategic problems that faced the new administration as it came to power in Peking and examines the military, industrial, and technical resources currently at China's disposal as well as changes that have been proposed, implemented, or that may be required in the future. Finally, he suggests some of the limitations circumscribing government policy in these areas and some of the choices that lie ahead.

Harry G. Gelber is professor and head of the Department of Political Science at the University of Tasmania, Hobart, Australia. He has taught at Monash, Harvard, and Yale Universities and at Nuffield College, Oxford. He conducted the research for this book as a visiting fellow at the Institute of International Studies, University of South Carolina.

*This volume is included
as Number 12 in the
Studies in International Affairs
of the
University of South Carolina's
Institute of International Studies*

Technology, Defense, and External Relations in China, 1975-1978

Harry G. Gelber

Westview Press / Boulder, Colorado

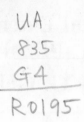

This book is included in Westview's Special Studies on China and East Asia and is Volume 12 in the Studies in International Affairs series of the Institute of International Studies, University of South Carolina.

Copyright © 1979 by Westview Press, Inc.

Published in 1979 in the United States of America by
  Westview Press, Inc.
  5500 Central Avenue
  Boulder, Colorado 80301
  Frederick A. Praeger, Publisher

Library of Congress Cataloging in Publication Data
Gelber, Harry Gregor.
  Technology, defense, and external relations in China, 1975-1978.
  (Westview special studies on China and East Asia)
  1. China—Defenses. 2. Technology—China. 3. China—Foreign relations—1976-
4. China—Politics and government—1976- I. Title.
UA835.G4   355.03'3051   79-12639
ISBN 0-89158-379-3

Printed and bound in the United States of America

For Susan, as Always

Contents

Preface

The period 1975-78 is one of peculiar interest for students of modern China. It saw the departure of the towering figure of Mao and the first major "changing of the guard" since 1949. In a system with few rules or institutions to guide such a succession, it created precedents. It afforded tests for competing theories about the development of the Chinese Communist Party and the balance among the competing elites in Peking. At the end of a period of anxious speculation about the likely principles and practices of post-Mao China, it provided some hard evidence of new policies. Indeed, it may have proved to be a formative period for the future policies and aspirations of China, not merely in the immediate aftermath of the changeover but for the remainder of the twentieth century and beyond. It is therefore a period that deserves particular attention.

One enters this field with some hesitation. Writing about China has been a major growth industry in recent years. Most of the literature falls into four unequal but fairly distinct categories. There are the works of China scholars proper, resting on a grasp of the language, culture, history, and politics of that great civilization. There are papers and articles written with an eye to policymaking in one capital or another. There is reportage, whether by academics, journalists, or other travelers. And there are works that attempt to bring a general grasp of economics or sociology or international relations to bear on the Chinese case. This book falls into the last category. It tries to consider the development of Chinese policies during the years 1975-78 not merely in the context of China's current history and proclaimed political and social principles, but in the light of a number of more general considerations of the balance of power, of problems of economic growth, and of the needs of technical development. In doing so, it relies on translations from Chinese originals, including official Chinese English-language documents, and on secondary sources.

Clearly, no such work could have been attempted without the help and counsel of friends and colleagues. I acknowledge with gratitude my very real debts to Michael Armacost, Doak Barnett, Robert Bowie, Richard Broinowski, Ross Cottrill, John Davies, Audrey Donnithorne, Paul Doty, Robert Furlonger, Alan Goodman, Hans Heyman, Jr., Harry Hinton, Samuel Huntington, Ellis Joffe, Chalmers Johnson, James Lilley, Robert Mathams, Makoto Momoi, Michael Nacht, Dwight Perkins, Richard Pipes, Uri Ra'anan, Pierre Ryckmans, Robert Scalapino, Thomas Schelling, and Harry Simon. My thanks not only for intellectual stimulation but for hospitality and support go to Gaston Sigur and the Institute for Sino-Soviet Studies of the George Washington University; and most particularly to Richard Walker and his colleagues at the Institute for International Studies of the University of South Carolina, where most of the study was prepared. Needless to say, any errors of omission or commission remain my own. I am further indebted to Mrs. Beth Lucas who saw to the typing of awkward drafts and, for prompt and efficient research assistance, to Mrs. Pam Clark.

But the biggest debt of any author is to his own family. To that rule I am happily no exception. Nicholas was helpful and, more important, kind. Christopher, Katharine, and Philippa were generous and forbearing when I was distracted, impatient, or downright unbearable. And without Susan the writing, proofreading, and much else besides would have been impossible, as she well knows.

Harry G. Gelber

Technology, Defense, and External Relations in China, 1975-1978

1
Political Change
and Foreign Policy

The year 1976 brought great changes to the ruling elites of the People's Republic of China. It saw the deaths of several of the Grand Old Men of the Revolution, including the three major architects of Communist China: Chou En-lai the administrator, Chu Teh the general, and Mao himself. Both as fact and as symbol it represented the disappearance of the whole first generation of revolutionary leaders, the men of the "Long March,"[1] and hence a change of habits and perspective that might prove to be of great importance. Appropriately, perhaps, the land and the seasons marked the occasion by a series of natural disasters—droughts, floods, and earthquakes— which did nothing to ease the problems facing the new leadership. And the policies espoused by that new leadership seemed to underline the quality of change in the conduct of China's affairs. The death of Mao on 9 September was followed almost immediately by the coup against his widow, Chiang Ching, and her associates in the Shanghai group known as the "Gang of Four," and by the most intense and sustained campaign to achieve rapid economic modernization that China had seen for twenty years and perhaps for the whole of the twentieth century.

Yet it is possible to interpret these events as only the latest in a number of dramatic shifts in policies and priorities that have occurred in China over the last century or more, representing recurrent swings among a very small number of approaches to the problems of China's political and social development. In a highly stylized way, one can suggest that the various ap-

1

proaches have clustered around five themes. One has been concerned with centralism versus localism. Another has had to do with nationalist and nativist principles versus some receptivity to foreign ideas and techniques. A third has focused on pragmatism in policymaking versus political and cultural fundamentalism. A fourth has emphasized statism and law and order versus populist and utopian principles. And the fifth has been concerned with the difficulties caused by the emergence of a new middle class of managers and technocrats for the balance between older classes of society. Political debates, and foreign analyses of them, have been greatly complicated by the fact that there have been few clear and consistent patterns about which persons or groups have supported which side and by the fact that, as always in China, the operational compromises have had to do with the interplay of personalities and the networks of personal associations derived from the politics of cities, provinces, and other groupings. Moreover, the areas of agreement often have been as important as the subjects of debate. Debates have taken place within a broad cultural and philosophical tradition ranging from the forms of Chinese language to assumptions about China's proper place in the forefront of human and cultural development. There has been broad agreement on the need for national unity and provincial and popular support for the central government as a condition for the achievement of any satisfactory set of internal and external policies. There has been no serious or lasting challenge to the role of a strong bureaucracy and the need for an extremely tight system of social controls. Nor, between 1949 and 1978, was any serious challenge allowed to arise to the dominant and all-pervasive role of the Chinese Communist Party (CCP) or to the formulation and development of the ruling political ideas within the framework of Maoist ideology.

That ideology has played a role of particular significance in several ways. In one sense ideology represents truth: unchanging, scientific, determined by history. In another, however, the interpretation of that truth and its application amid changing sets of practical circumstances can be negotiable within very broad limits. But the process of interpretation must avoid two equal and opposite dangers. Interpretation and policy formation must not decline into mere "ad hocery." Ideology provides a basic world view, a glass through which reality can be perceived, analyzed, and interpreted. It provides the concepts and the vocabulary of that interpretation. Policies, to be acceptable or even seriously debatable, must be formulated and presented in terms which accord with that vocabulary and with the main lines of that world vision. They must be defensible in ideological terms against objections deriving from other segments of currently accepted views. Ideology therefore obliges the leadership to formulate and defend policy in coherent and comprehensive philosophical terms, by close reference to basic principles. It also lends itself to distinguishing between right and wrong and to personifying that distinction in judgments on the participants in public debate at any given time. However, interpretation must also avoid rigidity and formalism, and suggest polarities of belief rather than fine boundaries. Interpretation lays down norms, but it also decides the range of permissible variations. Indeed, tactical maneuverability has been incorporated into the dogma as the dialectical unity of principle and practical flexibility. This has a variety of philosophical and practical implications.

Mao repeatedly denounced dogmatism and idealism apriorism and emphasized that theory must be subject to constant reexamination and, if necessary, revision in the light of experience. He went to some lengths to try to ensure that this "contradiction" between theory and practice, in the form of fruitful tension, would continue after his death, and, of the people around him, Chou En-lai and Chiang Ching may be said to have personified the dualism during the final period of Mao's life. On the practical level, too, the ideology not just allows but actually enjoins flexibility. Long ago Chairman Mao explained the need to use contradictions, to obtain majorities, to isolate and destroy opponents, and for such purposes to form temporary coalitions. Though the particular combination of theory and practice may be specific to the CCP, the tactics themselves are not particularly Maoist or even Chinese. Machiavelli would have felt entirely at home in such a universe of discourse. *Divide et impera* was a commonplace of

statesmen long before the days of the Roman Empire. And in
some corner of that seventh circle of the Inferno which Dante
tells us, is reserved for the violent, Mao and Palmerston have
doubtless exchanged sage comments on the need to have no
permanent friends or permanent enemies.

The ideology also plays a central role in legitimizing the
position of the CCP and, hence, in the maintenance of the
hierarchical state which is China. The official dogma provides
the sole permissible framework for rallying the public, in part
or in whole. On it rests the position of the Party which in turn
enunciates and assures the dominance and all-pervasive relevance of the ideology. No checks and balances against the Party
can be allowed to exist. They might suggest, intolerably, that
the dogma or the leadership were fallible. If institutionalized
and maintained, they might factionalize the Party, even create
alternatives to it. All representative bodies capable, however
remotely, of forming an alternative to total Party control had,
therefore, to be eliminated or emasculated. While this did not,
of course, eliminate dispute and factionalism, it tended to
confine it to the internal discussions of the Party and to permit
canonization of the beliefs while at the same time rendering
popular participation sterile.

It is at this point that the Party has been Janus-faced. On the
one hand, its purposes and operational habits have been built
on what Balasz[2] has called some of China's deepest traditions,
"totalitarian, state-centered, and bureaucratic." Complete
control over social activities, fear through the imposition of the
principle of kinship or other collective responsibility, mutual
surveillance, the assumption that an accused person is guilty
until proven innocent, and the invariable priority accorded to
state over individual interests—all these were phenomena of
Chinese life long before 1949. Similarly, the Maoist state found
some aspects of the Confucian traditions of behavior helpful to
it. Humility and subordination to authority on the part of the
individual citizen and a quasi-sacerdotal position for the
official of the omnipotent state were preferred characteristics
of the post-1949 regime, much as they were for its imperial
predecessors. Traditional emphases on bureaucratic authority,
law and order, and an absence of public dissent were reinforced

by mass organization and indoctrination and the modernized versions of Chinese legalism. It was a tradition that had many advantages, some of which were personified by Liu Shao-chi in the 1950s and 1960s and by Teng Hsiao-ping in the 1970s. It proved to be reasonably efficient and flexible. It provided a bureaucratic system which was in many ways intelligently moderate, pragmatic, and intent on faster advances toward economic and technical modernization.

Yet the system had profound flaws. It created a massive official apparatus for persuasion and coercion. This extended beyond the ubiquitous study meetings, the mutual surveillance, and kinship responsibility to the maintenance of a monopoly for official propaganda and a legal system in which there were mass arrests and unlimited pretrial detention, in which trials tended—and still tend—to be pure formalities with judgments frequently reached in advance and with no rights of appeal for the accused. There appears to have been fairly regular official use of torture,[3] and the authorities maintained a massive prison camp system. This system, used both for punishment and "reeducation," may have contained several tens of millions of people.[4] No less important was the large-scale loss of life. The authorities regularly resorted to exemplary executions.[5] There was large-scale killing during the various campaigns from the liquidation of counter-revolutionaries in the 1949-52 period to the disturbances of the mid-1970s. The Cultural Revolution amounted in some places to a civil war. And Western estimates of the number of deaths during the famines of 1959-62 range up to 50 million.[6] At the same time, the hierarchical structure of the system produced major inequalities of income and life-style amounting to nothing less than the creation of a new set of class privileges and distinctions.

The pressures for acquiescence in, and support of, the official line, supported by traditional social pressures for consensus, frequently produced a surface appearance of unanimity. The reality was otherwise. There were notable gaps between faith and practice, between the official picture and everyday reality, including its elements of fear and resentment. Cadre cynicism became common. Official condemnations of corruption, selfishness, black marketeering, official arrogance and arbitrariness, and worse crimes like theft and murder suggest that these events were far from rare. There was sporadic evidence of stealing and prostitution at times of shortage, of families hiding young people supposed to go to the country-side, of bribery, cheating, and a variety of personal "favors" to enable people to get or keep jobs, or to stay in the cities, or to mollify important cadres. Mass movements were almost in-variably events of organized spontaneity.[7] Even during the Cultural Revolution different Red Guard groups appear to have been organized by rival sections of the elite. But perhaps the greatest, and in some ways the most subtle, dangers for the regime arose from the difficulty of getting adequate and unbiased information on what was actually happening, for without such information the design of appropriate policies was and is impossible. Yet the very comprehensiveness of the official system of controls, combined with an absence of institutionalized constraints on official behavior, made it certain that senior officials would have difficulty in dis-covering what the practical realities of life were like for ordinary men. The repeated propaganda stress on "learning from the masses" was only one sign that the leaders were aware of the tendency for reports to be framed in terms of the leadership's own a priori assumptions or pronouncements, even in those areas where it might have been very willing to remedy problems if it had known about them.

It is not surprising that the Party should have had a utopian as well as a bureaucratic face. This went beyond the notion that Party discipline should suffice to prevent bureaucratic degeneration. It involved notions, going back half a century to Sun Yat-sen and beyond, that the people should be given some powers of response or control short of rebellion. After 1949, it involved emphasis on the genuinely popular and participatory elements of the Chinese revolution. Such tendencies re-appeared at irregular intervals; in the "Hundred Flowers" campaign, in the "Great Leap Forward," in the Cultural Revolution, and in some aspects of the activities of the Gang of Four in 1974-76. They were efforts to which Mao was especially sensitive, aimed at making a reality of the links between leaders and masses; of maintaining and harnessing mass enthusiasm; and of retaining the egalitarianism, brotherhood, and spirit of self-sacrifice of the revolutionary period. They were aimed at creating the "new man" on whom Maoist society would in the longer term have to depend. They aimed at the creation of a relatively decentralized, unbureaucratic China, without social stratification and class privileges. Proponents of these efforts claimed to be opposing corruption, feudalism, and bureaucratic arrogance, opportunism, formalism, and pedantry. In sum, the efforts were attempts to prevent the emergence of a Soviet-style revisionism and the consolidation of the CCP as a privileged elite and to curb the linked bureaucracies of Party and state. Though these views were in some ways romantic, they were also based on hard, pragmatic political realities. Certainly the growing gap between a sophisticated bureaucracy and an everyday reality increasingly marked by corruption and practical confusion is one of the classic dangers that have faced successive Chinese regimes.

Yet this aspect of the Party's approach had evident weaknesses also. It argued for egalitarianism, but in practice displayed a hard-nosed puritanism which led to rigidity and much discontent. It emphasized correct belief rather than effective economic action, with the result that economic activity became disorganized and many people were driven to needy desperation. It opposed bureaucracy but proved unable, most spectacularly during the Cultural Revolution, to create an alternative structure or even to develop a comprehensive theory on the basis of which one might be created. It insisted upon purity but, as so often with purveyors of secular notions of virtue, was willing to offer up hecatombs of victims in the name of abstract nouns.

A good deal of contemporary Western comment was puzzled by these various dichotomies. Confronted by the evident gap between national pretensions and pragmatically realistic policies, or by differences between ideological principle and practical compromise, many observers suggested that the pragmatism was a mere cover for revolutionary intentions or else that revolutionary slogans were a ritual disguise for policies explicable in normally pragmatic Western terms.

Neither view is entirely plausible. There has been a historic tendency for Chinese administrations to maintain assertive and bombastic language even at times of obvious and conscious political and military weakness.[8] Decisions to leave undisturbed the evident gap between declaratory language and the analyses on which practical policies had to be based may have served the purposes of domestic morale and cultural cohesion as well as those of maintaining external aims in principle, pending the achievement of the means to fulfill them. Similarly, the appearance of a gap between ideological principle and day-to-day policy did not of itself permit definite conclusions about whether either could be said to represent the "real" aims of the regime more than the other. Outsiders tended to divide the participants in Chinese policy debates during the 1970s into "moderates" and "radicals" along the lines suggested by the divide between pragmatists and utopians within the Party. But this was too simple, as was any analysis in terms of straightforward dichotomies. Policy pragmatism tended to be associated with administrative centralizers and emphasis on order. But utopians could be, and were, pragmatic on many issues. Populists could, and did, favor rapid economic modernization. Bureaucrats could be, and often were, fundamentalists. Nativism tended to be associated with populist groups, yet it would be hard to deny centralizing bureaucrats the character of nationalists.

Approaches to policy actually concerned clusters of views and groupings, with the composition of the clusters shifting somewhat in relation to particular issues and personalities. One of these clusters may be said to have had to do with nativism and political and cultural fundamentalism. From this point of view, China's nineteenth-century conservatives and the "radical" Gang of Four were brothers and sisters under the skin. The approaches favored by such groups emphasized cultural and educational policies centered on China's own traditions and designed to maintain a political and cultural system distinctive from that of the outside world. These views stressed correct values rather than technical competence, mass participation rather than elitist excellence, domestic notions of virtue rather than responses closely attuned to external challenges, and a distrust of material values as well as foreign influences. Another cluster included views shared by the nineteenth-century innovators as well as the "moderates" of the late Mao and post-Mao periods. These groups emphasized the virtues of pragmatic adaptation to contemporary realities, economic rationality, managerial competence, and technical advance. They wanted to expand China's economic base more rapidly and were sensitive to the needs of modern planning, especially in economic matters, and to the relationships among economic, technical, and security concerns. They tended to stress the connection between domestic development and China's ability to maintain her political and cultural position vis-à-vis the outside world, let alone her ability to exercise influence abroad. They tended to seek national unity through decreased emphasis on arguments about belief and greater attention to raising the standard of living of the Chinese people; less emphasis on nativism and more on using whatever means might be available to raise China's economic, political, and military capacities. Altogether, the debate a century earlier, between conservatives who opposed opening China to the world because such action would be likely to destroy her traditions and those who favored modernization as the only feasible road to national strength and independence, had at least some interesting parallels with debates between radical conservatives and moderate modernizers of the early and middle 1970s.[9]

In practice, neither approach prevailed wholly or for long over the other. Practical policymaking usually concerned some form of compromise between them. The end of the Cultural Revolution heralded the reestablishment of such a complex policy compromise. It is not possible to describe the details of the debates on these fundamental matters which took place in Peking, but the outcome suggests that the basic concerns were widely shared. They involved two sorts of problems. One was the creation of a basis on which to conduct China's affairs during the post-Mao era, which could not be much longer delayed. The other was the urgent and self-evident need to repair the damage left behind by the Cultural Revolution. Given the external dangers to which it had given rise, internal and external security alike demanded the restoration of an effective structure of CCP control, of civil administration, and of orderly governmental methods. No less important was the need to repair the economic damage, to remove the drag on modernization that the Cultural Revolution had created and the widespread misery it had caused. If Chinese socialism was to succeed, there would have to be a sharp rise in production and productivity. Equal distribution had been taken as far as it could reasonably go. Any improvements in the lives of ordinary men and women would have to come from improved economic performance and repairing the damage of past disruption. People would not go on supporting far-reaching revolutionary aims without some improvement in their own lives.

After 1969, and especially after the fall of Lin Piao in 1971, it was Chou who played the key role in forming the new government coalition. It was a delicate exercise. It was, perhaps, the alliance of state administrators, led by Chou, and leaders of the People's Liberation Army (PLA) that carried most weight.[10] In this group, Chou was able to gather around him many of the old administrators and planners who had been demoted or disgraced during the upheavals. They formulated the essential development plans to provide for rapid industrialization, a shift from output targets to profits, from management by factory committee to management by technocrats, from non-material to material incentives, from political discussion to harder work, from allocation to market socialism. But the details, methods, and costs of the Chou-Teng program aroused bitter objections from the Shanghai "radicals," led by Chiang Ching, who feared the damage to revolutionary values and the unity of the leadership and the masses that the program implied. These doubts found reflection in the campaigns to criticize Lin Piao and Confucius, which were oblique attacks upon Chou himself.

Mao refrained throughout this period from making any definitive choice between the two lines. Instead, he saw to it that the balance did not tilt too far in any direction. His position was not, perhaps, surprising. He must have accepted the need to achieve economic progress and modernization if socialism were to succeed. He may have been alarmed by the extent to which the Cultural Revolution aroused forces that moved beyond his control. No doubt he saw the need for the administrative genius and the practical reforms of Chou and Teng. But he was not prepared to renounce the aims of fundamental social change that had led to the Cultural Revolution in the first place. By 1965/66 he had concluded that China's progress was being obstructed by a number of factors inherited from the past. These included traditional rural conservatism, including the hankering after private property; traditional Chinese elitist values and bureaucratic habits; and a number of foreign influences, whether Western tastes in scholarship and art or Soviet theories of development, too thoroughly absorbed during the 1950s. It was he who had launched and sponsored the Cultural Revolution, and any rejection of it would involve his own position and philosophy. Consequently, he was not willing to abandon the utopianism of the Shanghai group which was likely to be essential for the healthy further development of the Chinese body politic.

The Cultural Revolution may be said to have ended in 1969. Within two years, the CCP apparatus had been sufficiently reconstructed for the Party to challenge the ascendancy of the PLA in the post–Cultural Revolution civil organs. By the latter half of 1971, Party reconstruction at the center as well as in the provinces was virtually complete. But within the Party the struggle between lines continued. At the Tenth CCP Congress in August 1973, it became evident that the utopian, pro–Cultural Revolution groups were once more gaining ground: young Wang Hung-wen emerged as the third most senior member of the Party and was clearly being groomed for higher things. Yet Chou's old lieutenant, former Vice-Premier Teng Hsiao-ping, was returned to the Central Committee and, in December 1973, to the Politburo. During the next two years Teng, who was evidently acceptable to Mao as well as to the older governmental and Party cadres and to the PLA, played an increasingly important behind-the-scenes role in planning and administration. By January 1975, he was returned to the vice-chairmanship of the CCP and had become senior vice-premier and a member of the Politburo Standing Committee. At the same time, the Fourth National People's Congress (NPC), under Chou's management, produced a series of documents and personnel changes that confirmed the impression that Chou's line was prevailing. Chou's own report on the work of the government stressed the need for modernization and out-lined a two-stage plan for achieving it. The first stage was to build an independent and relatively comprehensive industrial and economic system within fifteen years. The second was to achieve comprehensive modernization of agriculture, industry, national defense, and science and technology by the end of the century, to bring China into the front rank of the world's nations.[11] But Chou was also careful to stress that "only when we do well in revolution is it possible to do well in produc-tion," to make it clear that the drive for modernization would sustain, not replace, the drive toward socialism.

Mao himself, at the same time as approving Chou's new appointments in December 1974, issued a series of new instruc-tions on the continuing need to avoid bourgeois tendencies.[12] From this, the Gang of Four went on to argue that the forms of distribution and relations between men could play a decisive role in determining trends toward bourgeois forms or toward the dictatorship of the proletariat even after the systems of ownership had been collectivized or nationalized.[13] Material incentives could still lead to bourgeois forms. Empiricism had to be opposed.[14] Changes in the relations of production still had to be given priority over the development of productive forces.[15] And hence, making revolution continued to be more important than increasing production. Naturally the dis-semination of these arguments brought fresh disorder into plants and offices where people were encouraged to disregard rules and regulations, to denounce material incentives, and not to rely on foreign technology. Mao continued to try to hold the ring. He did not entirely agree with the Shanghai group's suggestions about priority for the relations of production over the development of productive forces, but neither did he entirely agree with their critics. In mid-1975, he seems to have produced a Delphic document that allowed both sides to claim that they had his support.[16] In the meantime, the group of CCP administrators gathered around Teng found it hard to see how the principle of greater pay for more work could be challenged and tried to speed up industrial development. Also in mid-1975, officials under Teng's guidance drafted three policy documents: "Several Questions Concerning the Work of Science and Technology"; "On the General Program for All Work in the Party and the Country"; and, perhaps most important, "Some Problems in Speeding Up Industrial Development."[17] In these, Teng continued his advocacy of more production and hard work, improved managerial authority, improved living standards for workers, and a technology import program.[18] Economic development had equal priority with making revolution, and the Shanghai group were guilty of ultraleftism.[19] What was needed in China was more professional expertise and less of a tendency to look for "capitalists" everywhere.

By the latter half of the year, Teng had taken charge of the work of the Central Committee, and the economy was making progress. On the other hand, Chou was visibly in ill health, and Teng's programs were running into increasing political difficulties. The Shanghai group stepped up their attacks. The December issue of *Red Flag* published a leading article entitled "The Direction of the Revolution in Education Must Not Be Tampered With,"[20] and Mao himself reiterated that class struggle was the key link on which all else depended.[21] By this time the affairs of the government and of the Party were in considerable confusion. As part of the factional conflicts of the previous years, each group had placed adherents in the areas dominated by its opponents. These adherents leaked information and stole documents in a way calculated to embarrass the other side. Normal bureaucratic channels and procedures were regularly subverted or circumvented.[22] It is difficult to see how such a situation could have lasted, and the death of Chou in January 1976 brought matters to a head. It had been widely expected that Teng would be Chou's natural successor as prime minister. But in the event, Mao finessed a Politburo Standing Committee decision on the matter and appointed a relatively unknown newcomer as "temporary and acting" premier.[23] The newcomer was Hua Kuo-feng who, after a relatively inconspicuous career in provincial administration and the central security apparatus, had become one of half a dozen vice-premiers only a year earlier. In the weeks that followed, Teng's program came under even sharper criticism. The turning point came with the April 5 riots by supporters of Chou and Teng in Tien Anmen Square in Peking, which resulted in a considerable strengthening of Hua's position and the renewed demotion of Teng. Two days after the riots the Politburo met and passed two resolutions.[24] One promoted Hua to permanent premier as well as to the Standing Committee as first vice-chairman. The second dismissed Teng from all his posts (though it did not deprive him of Party membership). It seems that both resolutions were proposed by Mao,[25] Teng's dismissal being based on the proposition that his general behavior had made his problem one of "antagonistic contradiction."[26] The circumstances of the decisions make it clear that, while Mao was not making a definitive choice in favor of the Shanghai group and against Chou's veteran administrators, the anti-Teng moves would not have been possible if the Shanghai group and Mao had not supported each other.

Yet Hua found himself presiding over a government that was deeply divided. On April 30th Mao, in failing health, wrote out three instructions for Hua: "carry out the work slowly, not in haste"; "act according to past principles"; "with you in charge, I'm at ease."[27] Hua transmitted the first two instructions to the Politburo but kept the third in reserve. The documents were important in strengthening Hua's claims as designated heir, but were not necessarily decisive. Quite apart from questions of authenticity which might later be raised, there were certain to be objections to any suggestion that an expression of Mao's wishes should override Party procedures for the choice of a leader. But in June, Hua's position was further strengthened. Mao's increasing physical incapacity enhanced Hua's role, both in public and with foreign visitors[28] and in the inner councils of the CCP. And the earthquake at Tangshan at the end of the month, in which between half a million and a million people died, created major problems of relief and rehabilitation in whose solution Hua played a prominent leadership role. In the meantime, the Shanghai group's denunciation of foreign technology, technical criteria, material incentives, and bourgeois tendencies, not to mention Teng, was reaching a crescendo.

The deaths of Chu Teh in July and of Mao at the beginning of September brought the question of the leadership, and of Hua's role in it, to the point of decision. The details of the leadership discussions which took place during September remain obscure. But it seems likely that, in general terms, Teng was out of the running (indeed, the campaign against him continued unabated), Yeh Chien-ying was not seriously considered, and neither Hua nor Chiang Ching could muster the required majority support in the Politburo. Subsequent events suggest that Hua and Yeh then agreed to eliminate the Gang of Four, who were arrested by military and security forces at the beginning of October. On October 7, Hua, Yeh, and Wang Tung-hsing reported to the Politburo on the fall of the group.[29] Within two weeks, Hua had formally been elected to the chairmanship.[30] Opinion in the Politburo may have been swayed by Hua's existing power and recent record, by the weight of Mao's "third instruction," which Hua now revealed, by the absence of any generally acceptable alternative candidate, and by the undesirability of prolonged leadership disputes which might encourage further internal or external difficulties. It may well be that Hua gave certain undertakings about his support for a revision of economic and developmental policies. Since the group that elected him included supporters of Teng, it is also possible that Hua gave some general undertakings about Teng's eventual rehabilitation.

During the six months that followed, the outlines of the new governing coalition, and its major policies, began to emerge. The supporters of the Gang of Four were purged in a campaign which continued through 1977 and 1978. The economic policies of the new regime were developed and enunciated in a series of economic and political conferences. The way was prepared for Teng's return. And the various groups composing the coalition tried to insert members of their own networks into key provincial and central government positions, partly by filling posts whose previous holders had been purged and partly by personnel changes at one another's expense. Hua associated himself closely with the new policies for industrialization and technical development, but did so in a way that strengthened his claim to Mao's mantle. As editor of Mao's selected works, he was in a good position to interpret the political and ideological inheritance in the light of contemporary circumstances. In December, he published most of Mao's address "On the Ten Great Relationships," originally delivered on 25 April 1956.[31] It was to prove a document of major importance in the design of the new coalition's policies. In it, Mao argued inter alia for more emphasis on agriculture and light industry, not instead of but as the indispensable basis for the better and faster development of heavy industry. Yet emphasis on industrialization, whatever its theoretical framework, meant greater reliance on the network of veteran administrators, like Li Hsien-nien, who supported Teng, and, indeed, on Teng himself. The PLA and Yeh, too, probably saw that their wishes for the continued suppression of the Gang of Four and for greater attention to the needs of military infrastructure and equipment required the kind of administrative reforms and industrial renovation in which Teng's supporters were bound to play key roles. Toward the end of 1976, Hua agreed that the issue of Teng's rehabilitation should be discussed at the Third Plenum, and in December an internal CCP document informed members that the Gang of Four had exceeded Mao's instructions in attacking Teng.

During the early months of 1977, while Hua was playing an increasingly prominent public role in a series of national economic conferences, the problem of Teng was moving toward a resolution. In January 1977, following an investigation conducted by Yeh, the Politburo decided to downgrade Teng's case from an "antagonistic contradiction" to a "contradiction among the people,"[32] a step that clearly made rehabilitation possible. In March, the Politburo appears to have agreed that Teng should be restored to his former posts, but that the timing of Teng's return should be for Chairman Hua to decide.[33] If Teng's supporters made a bid for his appointment to the prime ministership, it failed. In April, when volume 5 of Mao's *Selected Works* appeared (edited by Hua), it was found to be complete with references to Teng. There followed an exchange of correspondence between Teng and Hua. Teng recognized Hua as the legitimate successor to Mao as chairman. He expressed support for the suppression of the Gang of Four. He expressed his appreciation to Hua for

Hua's willingness to rehabilitate him. He acknowledged that he had committed errors which justified criticism of him during 1976, and he expressed the wish to serve under Hua.[34] Hua reiterated that Teng had indeed made mistakes[35] but recommended rehabilitation to the Third Plenum of the Tenth Central Committee in July. The Plenum duly confirmed Hua as chairman; reinstated Teng as deputy premier, vice-chairman of the CCP, vice-chairman of the Military Affairs Commission, and chief of staff of the PLA; and expelled the Gang of Four from all Party posts.[36] The Eleventh Party Congress, convened in mid-August, confirmed these decisions.[37] It also made major personnel changes. The Politburo was augmented by ten new members, about equally divided between the networks of Hua, Yeh, and Teng. Both there and in the Central Committee new appointments or reinstatements went principally to CCP veterans, soldiers, or people with technical or organizational skills. The new Central Committee consisted of 201 full members and 132 alternates, with only 56 percent of the members of the Tenth Central Committee remaining members of the Eleventh.[38]

Altogether, the new regime was aptly described as an amalgam of the moderate beneficiaries of the Cultural Revolution, led by Hua; the survivors, led by Yeh; and the rehabilitated victims, led by Teng.[39] And though the chief protagonists may have been Hua and Teng, it seems likely that the PLA played a role of particular importance in the creation and maintenance of the new regime. Between 1971 and 1975, its political influence had steadily declined. In December 1973, seven of the eleven commanders of military regions were moved to new posts, depriving them of their control of provincial administrations and local revolutionary committees. By 1975 only two out of thirty-nine regional and provincial military commanders still held key political posts. Yet it was the PLA's anxieties about the radicals that helped Hua to muster a majority in Peking for the anti–Gang of Four coup, and it was the PLA that played a major role in carrying out the coup.[40] It played a major role in subsequently strengthening Hua's position,[41] while its interest in modernization and effective administration contributed to Teng's return to office.

Altogether, its resources proved essential to the restoration of order and the suppression of radical influence by the new regime. Hua himself made a point of relying on Yeh, the minister of defense;[42] wore a uniform in public, as did Teng, for example, at the Fifth National People's Congress; and, at the end of 1976, was proclaimed supreme commander of the PLA. Moreover, the role of the army increased once more in the politics of the provinces as well as at the center. And Chairman Hua was at pains to indicate that the new coalition could be regarded as stable and that it was time for people to get on with social reconstruction and economic development rather than faction fighting. "The Cultural Revolution," as he put it to the Eleventh Congress, "is over after eleven years." What China needed now was a period of tranquillity and national unity. Civil order had to be restored to "bring great order across the land."

The slogan of "great order" applied as much to the internal affairs of the coalition as to the country at large. The coalition's new policies implied sweeping changes, yet their feasibility was bound to depend largely on general confidence in the permanence of the new line and on the balance of compromise and power within the government. The new policies therefore made compromise at once more urgent and more difficult to achieve. What the government offered was a prospectus for reforms across the whole spectrum of China's social, political, and economic life. Central to it were economic recovery and growth. This was to be based on a rise in labor productivity, expanded investment, more flexible pay, and incentive policies. Sharp rises in output were planned for every major sector from steel to agriculture, from petrochemicals to transport. There was to be stress on managerial enterprise and efficiency, financial discipline, and hard work. The education, scientific, and research systems were to be drastically overhauled, with a return to emphasis on examinations and on merit, more teacher authority in the classroom, competition for university entrance, and more freedom and prestige for teachers and researchers. The CCP apparatus was to be strengthened, made more efficient and disciplined, and insulated from interference by the public security organs. Such reforms were sure to depend, inter alia, on the willingness of large numbers of people across the country to take initiatives and accept responsibility for changes, not all of which would be universally popular. Yet Party officials, industrial managers, scientific administrators, and military commanders had experienced a period of twenty years or more during which uncertainty was a dominant fact of political life. Indeed, the personnel shifts and internal disputes of 1977/78 suggested that in many ways it continued to be so. Strong adherence to any line was likely to be penalized after the next turn of the political wheel. Personal responsibility for major decisions or unambiguous adherence to any single policy line was almost certain, sooner or later, to mean political and social vulnerability. The wisdom of cautiously bending with the prevailing wind must have been one of the chief lessons taught by the evolution of domestic politics.

Under the new regime too, policies, or their application, were bound to vary with the ebb and flow of the Byzantine politics of the Chinese establishment. Group loyalties and the interplay of passion and ambition, of personalities and principles, would as always play important and perhaps decisive roles. The official emphasis might be on efficiency, but bureaucratic politics would sooner or later impose its own limitations. Moreover, the particular composition of the coalition might not last. Personnel changes at the center and in the provinces might affect its internal balance. Teng might design economic reform policies in 1978, but the doubts about him could easily grow stronger. The age of some of the leading figures was itself enough to suggest that there must be leadership changes in the not too distant future. And it could scarcely be assumed that such changes would involve no changes of policy or official line.[43] At lower levels, the administration had lost at least some of the skills available to its predecessors. The generational changes in politics and bureaucracy meant older, well-trained men with some experience of the outside world had been replaced by younger men, frequently less well trained, with the quite different perspectives and sometimes parochial outlook originating in provincial or economic administration.

Moreover, even if the regime did persist in something like the form of 1977/78, it was not clear that its priorities and policies would necessarily remain unchanged. There were social problems, among them the difficulties of the unemployed young, including those millions of students and young workers who had been sent to the countryside during the 1960s and early 1970s and might someday make their claims vocal. Or again, there were the older and physically weaker workers who might suffer as a result of an emphasis on incentives that could favor the young and the strong. Not least, there would be the difficulties produced by the very successes for which the administration hoped. A transformation from an economy based on labor-intensive agriculture to a largely industrial economy seemed bound, in China as elsewhere in the world, to produce great changes in men's perceptions of their role in the universe, their relations to each other, and the relationships between their lives and their society. As people came to be uprooted from accustomed ways, the difficulties caused by such social and psychological changes would be likely to grow. At a different level, again, there were bound to be contradictions and tensions among the segments of such far-reaching policies of reform. The administration would have to try to increase agricultural output faster than population growth but without allowing material incentives to undermine established social relationships too greatly. It would have to raise wages enough to avoid undue discontent among workers but not enough to divert too great a proportion of economic gains from investment to consumption. And it would have to achieve such gains while overcoming the heritage of educational disruption and industrial maladministration that had been bequeathed by the previous fifteen years.

Nor could the advent of a new administration resolve the more profound problems with which Chinese leaders had grappled for so long. These had to do with the functions of the Party, the analysis of the nature of economic and political development, and the questions of not just what kinds of development were desirable but at what speed and at what cost to which segments of society. Since these arguments had to do with the basic values of the Chinese revolution and most major facets of the government's philosophical and policy position, it was hardly surprising that there should have been differences about them within the coalition. Inevitably, these differences involved the proper interpretation of Mao and the extent to which the government's new policies could be represented as conforming to, or diverging from, the Maoist inheritance. These arguments were bound to extend to competing interpretations of China's recent history, including the rights and wrongs of past purges and the role of the Gang of Four.

Throughout 1977 and 1978, there were clear differences of emphasis between Hua and Teng on these issues. Almost invariably Teng, siding as he did with modernization and more rapid economic growth, with stress on scientific development and greater freedom for experts to develop expertise, within fewer political constraints, tried also to reduce what he saw as the inflated role of Mao. He and the groups associated with him argued pointedly that it was Mao who had initiated and led the Cultural Revolution,[44] and hence, by implication, was responsible for its injustices and disasters. Innocent people had suffered in various Maoist campaigns.[45] A number of previous campaigns and decisions had been mistaken, and a number of people and actions unjustly condemned.[46] In any case, exaggerated respect for any individual was inappropriate and reactionary.[47] Some of Mao's more self-critical remarks were published.[48] The government even withdrew the "little red book" of *The Thoughts of Chairman Mao*—allegedly because it had been edited by Lin Piao and, hence, had distorted Mao's true meaning.[49] Though Teng and his associates had suffered especially at the hands of the Cultural Revolutionary radicals, it seems likely that their line in 1977/78 had less to do with personal vengeance than with two other considerations. One was the need to distinguish between those aspects of the Maoist inheritance that remained essential to the regime and those other aspects that seemed an obstacle to rapid modernization. The other consideration was the need to hurry, while Teng and his friends, all elderly, remained on the scene, and create faits accomplis from which their successors could not greatly deviate.

Chairman Hua, on the other hand, stressed continuity, reconciliation, and his own apostolic succession from Mao. As early as August 1977, he attempted to draw a clear line between Mao and the Gang of Four, whose influence would have to be purged. Mao had initiated the Cultural Revolution, but he had done so for the purpose of opposing Soviet and Soviet-style revisionism.[50] By November 1978, the *People's Daily* was warning that the campaign to reevaluate Mao must not be turned into a weapon for "anti-Party adventurers."[51] Though no less keen than Teng on economic development, Hua also argued that emphasis on political work should be strengthened, not weakened. "Politics is the commander, the soul in everything,"[52] even for scientific personnel. Where Teng was prepared to encourage the scientific elite, Hua thought that scientific advance must be reached through the integration of scientists with the masses and the raising of levels of knowledge and culture for everyone. Where Teng wanted China to learn more intensively from abroad, Hua stressed the abilities of Chinese to learn anything and to master any problem.[53]

Ambivalences of this kind extended into the interpretation of the role of the Gang of Four. Their position came to be officially classified not as radical but as right wing. The charges in support of this interpretation were several. The group had failed to understand Mao's principle of the unity of theory and practice. By putting theory first, they had fallen into the errors of metaphysics. Their program was so far removed from reality that its implementation would have caused severe political and economic setbacks. Members of the group had adopted ultra-right-wing political methods and, not least, life-styles. The implications of these charges were interesting. They might, but need not, allow the government to put primary emphasis on economic growth. The new regime could offer fresh explanations for the various political and social disruptions that had taken place since the late 1960s and could use the four as scapegoats to appease public discontent. But the charges also suggested a certain sympathy, if not for the Gang of Four, then for some of the ideas for which the Gang of Four had stood. To label the Gang rightist meant keeping open options for the revival or maintenance of some leftist ideas which could be associated with the Maoist inheritance. As Yu Chiu-li put it in May 1977: "It is not enough to have only a revolution in the system of ownership of means of production. The socialist revolution on the political and ideological fronts must continue to be carried out thoroughly. Those parts of the relations of production which do not fit the forces of production and those parts of the superstructure which do not fit the economic base must also be reformed without interruption."[54] The campaign against the Gang of Four continued unabated through 1977/78 only to be wound up at the end of the second year. The vehemence and duration of the campaign did not suggest that the principles and arguments of the Gang of Four had been everywhere abandoned. And the announcement that the campaign would end did not make it clear whether the ending meant final victory or a move toward some tolerance of or even practical compromise with the remaining disciples of radicalism.[55] But it was clear that if these various groups and leaders differed, it was no mere vulgar struggle for personal power, even though personal power considerations were greatly involved. There were genuine differences over questions of great difficulty and far-reaching importance.

It was in relation to such questions that the various groups and networks composing the administration tried to expand their base and their relationships with various constituencies. There were a number of signs of contention, especially between Teng and Hua.[56] During the weeks preceding the Fifth NPC, which met in Peking in March 1978, there appear to have been moves to promote Teng to the prime ministership. Yet if such ambitions existed, they suffered an unexpected reverse. Teng was largely excluded from the proceedings of the conference[57] and had to content himself with a major role in the much less important Fifth Meeting of the Chinese People's Consultative Conference. Hua retained the post of prime minister. The long-dormant state presidency was not revived as had been widely expected. Instead, Yeh was appointed to the chairmanship of the People's Congress, the pro forma post of head of state, while his former post of defense minister was transferred to Hsu Hsiang-chien. A member of the Teng network, Yu Chiu-li, became chairman of the State Planning Committee, and Fang Yi became head of the Committee on Science and Technology. A Hua supporter, Wu Teh, was removed later in the year from the Politburo.[58] In November/December 1978, there was a remarkable wall-poster campaign in Peking, apparently designed both to let off some reformist steam and to confirm support for Teng. It was, perhaps, not entirely coincidental that the support was expressed in ways especially accessible to foreign correspondents. The posters called for a freer political system and a variety of reforms. At higher levels, Teng himself showed he could be as populist as anybody by airing the notion of election of officials by secret ballot. Senior law officers promised a review of the judicial system with the aim of making some rights and civil liberties enforceable. Yet the impact of the campaign was kept limited. At the beginning of December, internal orders went out banning criticism of Mao and Hua as well as street rallies.[59] Teng said to an American visitor that some of the criticism of Mao was unfair, that he and Hua were in entire policy agreement, and that he, Teng, had once again refused an offer of the premiership as he had refused it in mid-1976.[60]

The official verdict on it all came at the end of six weeks of hard bargaining within the Party leadership, in the form of a communiqué on 22 December 1978.[61] This approved the rehabilitation of a number of old leaders disgraced during the 1960s; the establishment of a new commission for Party discipline, headed by the newly rehabilitated vice-chairman of the CCP, Chen Yun; and a range of Teng's economic and administrative reforms. Yet it also upheld Hua's own status and approved a suggestion by him that Chinese publications should stress the Party's collective leadership rather than give undue prominence to any individual. On the whole, therefore, though there were shifting tides of influence among networks and schools of thought, the personnel policies and movements of 1978 suggested a desire to maintain the basic balance and compromises of the coalition and not to allow any of its major components to become overly dominant. Whether that balance would prove to be sustainable in the face of the very far-reaching economic changes being introduced by Teng toward the end of the year remained to be seen.

Of necessity, the connection between the operational principles of domestic policy and of foreign policy were close. This means more than that in China, as elsewhere, domestic needs and wishes are reflected in attitudes to the outside world. Foreign policy, like its domestic counterpart, has been shaped by Chinese customs and traditions, including traditional views about China's place in the world. The historical continuities of two thousand years of a self-contained cultural and political system in which Peking played an unquestioned leading role have left their mark on Chinese international behavior. Policymakers have inevitably reflected consciousness of the special and, *ex hypothesi*, superior qualities of Chinese culture, the China-centeredness of most Chinese attitudes, and the automatic assumption that China, as a matter of course and of right, must play a central role in the affairs of the world. It is an assumption whose implications have differed from those of most past Western empires or movements claiming to have global significance. The Western tradition—including, in this context, the Russian one—has tended to imply that universal validity meant, or should mean, universal adherence, even conversion. The Chinese view, while according a special role to China, has implied no wish to convert, or even directly to control, lesser breeds who could not by definition be members of the Chinese polity. But there was an obvious discrepancy between such views about China's special status and the role that China actually played in world politics between the mid-nineteenth and the mid-twentieth centuries. The discrepancy may help to account for some of the nationalist strains which accompanied China's international reassertion. These included markedly chauvinist interpretations of recent history, with their notions of a "century of shame," as well as the evident determination of administrations in Peking to lead China out of her position of relative weakness and not to compromise any aspect of her sovereignty.

At the same time, China's leaders recognized that, whatever their specific wishes in the international arena might be, they must be pursued in a world of Western-style nation states. The principles of modern international politics and diplomatic and international legal forms, as well as the chief political and organizational ideas which influence world politics, stem from Western political traditions and concepts. The very notions of formal equality between nations, competition between the interests of nationally defined entities, and balance-of-power aims to which Chinese policy must be attuned derive from non-Chinese traditions and form an intellectual and political framework which China can hope to influence but hardly to control. On the other hand, the foreignness of these concepts may also have made it easier for China to formulate or make use of political principles, such as class differences or "the revolutionary struggle of the world's people," that cut across national distinctions but that, for all their modern vocabulary, aroused echoes of older and more traditional Chinese views of the world. It may also have made it easier for the Chinese government to retain the traditional notion that, irrespective of formalities and legal norms, states are not equal in size or power or cultural weight and that practical international politics must therefore find some acceptable way of dealing with relations between superiors and inferiors.

It is in light of these international conditions that China attempted to pursue more specific aims. In a highly generalized way, these can be classified under several headings. There was the overriding aim of safeguarding national security. Where basic security interests were at stake, most administrations of the 1960s and 1970s showed themselves willing to relegate ideological niceties to a secondary role and to proceed by the hardheaded rules of realpolitik. Another aim concerned the need for power and prestige, the establishment and maintenance of China's great power status. This meant working from the position, attained by the mid-1960s, of a nation that must be consulted on all major questions of East Asian politics toward one where China would be consulted on all, or most, of the great questions of concern to the global community. Similarly, it was necessary to assert China's claim to a preponderant position in East and Southeast Asia, at least in the sense of an ability to deny dominance to any other state and to exclude, or maintain at minimal levels, the influence of her adversaries. The government wished to rectify China's borders, secure the return of Taiwan, and to make good China's claims to a series of offshore rights. At the same time, the administrations of the 1970s emphasized the management of trade and financial relationships with the outside world so as to maximize the drive for domestic development and modernity and for China's external political influence, while minimizing the extent and duration of foreign influences upon China. They also maintained China's claim to the leadership of all true Marxist-Leninist forces in the world. Though this side of Chinese policy received less stress from Mao's heirs, there was no sign that they were unaware of the universal features of Marxism-Leninism or failed to understand that the revolution must in principle be global. The nature of historical change cannot be understood or China's role fulfilled in a solely Chinese context. From this point of view also, it was logical that China should display relentless declaratory, and mostly practical, hostility to imperialism, social imperialism, and what she termed superpower hegemony. China herself, her leaders insisted, would never be a superpower, a term denoting not just economic size and political weight but certain patterns of behavior. For in the Chinese view, a leadership role was to be derived from acceptability and right, not mere might, and conferred duties and obligations as much as benefits. In sum, China, being involved in world affairs, wanted to help shape that environment to suit her own desires.

In pursuing such objectives, the Chinese leaders held that the correct analysis of the basic characteristics of the contemporary era was of cardinal importance. Policy could only be sensibly derived from a proper understanding of the world situation, from a particular cosmology. That cosmology should be coherent, comprehensive, and, within its terms of reference, internally consistent. Only such an analysis of the world situation could form an agreed basis for policy design by the entire government and Party apparatus. The cosmology assumed conflict as a fundamental and permanent feature of the international scene. It was therefore necessary to identify the "major contradictions" of any given period or particular situation. Only after that had been done, and the main and lesser opponents had been correctly identified, could appropriate policies be devised. In devising them, maximum tactical flexibility was not just permissible but desirable. The government could form a united front with any group, including

lesser opponents, with whom cooperation proved to be feasible. Two kinds of united front might then be possible. One
was a united front from above, involving cooperation with
other governments, including, where necessary, military
dictatorships or monarchies, against such opponents as
"superpower hegemony" or "zionist imperialism." The other
was a united front from below, involving alliances with
workers, peasants, intelligentsias, and revolutionary groups
against these same national governing systems.

The basic world view underwent several changes during the
first twenty-five years of the People's Republic. After they
achieved power in 1949, Mao and his colleagues emphasized
the simple dichotomy of the revolutionary struggle between
the capitalist and the socialist camps. By the mid-1950s that
interpretation had given way to a more complex one in which
neutralist nations were regarded as potential allies and united-
front tactics as desirable. In the 1960s the analysis changed
again, in line with changes in the world balance of power.
Peking now saw herself as waging a two-front struggle, on behalf
of genuine Marxist-Leninist revolutionary forces, against the
imperialists led by the United States on the one hand and
against the revisionists led by the Soviet Union on the other. By
the later 1960s the role of the Soviet Union had changed from
that of deviant socialist state to one of social imperialism,
even social fascism. By the beginning of the 1970s the official
view saw the world in three tiers. The first consisted of the
two superpowers, the major oppressors. They were classified as
imperialists and hegemonists, endangering the world by their
collusion at some levels and contention at others. The second
tier consisted of the rest of the developed world, apt to exploit
the Third World but struggling jointly with it against the still
greater oppression of the superpowers. The third tier was that
of the developing world, including China herself. It was an
analysis with highly important implications. The lines of
division between the three tiers cut across the old demarcation
lines between socialist and capitalist forces. Peking continued
to argue that the basic struggle in the world was between
revolutionaries and imperialists, but it was clearly the underdeveloped who were the revolutionary force while the defini-

tion of imperialists had come to include the Soviet Union. At the same time, the diminished emphasis on the older ideological categories made it easier to cultivate relations with advanced industrial countries. The interpretation emphasized relations between states and governments, rather than relations with parties. It therefore tended to diminish China's role as a supporter of revolutionary movements within other countries while associating China with the governments of the less developed as the crucial revolutionary force.

As China emerged from the Cultural Revolution, the outlines of the government's world position were sketched by Lin Piao. Addressing the Ninth CCP Congress in April 1969, he promised China's support for revolutionary struggles waged by oppressed peoples. Though the United States was still named as principal enemy, the Soviet Union was now accused of social fascism as well as "revisionist social imperialism." The two superpowers were accused both of collusion and of contention, but the world war threatened by the latter might be avoided if revolution were strengthened. The most important contradictions in the world were four: between the oppressed nations and imperialism and social imperialism; between the proletariat and the bourgeoisie in the capitalist and revisionist countries; between imperialists and social imperialists as well as among imperialists; and between socialism and both imperialism and social imperialism.[62] By the time Premier Chou reported to the Tenth Congress in 1973, the analytic and declaratory emphasis had shifted somewhat. The international situation was one of "great disorder." Though superpower contention might yet produce a great war, revolution was the "main trend" and might be able to prevent this. Between the United States and the Soviet Union, the latter was now the greater threat, creating a need for "necessary compromises" between revolutionary countries like China and imperialists like the United States. Yet Chou also shifted the focus of debate away from emphasis on class and revolution and toward emphasis on interstate relations with the sequence of his declaration that "countries want independence, nations want liberation, and people want revolution."[63] This basic position was to be reaffirmed and elaborated by Vice-Premier Teng at the United Nations and by Chou himself at the Fourth NPC in January 1975.[64] There no longer existed a socialist camp. China belonged to the Third World, was committed to struggle with it against the two superpowers and the dangers of war which they represented. "History," as Teng explained, "develops in struggle and the world advances amidst turbulence."

The development of the cosmology and of the tactics derived from it were linked to the shifts of domestic politics. During the early and mid-1970s, the cluster of views associated with the Shanghai group admitted that China faced external dangers, especially from the Soviet Union, but argued that the chief dangers were internal ones.[65] These were, it was argued, of two principal kinds. One had to do with erroneous analyses of the outside world and the dangers it posed, or might pose, for China. This approach overemphasized the power disparities between China and others, thus encouraging defeatism. It overemphasized material means rather than men. It disregarded the fact that imperialism and social imperialism were aggressive for reasons internal to these systems and, hence, no Chinese concessions could reduce the dangers from them. It underestimated the rate of change in the world and the possibilities open to physically and economically weaker but politically more mature groups and societies. The other chief danger, according to this view, lay in weakening the political enthusiasm and unity of the Chinese masses. Material incentives would increase inequality and raise internal tensions. Domestic opponents were liable to make common cause with external adversaries. Only vigilance and political struggle at home could produce true unity, discourage bourgeois elements at home and their supporters abroad, and, hence, also ward off external dangers. There were a number of standard difficulties about all such views. In economic terms, they would tend to keep growth rates down, delay industrialization, and extend the period of China's uncompetitiveness and dependence. In technical terms, they tended to confirm China's relative isolation from the intellectual and informational intercourse of the rest of the world. In political terms, they tended to underline China's irrelevance to many of the key global issues of the day, an irrelevance which was arguably no less in an age of space exploration, of the exploitation of manganese nodules on the ocean bed, and of the management of global capital movements than it had been at the time of the Crimean War or the Congress of Berlin. In strategic terms, such views confirmed China's position of relative weakness.

The opposite school of thought was that roughly associated with political "moderates" and economic modernizers. Such groups tended to stress the links between domestic development and influence abroad. They tended to see the threats to China as mainly external and largely military. They were inclined to argue that China was falling further behind her adversaries in defense matters and must reverse that trend. A program to achieve this must include a foreign policy capable of playing off China's opponents against one another. It must emphasize the import of defense equipment and technology from abroad, while maintaining the initiative in such exchanges in Chinese hands. It must stress economic development and military production at home, encourage discipline and performance, and do away with the attitudes of the Cultural Revolution. It must encourage material incentives and sound management at home. These views, also, were not free from difficulty. They necessarily implied the acquisition of foreign knowledge and technology, and more intimate relationships with foreign things and powers, in ways that might be at odds with Confucian traditions no less than with Maoist principles. They may also have underrated the difficulties of political mobilization and unification in so vast a society as China. If so, they might sooner or later be open to the charge that their implementation could require, at minimum, a sharply expanded role for the bureaucracy. But given China's administrative, geographic, and communications conditions, such an expansion might make it too cumbersome, too unresponsive, and too ineffective.

Here, too, policy rested on compromise: a compromise between various domestic groups and schools of thought, between Chinese preferences and unrelenting external facts, and between alternative interpretations of, and conclusions drawn from, the general cosmology. It was a unique amalgam of traditional Chinese tactics in playing off barbarians against

one another, of Marxist-Leninist united-front tactics against
the major enemy, and of classical balance-of-power policies.
And during the period 1969-73 the results were brilliantly
successful. In 1969-71, China adopted united-front tactics
against the Soviet Union together with an attempt to keep the
Soviet Union and the United States in conflict, as Mao had
done thirty years earlier with the Kuomintang and the
Japanese. With skill and subtlety, Premier Chou led China out
of the trough of the Cultural Revolution to the establishment
of a regional deterrent against the Soviet Union, the achievement of an opening to the United States, China's entry into the
United Nations, and her recognition by the bulk of the international community. The internal and external conditions
which made these successes possible were unusually favorable.
There was the special relationship between Mao and Chou,
which enabled the government to combine a foreign policy line
congenial to "moderates" with sufficient adherence to the
domestic policies of the "radicals." The virtual abandonment
of foreign policy during the Cultural Revolution presented
Chou with an opportunity, surely unique, to redesign foreign
policy to some extent from scratch, with a minimum of prior
commitments or entanglements and hence a maximum of
maneuverability. The danger from Moscow was urgent enough
to bring together a number of groups who might not have
achieved agreement under less-stringent conditions. And the
Cultural Revolution followed by the fall of Lin Piao weakened
just those powerful civil service, CCP, and PLA bureaucracies
which might, in other circumstances, have claimed a veto on
diplomatic flexibility. Meanwhile, abroad, events were also
moving China's way. The concluding phases of the Vietnam
war put China in a position to put pressure on an America
extracting herself from an unpopular war, while U.S. and
European opinion showed a profound distrust of the anti-
Chinese and anti-Communist rationale that had helped to
involve the United States in the first place. The Soviet invasion
of Czechoslovakia in 1968 alarmed the Communist world and
the West alike, while the movement of opinion in the United
Nations increasingly favored Peking's membership.

Between 1976 and 1978, the new regime did not introduce

any major declaratory or categorical change in the prevailing assessment of the world situation. Rather, it continued to follow the logic of Chou's policies of closer links with the West, a united front against the Soviet Union, and a rapid strengthening of China's material infrastructure, all culminating in the annus mirabilis of Chinese diplomacy, 1978. The new government's line and the rationale for united-front tactics and links with the West were set out unambiguously by Chairman Hua in his political report to the Eleventh CCP Congress on 12 August 1977:

> The two hegemonic powers, the Soviet Union and the United States, are the biggest international exploiters and oppressors of today and the common enemies of the people of the world. The third world countries suffer the worst oppression and hence put up the strongest resistance; they are the main force combating imperialism, colonialism and hegemonism. The second world countries have a dual character; on the one hand, they oppress, exploit and control the third world countries, and on the other, they are controlled, threatened and bullied by both hegemonic powers in varying degrees. Chairman Mao's thesis differentiating the three worlds gives a correct orientation to the present international struggle and clearly defines the main revolutionary forces, the chief enemies, and the middle forces that can be won over and united, enabling the international proletariat to unite with all the forces that can be united to form the broadest united front in class struggles against the chief enemies on the world arena.

And he went on, quoting Lenin:

> The more powerful enemy can be vanquished only by exerting the utmost effort and most thoroughly, carefully, attentively and skilfully making use without fail of every, even the smallest, "rift" among the enemies, of every antagonism of interest among the bourgeoisie of the various countries and among the various groups or types of bourgeoisie within the various countries and also by taking advantage of every, even the smallest, opportunity of gaining a mass ally, even though this ally be temporary, vacillating, unstable, unreliable and conditional.[66]

That the diplomatic and economic arrangements of 1977/78 should continue to be seen in the context of united-front tactics and strengthening China against the possibility of war was made clear in the Central Committee communiqué of December 1978.[67] If that perspective was accepted, it was logical for Teng to argue that the arrangements did not amount to a new axis or alliance between China, the United States, and Japan.[68] But whatever the interpretation, it could scarcely be doubted that they amounted to a major shift in the world balance of power and especially in Pacific relations. The component parts were the existing political and security agreements between Japan and the United States, to which were now added a treaty of peace and friendship between China and Japan and, in December, the full normalization of relations between China and the United States. Together with the agreement between the Soviet Union and Vietnam in November, they suggested a pattern of opposing entente blocks of a classic kind. From Peking's point of view, the core problem was clearly that of the Soviet Union. It was important because it affected almost every aspect of China's foreign relations. It was important because it reflected so many historical and cultural fears and resentments. And it was vital because it posed the most urgent foreign threat as well as the greatest danger to the ideological position, and hence the political legitimacy, of the Chinese regime. Chinese policies not just vis-à-vis the United States and Japan but in Europe, Africa, and elsewhere were strongly influenced if not dominated by the wish to contain Soviet power, to constrain Soviet freedom of maneuver, to create or encourage countervailing politico-military arrangements, and to compete successfully with the Soviet Union both within the Communist world and outside it. The Soviet threat was a main driving force not just in external affairs, but in domestic modernization. And the domestic political constellation depended to an important degree on the political rejections of the Soviet Union and of Soviet ideas.

At the same time, within a governing elite strongly associated with the notion that China's main dangers were external, there were occasional signs of ambivalence about the USSR. These may have reflected differences of tactics rather than strategy. At any rate, there were signs of disagreement between those who seemed prepared to reduce the Soviet danger by making limited arrangements with Moscow and those who were opposed to any concessions lest the Russians interpret any such moves as weakness and hence be more, rather than less, likely to move against China. The first attitude was suggested by a series of minor gestures. In December 1975 the Chinese released a Soviet helicopter pilot who had strayed across the Chinese border in the previous year.[69] In November 1976, just after the coup against the Gang of Four, the head of the Chinese Mission in Moscow for once failed to walk out of the celebrations of the Soviet October Revolution. The Sino-Soviet border talks were resumed. In October 1977 the two sides signed a border river-navigation agreement, and in the following month the foreign minister, Huang Hua, himself attended a reception at the Soviet embassy. There were signals in the press, for example, by the military.[70] And with the rehabilitation of those disgraced during the 1950s and 1960s, some must have recalled that Peng Teh-huai had wanted to mend the quarrel with the Russians in the interests of the PLA and a strengthening of China's security. In any case, the logic both of China's security problems and of the needs of balance-of-power politics might well suggest an attempt at some point to improve relations with Moscow.

Yet on most public occasions, Chinese ministers maintained a high level of declaratory hostility, and Chinese external policies were relentlessly opposed to the Soviet Union on almost all issues. Such a line was encouraged by a number of considerations. Any concessions to the Soviet Union would be damaging alike to national pride and ideological principle, at best causing acute domestic dispute, damaging cohesion and discipline. If continued, it might even permit the exercise of Soviet influence among China's provincial elites or middle-level CCP cadres. Other dangers would arise for China's external position, including her ability to win friends in the Third World and among the discontented within the Communist family. More basic still were the traditional hate, fear, and resentment of the Russians, deep popular feelings strongly reinforced by the national experience since 1960 and not lightly to be challenged by any government. At any rate, the political and theoretical rationale for maintaining hostility was reiterated.[71] Chairman Hua's visits to Eastern Europe and Teng's to Japan, Southeast Asia, and a little later, to the United States stressed implacable hostility to Soviet "hegemonism" and the desire to strengthen political links with nations and forces similarly opposed to Soviet dominance. Chinese help was given to anti-Soviet forces in Africa and the Middle East. Soviet and Vietnamese gains in Southeast Asia were opposed to the point of confrontation (and later war) with Vietnam. And Chinese warnings to the United States and Western Europe against weakness and appeasement of Soviet power[72] became, if anything, more strident.

That China had a number of interests in common with the United States was evident. The United States remained the principal competitor of the Soviet Union on the world scene, could impose major constraints upon the Soviet rulers, and hence increase China's security and freedom of maneuver. The successes that Soviet foreign policy had achieved in Africa and the Middle East in 1977/78 merely underlined the need to bring U.S. power more actively into the ring. The United States was the largest and best supplier of many of the technologies China wished to import, and U.S. acquiescence was desirable and in some respects necessary even for imports from other parts of the Western world. Direct U.S. help in supplying certain kinds of information was of even greater importance. U.S. arms and political support protected Japan while the U.S.-European alliance limited Soviet influence and increased pressures on the western borders of the Soviet empire, at the same time as setting conditions for the expansion of China's own links with the advanced industrial democracies. It was not surprising, therefore, that China should endorse and support not merely NATO and general U.S. military preparations vis-à-vis the Soviet Union, but the strengthening of U.S. naval and other forces in the Pacific,[73] and the maintenance of U.S. bases in the Philippines, and regard with equanimity the slowdown or halting of withdrawals of U.S. forces from South Korea.

On the U.S. side, also, there were important geopolitical reasons for a Sino-American arrangement. President Carter's national security assistant, Zbigniew Brzezinski, stressed the desirability of Sino-American cooperation against Soviet power during his visit to Peking in June 1978. Shortly afterward, the assistant secretary of state for Far Eastern Affairs pointed out that China, Japan, and the United States had a common interest in Pacific stability and that it was an advantage for the United States no longer to be compelled to choose between China and Japan. In the economic sphere, it was desirable for the United States to participate in the Chinese modernization program. Modernization would strengthen China as a balancing factor against the USSR. Its requirements would bring China into closer contact with the outside world in general and the West in particular. It would begin to tie her into an international economic and political network whose benefits she would continue to need but whose workings she could not control. At the same time, closer U.S.-China arrangements and direct commercial dealings between them could increase U.S. economic leverage against its competitors within the advanced industrial world. Though it was true that closer relations with China depended on the abandonment of political and defense relationships with Taiwan, it could not be argued that the Taiwan incubus on U.S. policy in the Pacific should be sustained forever. In the American official view, Taiwan had been given ample opportunity to change its posture from that of the pretended government of China to that of an independent Republic of Taiwan. That it had failed to do so was not an American responsibility. Last, but by no means least, there were President Carter's domestic political needs and the requirement for what U.S. opinion would regard as a resounding diplomatic success. These suggested that a move should be made by the first quarter of 1979, before the opening of the U.S. presidential election season. The final steps toward a "normalization" of Sino-U.S. relations, therefore, appear to have been taken largely at American initiative. In September 1978, President Carter suggested fresh talks to Peking, with a proposed deadline of the end of the year. The final questions were cleared up in a few days in December, with the joint communiqué on normalization being issued on 15 December.[74]

From the Chinese point of view, these events must be

accounted a remarkable success. In general, relations with the
United States could and did affect the progress of U.S.-Soviet
relations. The relative coolness of Sino-American relations had
given the Soviet Union a diplomatic advantage of which it was
now deprived. Of even greater immediate importance was the
conjunction of the new diplomatic relationship with the
strengthened political and economic links between China and
Japan. This created a mutually supporting tripartite pattern.
There were large possibilities for the expansion of Sino-
Japanese ties. There were hints about possible military
cooperation between China, Japan, and the United States.[75]
Such cooperation might well prove to be in the logic of the
situation if the political disturbances produced by events like
the 1979 Sino-Vietnamese conflict proved to be temporary. At
the commercial level, greater Chinese access to U.S. technology[76] and a greater propensity to accept imports from Japan
would march together with greater competition among
China's suppliers.

There was also the resolution of the problem of Taiwan.
Throughout 1976-78, China, aware of the fact that on general
geopolitical grounds the cultivation of U.S. relations had to
have priority, had made it clear that resolution was not an
urgent matter. Now it was settled and very largely on China's
terms. The United States agreed to end diplomatic relations
with Taiwan. The remaining U.S. troops would be withdrawn
from the island. And Washington undertook to abrogate the
U.S.-Taiwan defense treaty as from the end of 1979. There were
certain qualifications. In spite of formal Chinese objections,
the United States would maintain economic and cultural relations with the island and continue to sell arms, as well as
nuclear reactor fuel, to the Nationalists on it. The United
States accepted Peking's hints that it had no intention of
attacking the island, and China remained resoundingly silent
when President Carter asserted that the United States retained
an interest in the peaceful resolution of the differences between
Peking and Taipei. But although it was true that Taiwan's
forces were much better armed than the PLA and that the
means for an effective attack from China did not exist, it was
also true, as the U.S. secretary of defense put it in mid-

December, that Taiwan would in future have to rely on itself. Peking, having won its main point, was generous on lesser details, though most notably so in ways designed to support existing foreign and modernization policies. Teng stopped the threat to the offshore islands of Quemoy and Matsu. It became easier for China to move troops toward the Vietnamese frontier and launch the 1979 punitive expedition. Teng offered Taiwan internal autonomy, said the island could continue to have its own economic system, and suggested direct postal services and mutual visits. Trade Minister Li Chiang spoke of China-Taiwan trade.[77] It was made clear that Taiwan would even retain its own armed forces and that full unification would take a long time to come about. Altogether, what was being suggested seemed, by the end of 1978, to offer a variety of future possibilities, including that of allowing Taiwan to become another Hong Kong. What was also clear was that such a development could greatly stimulate China's own modernization program. If Taiwanese skills and resources, Taiwan's foreign links and financial arrangements with the Western world, and her nuclear power capacity and proven economic dynamism could be harnessed to Peking's general plans for China, her industrial and technical development could be greatly advanced. It was a prize worth some political moderation.

Most remarkable of all, China does not appear to have had to pay any major price for these achievements, or even to have formally altered the cosmology which guided her attitudes to the outside world. If anyone's position had suffered, it was arguably that of the United States rather than that of China. Indeed, the more fully the new arrangements were exploited, the more could U.S. credibility be in question, at least among those governments that desired a counterbalance to Chinese power. Yet for China herself, in a formal sense the United States remained the chief imperalist power, defined as fundamentally hostile, an enemy second only to the Soviet Union. Washington remained a major obstacle to revolutionary struggle and to liberation movements. But the United States was also a declining power, her military capacity in the process of being overtaken by the Soviet Union.[78] Politically, the United States was unreliable, apt to veer erratically between aggression in Southeast Asia, gullibility in the face of Soviet siren-songs about détente, and greed in seeking hegemony with the Soviet Union in such matters as strategic and nuclear arms,[79] while desiring dominance over the Third World. Even in the first flush of the Sino-American rapprochement, therefore, the Chinese attitude—and certainly the explanations offered to private domestic audiences[80]—remained cool and suspicious. At no point during the early and mid-1970s did China find it necessary to make any major concessions in return for American assistance, and the pattern was repeated in 1978.

The other side of this triangular pattern was China's relationship with Japan. By 1978, Japan was one of the most promising sources for China's technology acquisition policy, China's largest trading partner, and a power of considerable strategic importance. Japanese political and economic elites were sensitive to China's needs. The historical links between the two societies, the strong attraction which Chinese culture and Chinese ways have always had for Japan, and the ways in which the structural complementarities of the two states and economies might be exploited to their mutual benefit, all made the relationship ripe for further development. Resentment in Tokyo of Soviet behavior, and encouragement from the United States, proved decisive. So, no doubt, did the prospect for Japanese leaders of new markets in a period of world trading difficulties, of a diversion from certain domestic political difficulties, of the possibilities of a prestigious and popular political alignment, and, not least, of the assuaging of Japanese guilt-feelings about their country's behavior in China during the 1930s and 1940s.

Preliminary negotiations had begun as long ago as November 1974, during a visit to Tokyo by China's deputy foreign minister, Chao Nien-lung. Progress had been delayed both by internal political changes in Japan and by China's insistence that the new treaty should incorporate an "anti-hegemony" clause, understood by everyone to be pointed at the Soviet Union. But during 1976-78 opinion in Tokyo moved. The arrival in Japan in September 1976 of a Soviet MIG 25, whose pilot asked for political asylum, created alarm about the adequacy of Japan's radar and air defense systems. Soviet naval deployments in Japanese waters increased. So did Soviet harassment of Japanese fishing vessels and Soviet verbal and propaganda attacks on Japanese policies and leaders. The Soviets remained immovable on the sensitive subject of Japan's northern islands, insisting, when Foreign Minister Sunoda again raised the subject in Moscow in January 1978, that the matter was settled and had been since 1945. Indeed, in the following month, the Soviet government submitted a draft treaty of friendship whose terms seemed remarkably akin to those applying to Moscow's East European satellites. For Japan's leaders, a move toward China seemed an obvious response. This reaction was further strengthened, at first by the general confusion surrounding U.S. policies during the first year of the Carter administration, and later by positive U.S. encouragement to deepen Japan's relations with Peking. A Sino-Japanese trade agreement in February 1978 provided for $20 billion worth of trade over seven years.[81] Before the year was out, trade not covered by the agreement had doubled this figure and there were suggestions that it might be doubled again.[82] China had also approached Japan for loans on the order of $35 billion.[83]

In May 1978, the Sino-Japanese political discussions were resumed, it being clearly understood both in Washington and Tokyo that the proposed agreement would be the precursor for normalization of relations between the United States and China. On 12 August, the two foreign ministers, Huang Hua and Sunoda, signed the Treaty of Peace and Friendship in Tokyo. When Teng visited Japan in October for the ratification, the journey turned into something not far short of a triumphal procession. The treaty included—in Teng's view as its very essence and nucleus[84]—the antihegemony clause. Article 2 read: "The Contracting Parties declare that neither of them should seek hegemony in the Asia-Pacific region or in any other region and that each is opposed to efforts by any other country or group of countries to establish such hegemony."[85] It was true that the Chinese and Japanese language versions of the antihegemony clause carried somewhat different nuances. It was also true that, at Japanese

insistence, the treaty incorporated an Article 4, stipulating that
"The present Treaty shall not affect the position of either
contracting Party regarding its relations with third countries,"
and that Chinese officials argued that the antihegemony clause
stated a principle intended to apply to everyone. But the
political effect was clearly that Japan had accepted wording
that implied association with some of China's sharper
criticisms of the Soviet Union. What had been created was,
despite remaining reservations in both capitals, a Sino-
Japanese entente. Moreover, it had been created in circumstances where it could rely on U.S. benevolence. Indeed, the
further development of the Sino-Japanese relationship could
plausibly be presented as merely a development of policies
based on U.S. support and encouragement. Japan's strategic
reliance on the United States, the importance of her economic
links with Western markets and financial centers, and the
policy of global relationships and diversification espoused by
the Japanese foreign office and economic authorities suggested
that the new links with China would not be allowed to play a
disproportionately important role in Japanese policymaking.
On the other hand, given the historic links between the two
parties, including the economic possibilities created for Japan
by close association with China's modernization and the
developmental and strategic value of Japan for China,[86] it was
entirely possible that in the longer term the Sino-Japanese leg
of the triangle would prove the strongest of the three. If so, the
effects upon world politics were likely to be substantial.

For the moment these considerations did not seem urgent.
Peking showed itself willing to adjust other concerns to the
needs of the new power relationships. In Korea, the Chinese
government was concerned to avoid both a consolidation of the
division of the peninsula and military adventures by either
South or North Korea.[87] The new Sino-Japanese relations
even suggested the possibility of certain future economic links
between South Korea and China. Japan and China were clearly
not willing to allow Peking's ocean resource claims to become
an obstacle to closer political relations. On the contrary, by
the end of 1978, the indications were that Japan had achieved a
particularly favored position in relation to the exploration and

exploitation of China's offshore oil. Peking's offshore claims were based on a combinaton of historical precedents and modern, United Nations–sanctioned principles. Like other states, China claimed that her sovereignty extended beyond her shores to the adjacent continental shelf. She also claimed, like others, the so-called 200-mile economic zone. And combined with this were her territorial claims to a number of small islands, reefs, and shoals in the South and East China seas, among which the most important were the Spratlys in the south and the Senkakus northeast of Taiwan. Taken together, these claims brought Chinese interests into potential conflict with the interests of Vietnam, Malaysia, the Philippines, Korea, and Japan. If and when they were made good, they would give China not merely very large raw material and other resources but strategic assets of some consequence. Assuming an expansion of her already large, if obsolescent, navy, China might dominate the sea routes through the South China Sea, dispute Soviet access through Southeast Asian waters to parts of the archipelago and the Indian Ocean, and influence many of the more important access routes to the states of Southeast Asia. The timing and manner in which these claims were pressed and adjusted would no doubt continue to depend on the tactics of managing larger political relationships.[88]

Relations with Europe were also of considerable importance for the new administration. In Eastern Europe, they were important because they could be used to weaken Soviet dominance, constrain Soviet freedom of maneuver, and increase the claims on Soviet material and political resources. Chairman Hua's visits to Rumania and Yugoslavia in 1978 were evidently made with an eye to such an outcome, as well as more direct if lesser gains to Chinese diplomacy. It seemed possible that the new Chinese relationship with Yugoslavia could prove of especial importance, both because of the possible relevance of Yugoslav industrial management and workers' control schemes for China's modernization program and because Yugoslavia might become a source of access for some Western military-related technology as well as the know-how associated with its use. But of altogether greater significance were Chinese ties with Western Europe. They were

significant partly because of the political and strategic links
between Western Europe, the United States, and Japan. The
Chinese government showed a constant concern for encouraging Western Europe's ability and willingness to resist
Soviet influence and to maintain a military preparedness
which would at one and the same time prevent any Soviet
westward expansion, divert Soviet resources away from China's
own borders, and diminish the dangers of Soviet-Western
collusion. Western Europe was also a major source of technology and capital goods, not to mention of weapons and
military equipment. (From America's point of view, Chinese
military procurement in Western Europe might produce less-
damaging reactions in Moscow than would procurement
directly from the United States.) Europe was also an area
where Chinese scientists, students, and industrial delegations
could expect to gather knowledge of great and direct importance to the Chinese industrial and scientific development
effort. During 1978, in addition to various scientific and
technical cooperation agreements with West European countries, China signed a $13.5 billion trade and cooperation
agreement with France, a $4 billion deal with West Germany,
and had several billion dollars worth of trade under negotiation with West Germany and Britain.

Chinese attitudes to the Third World, to the problems of
Southeast Asia and of Africa, and to revolutionary struggle
continued to be composed of several separate and occasionally
contradictory strands. The first consisted of the diplomatic
and major economic interests of the Chinese state as defined in
current major policies. The second comprised the needs of
China's anti-status-quo posture. In Chairman Mao's words,
"The current international situation is excellent; there is great
disorder under heaven." Together with this ran the slogan that
antihegemony tendencies were the mainstream of the contemporary global struggle and in that struggle China, while a
powerful member of the club of the less developed, would never
be a superpower in behavior and attitudes, however strong her
political, economic, and military position might become. The
third had to do with Peking's claim to be the center of true
Marxist-Leninist and socialist thought, one of whose major

obligations in the world was to combat revisionist thought, policies, and influence at every point. Though the first attitude was normally dominant, there was no sign that the other aims had been abandoned rather than subordinated or postponed.

At the same time, it was clear that as China became more deeply involved in multiple relationships in a great variety of circumstances and in many forums, so her diplomacy was becoming less flexible and she was experiencing problems of coherence and orchestration. Her ocean resource claims, for example, dovetailed with larger claims of many poorer countries but were liable to create difficulties vis-à-vis countries like Japan and the Philippines, with whom China desired amicable relations on other grounds. Her tendency on arms-control questions was to suggest that the United States was in collusion with the Soviet Union; yet, in general, criticism of the United States needed to be restrained. Southeast Asia might be a natural sphere of Chinese influence, but the need to oppose Soviet influence there made it desirable to conciliate Southeast Asian governments even at some cost to Chinese support for local revolutionary movements. During 1978/79 this became an especially acute issue. Relations between Vietnam and China had begun to deteriorate in the concluding stages of the Vietnam war, when the Soviet Union assumed the burden of supplying North Vietnam with the highly sophisticated equipment needed to win. Hostility between Peking and Hanoi can be traced back at least to October 1975, when Le Duan visited Moscow and signed a communiqué associating Vietnam with Moscow's policies. In mid-1978, Vietnam became a member of COMECON, and on 2 November Vietnam and the Soviet Union signed a twenty-five-year treaty of friendship and cooperation under which they agreed to defend the achievements of socialism and oppose imperialism. The Soviet Union also offered certain security guarantees to Vietnam.[89] The treaty complicated another Chinese problem, that of opposing Vietnam's expansion in general and its designs on China's embarrassing ally, Kampuchea, in particular. In the event, China proved neither able nor willing to prevent Vietnam's conquest of that ally,[90] though China subsequently responded forcibly and at considerable risk not merely by stimulating and supporting anti-Vietnamese guerilla activities in Laos and Kampuchea but by direct military action of a kind, and on a scale, that was bound to incur risks of a Soviet military response.[91]

Support for Kampuchean independence, for all the crimes of the Pol Pot regime there, seemed to dovetail reasonably well with China's general attempts to win the confidence of Southeast Asian governments. Teng's visits to Malaysia and Thailand were used to consolidate that confidence.[92] As Teng explained in Thailand, the People's Republic could not cease to support Communist parties or to conduct Party-to-Party relations without itself ceasing to be a socialist country. But this need not affect the development of relations between states.[93] Throughout Southeast Asia, Chinese spokesmen maintained that China desired nothing more than the friendship of local states and the cultivation of joint resistance to the Soviet Union and its regional lackey, Vietnam. Arms transfers to some states and revolutionary movements in various parts of the world continued and propaganda and communications support, training, and "rear area" facilities were still offered, but it became a low-key effort, clearly subordinate by 1978 to China's major diplomatic interests.

There was, however, one other issue on which Southeast Asia was especially sensitive: that of overseas Chinese. It was a group that the Chinese authorities wished to cultivate and support, not merely for their potential economic contribution to China's development but for obvious reasons of ethnic and national solidarity. Official statements spoke of China and overseas Chinese as patriots belonging to "one family" and called on them to make "joint and positive contributions to the reunification and construction of their motherland."[94] Not surprisingly, Hanoi and Moscow identified these groups as actual or potential agents of Peking. The Chinese government could only protest good intentions and urge overseas Chinese to accept the citizenship of their countries of residence and obedience to their laws. But given the combination of local resentments of Chinese residents[95] and China's inability to disown these Chinese communities, it was a problem without a solution, containable but not to be resolved.

In sum, the history of Chinese policy from the late 1960s to the late 1970s can be said to have been a successful and continuing adjustment to the realities of a changing world, rather than simply a response to the fluctuations of domestic politics. By 1978 these changes had greatly strengthened China's position and had created the basis for further developments of considerable potential importance for global politics. Yet the problems of relations with the USSR remained unresolved as did those of national security in general. A deliberate Soviet attack upon China seemed unlikely; but it was not the only possible cause of a Sino-Soviet conflict, let alone the only possible danger to China. Even if the likelihood of such dangers becoming real was less than the official pronouncements of the Chinese government were prepared to concede, a prudent administration could hardly avoid going beyond diplomatic rearrangements in planning for any conflict which might nevertheless occur.

2
Defense

In the Chinese view, the coming of war was inevitable. "War," in the words of the minister of defense, Hsu Hsiang-chien, "is a phenomenon between two periods of peace when classes still exist in society. War is a continuation of politics and hence of peace. A new world war can only be postponed, but not averted." So long as the social systems of imperialism and social imperialism did not change, war was bound to come. That did not mean, Hsu maintained, that it was imminent; but neither did postponement mean an end to dangers which had to be realistically faced.[1] More particularly, the general competition between the United States and the Soviet Union could not help but lead to war.[2] The likeliest cause of a world war was in Europe, where Soviet aggressive action might follow the achievement of a clear nuclear superiority over the United States. But however a war started, it was bound to involve China sooner or later. Though she would like to avoid it, a surprise attack could "come from any direction"[3] and China must not be afraid of it "because to be afraid gets us nowhere."[4] China must not allow herself to be disarmed by fear itself. She must rather be prepared for the hard but eventually victorious struggle which would have to follow. She would never be the first to use nuclear weapons, but with proper planning and preparation China could emerge successfully even from a great war. "All our work should evolve around preparations for war. We should proceed from the needs of war, do every job well and with a high sense of responsibility, as if everything we do is preparation before war."[5] Nor, of course, were world war and Sino-Soviet conflict the only security concerns of the Chinese leadership.

Forces

The armed forces which China had available to meet these concerns, though substantial in size, were in 1977/78 distinctly old-fashioned and underequipped. Of the 4.3 million men under arms, some 3.6 million were in the army, most of which was an infantry force. Of the 190 or so divisions in the PLA's order of battle in 1978, 121 were infantry, 12 armored, and 3 airborne, while another 40 were artillery divisions and 15 were railway and construction engineer divisions.[6] The core of the army's fighting power therefore consisted of the 136 or so main force divisions of regular troops under central PLA command and available for operations in any part of China. In those operations, they could expect to be assisted by local forces and border defense units of greatly varying quality and equipment. In 1978 these local forces included 70 infantry divisions and 130 independent regiments. They could also expect support from a people's militia numbering some 5-8 million.

The regular Chinese soldier of this period was highly motivated, physically fit, well disciplined, and well trained in basic skills and small unit actions. His mobility and performance in difficult country was thought to be good. But he was not well armed or equipped and poorly trained for complicated operations. In fact, the army appeared to be deficient in almost every major category of weapons and equipment. Artillery and armored forces had received special attention during the earlier 1970s with the strengthening of deployment in the north.[7] But the 9,000 tanks and 3,500 personnel carriers and fighting vehicles which the PLA possessed were greatly inferior in both numbers and quality to those of China's competitors, notably the Soviet Union.[8] The standard Chinese tanks appeared to be Soviet T-54s and Chinese-produced T-59 medium tanks, much less advanced than the Soviet models of the mid-1970s such as the T-72 or the older American M-60. The T-59 main battle tank, a simplified version of the older Soviet T-54, was originally built without power traverse, gun stabilizer, or infrared range finder, though these were probably incorporated in later models. Chinese-designed replacements for the T-59 were under test in the two main Shenyang tank arsenals but had not entered series production by the end of 1977. Altogether, the tank force lacked fire direction electronics and servo ancillaries. The armored divisions also lacked tank transporters and hence road mobility. A Chinese-made Armored Personnel Carrier (APC) based on older Soviet models had been in production since the mid-1960s, but very few seem to have reached deployment. Consequently, they were in use as command vehicles or light tanks and sparsely distributed even among elite units. The lack of armor and mobility had important consequences for deployment. Concentration in the north was dictated as much by lack of mobility as by immediacy of danger from the USSR. Nor could the armored units be supported by any substantial motorized infantry or SP Artillery force.

Most of the Chinese army's eighteen to twenty thousand field guns and rocket launchers and its five to six thousand heavy mortars were relatively obsolescent, without modern sighting devices. The antitank units relied at this period on 82-mm recoilless guns and rocket-propelled grenades as well as a variety of antitank guns. They appeared to have few remote-control systems, and laser sighting mechanisms were only entering service. There were no antitank guided missiles (ATGMs) or production facilities for them, though the Chinese authorities had expressed great interest in acquiring them from abroad.[9] Battlefield antiaircraft methods were equally outdated. China disposed of a number of antiaircraft weapons up to 100 mm, but the rudimentary character of the supporting radar systems and the absence of remote control or modern sighting devices, as well as the absence of surface-to-air missiles, were bound to make the army highly vulnerable to hostile aircraft. Helicopter support was negligible. Battlefield electronics were not available. Logistics were tenuous: many railways were single-tracked, many roads still unsurfaced with movement constrained by fords and ferries, and few trucks had cross-country capabilities. Communications were poor. There were even some reports of communications between companies and regiments by means of signal drums. Though these were doubtless extreme examples, command, communications, and electronic systems were bad throughout the services. Particular problems were posed by topography that made it difficult to construct and maintain land lines and ordinary radio links in some areas. On the other hand, some areas of electronics were given considerable priority after the Cultural Revolution. The first Chinese-made computer relying on integrated circuits was built in Shanghai in 1972, and three years later the experimental development of fourth-generation computer technology was under way,[10] a growing use of transistors in radar and communications could be observed, and Chinese-designed digital computers were being employed for fire control and target analysis.

The air force also combined substantial basic numbers with serious qualitative weaknesses.[11] Indeed, given the high-technology environment in which modern aircraft had to operate, it may be that this arm suffered even more than the others from China's adverse technology gap. In 1978, China appeared to have well over five thousand combat aircraft. Though this made it the third largest air force in the world, 80 percent of the planes were obsolete MiG-17 and MiG-19 fighter aircraft. The force also included under one hundred locally built MiG-21s and the Chinese-designed and manufactured version of the MiG-19, the F-9, some configured as fighters and others as fighter-bombers, possibly with some potential as tactical nuclear-weapons carriers. Several hundred F-9s were believed to have been deployed. The fighter force had relevance both to home defense and to tactical ground support: some interceptor units participated in ground-support training. In addition to the fighters, the Chinese air force disposed of a number of bombers of 1950s vintage design: over eighty TU-16s and a few TU-4s, together with about three hundred IL-28s and one hundred TU-2s. There were some four hundred transport aircraft and approximately three hundred fifty helicopters, mostly of older types. In all, the Chinese air force at this period lacked an all-weather interceptor capability—though prototype all-weather interceptors had been test flown—modern air-to-air missiles, or equipment for accurate ground strikes. It lacked electronic countermeasures. Air control and coordination were said to be poor. So was maintenance, with the engines of Chinese MiGs requiring overhaul after only one hundred hours, compared to the approximately one thousand hours between overhauls for F-4s in the West. There was said to be too little fuel for adequate training, and the general supply situation was unsatisfactory. There were morale problems, including repeated complaints about political promotions within the force.

There were also more fundamental complaints about neglect of the air force at research and development (R and D) levels. The aeronautical institute set up in Peking in 1956 did not appear to be producing new designs. Indeed, China had not by 1978 produced any original airframes or engines, and there were said to be, inter alia, unresolved metallurgical problems in the way of producing them. Partly in consequence, the latest Chinese Shenyang F-9 was said to be inadequate and underpowered. To overcome the engine difficulties, China bought fifty Rolls-Royce Spey engines from Britain in 1976, in a deal that included technical assistance to manufacture Spey 202 jet engines under license, without restrictive clauses in the contract regarding the military use of the Chinese-produced engines. But it seemed that the Spey could not usefully be built into the F-9 but rather required an entirely new aircraft to be built round it. A new delta-winged combat aircraft was understood to be on the drawing boards, but it would probably not be deployed before the early or middle 1980s.

The lack of all-weather interceptors and of an effective command and control network was bound to imply major weaknesses for China's entire air defense system. To this system approximately four thousand of the available fighter aircraft were assigned. China also had one hundred or so CSA-1 surface-to-air missiles, a Chinese variant of the Soviet SAM-2, as well as ten thousand antiaircraft guns of various calibers. This force was supported by some fifteen hundred radars, mostly of fairly short range, though more modern ones were being designed and some reports suggested that a new surveillance radar of Chinese design, with a range of five hundred kilometers, may have become available.[12] But most of the surveillance, communications, and control facilities were obsolescent and slow. The force may have been capable of giving limited defense to selected industrial and military complexes but, by the end of the 1970s, was in danger of being increasingly outclassed by the new Soviet medium and heavy bombers which were reaching deployment, like the Backfire or the SU-19. Existing Chinese interceptor forces could be evaded through night bombing, while SAM-2 defenses could be dealt with by on-board electronic countermeasures combined with jamming, deception, and suppression measures against Chinese radars.

Considerable attention was being devoted to naval developments. This was perhaps inevitable, given China's long coastline, the importance of coastal shipping and offshore activities to the Chinese economy, the vulnerability of many of her cities to seaborne attack, and the naval strength of her actual and potential competitors. With a total of over one thousand combat vessels, the Chinese navy was by the end of the 1970s the third largest fleet in the world. It was a substantial coast defense force, adequate to deal with most inshore threats by relatively unsophisticated surface opponents. It could probably not offer an effective counter to modern conventional submarines, still less to nuclear boats. The navy included a variety of vessels of foreign origin, mostly Soviet or American, but also a growing number of Chinese-built ships. By 1978 it had eleven destroyers, seven of them Chinese-built Luta craft, the others ex-Soviet ships. All of them were equipped with Styx ship-to-ship missiles or with a Chinese derivative of it named the CSS-N-1. The navy also had twelve destroyer escorts and fourteen patrol escorts.[13] All the ships were reported to be short on modern air-defense methods and antisubmarine warfare (ASW) devices. In addition, there were approximately forty submarine chasers and a force, well over a hundred strong, of Osa- and Komar-class missile attack boats equipped with the CSS-N-1. These forces were supported by a shore-based naval air force of some seven hundred aircraft, including some TU-16 bombers, about one hundred thirty IL-28s configured as torpedo bombers, some five hundred fighters, and a few helicopters. By 1978, China also disposed of over eighty fleet submarines. Most of them were Soviet R– and W–class diesel-powered boats. The majority were too noisy to be very effective in an ocean environment dominated by modern Soviet or U.S. submarines. There was, too, an amphibious capacity about which estimates varied greatly. But assuming a regional or short-range assault and the provision of adequate air cover and local naval superiority, China seemed to have the conventional amphibious capacity, supplemented by merchant vessels, to transport ten to twenty thousand men and their equipment.

The Chinese authorities appeared to be devoting some effort to naval construction through the 1970s, with a steady program of construction of destroyers, submarines, and missile patrol boats. In all these categories deployment figures were steadily rising. Indeed, there was evidence of a general increase in China's shipbuilding capacity. Between 1970 and 1976, for example, China's production of merchant shipping rose from about 121,000 tons to 319,000 tons, while her total holdings of merchant vessels rose from about two hundred seventy, totaling just under 2,000,000 tons, to over five hundred fifty, totaling over 7,000,000 tons.[14] While these totals, both of naval vessels and of shipbuilding capacity, were not impressive in absolute terms, the trends were suggestive. Against this, there were signs of both qualitative and quantitative problems in the Chinese naval program. There were unconfirmed reports of difficulties in getting the Luta destroyers to meet all design specifications. Further reports spoke of newly built Osa boats which were little more than copies of old ones, with few, if any, improvements.[15] Other indications suggested that China had more naval shipyard capacity in the mid-1970s than she could use, for reasons that ranged from a shortage of high-quality steel to shortages of skilled ship-construction manpower, both no doubt due in part to the effects of the Cultural Revolution.[16] Shortfalls in ship design capacities may also have played a part. And if China desired an effective ASW capability, this was likely to be an expensive business. Even a coastal system would require seabed sensors and other new weapons and equipment, including methods for dealing with the minelaying capabilities possessed by Soviet attack submarines.

At the nuclear and strategic level, China had made considerable progress in the two decades since she had decided to acquire an independent nuclear capability. By the mid-1970s, she had become the world's third nuclear weapons power, deploying a theater deterrent capable of reaching large parts of the Soviet Union and Asia. Her testing program had continued, even intensified, during the mid-1970s. By the end of 1978, she had conducted some twenty-three weapons tests, mostly in the twenty-kiloton to three-megaton range,[17] suggesting a combination of small devices for possible tactical use and large ones for use against area or hardened targets. All the tests had taken place at Lop Nor, in Sinkiang, and, of the twenty-three, three had been underground tests, the rest surface bursts. The stockpile of weapons had by 1978 probably reached several hundred and was generally expected to increase fairly rapidly. There were reports that the stockpile included approximately two hundred tactical warheads as well as a few atomic mines for air delivery. The means of delivery did not, by 1978, appear to include any portable missiles for battlefield use. The CSS-1 MRBM, with a range of approximately six to seven hundred miles, was a single-stage, road-transportable missile with a CEP[18] possibly as high as four kilometers. Some thirty to forty appeared to have been deployed, though deployment seems to have ceased around 1972 and there were suggestions that the CSS-1 might be in the process of being phased out in favor of the CSS-2 IRBM.[19] Where the CSS-1 was based on the old Soviet SS-3 and presented considerable difficulties of readiness and deployment,[20] the CSS-2 was based on the—also obsolescent—Soviet SS-4 and SS-5. It had a range of some fifteen to seventeen hundred miles, carried a one-megaton warhead, and approximately thirty were believed to have been deployed. The CSS-3 multistage limited-range ICBM, with a reach of approximately thirty-eight hundred miles, was flight-tested in 1976. This weapon was capable of reaching targets in Asia, Alaska, Australia, the Middle East, and the European parts of the USSR, including Moscow. A few had been deployed by 1978. The CSS-X-4 multistage, full-range ICBM, with a presumed range of seven to eight thousand miles, had not become operational by 1978 but was clearly under development.[21] Full-range testing would presumably require the use of impact areas in the Pacific or the Indian Ocean. When the weapon came into service, it would be able to reach the continental United States and Europe. The ICBM booster had already been used successfully in China's satellite program, and Western expectations were that some of the missiles would be deployed, in silos, by 1980.[22] It was not clear whether the apparent delays were due to technical difficulties, to political hesitations, or to some mixture of both.[23] All systems deployed by 1978 were liquid-fueled,[24] though solid fuels and systems based on them were under development. The missiles were dispersed and frequently hardened, though other ingenious basing methods seem to have been used, including emplacement of missiles into the mountainsides of narrow valleys, whence they could be brought out for firing but where they would be difficult to hit or put out of action.[25] The force was controlled by the missile arm of the PLA, the Second Artillery.

The PRC also had its TU-16 medium bombers, with a radius of action of fifteen hundred to two thousand miles, available for strategic missions. Though China began to produce these aircraft in 1968, they did not by 1978 appear to have been equipped with electronic countermeasures, air-to-surface missiles, or air tanker support. There were also the IL-28s and TU-2s and a fighter bomber force, a part of which could carry nuclear devices on tactical missions. The survivability rate of all these aircraft against modern air defenses, such as Soviet ones, was likely to be low. Their range confined them to effective use either on Chinese territory or in areas close to China's borders. But their utility in tactical battlefield strikes, counter-city retaliation—for example, against the Soviet maritime provinces—or in conflicts with smaller neighbors, was potentially substantial. And on the naval side, China had perhaps the prolegomenon for a sea-based deterrent. The Chinese navy continued to operate one G-class diesel-powered ballistic missile submarine as an R and D platform for SLBM developments. The boat had missile tubes but was not equipped with missiles. The navy also had two Han-class nuclear-powered submarines. One of them was operational. These were attack boats, equipped with conventional torpedoes. Western estimates were that substantial progress toward an operational sea-based missile force would await the development of solid fuels and that deployment might be expected during the 1980s.

A missile warning system, equipped with mechanical radars and capable of covering most of the potential Soviet strike arc, was operational. A major phased-array radar installation was under construction in northeastern China.[26] By the late 1970s, China had developed a small satellite program with both military and civilian applications. In the communications satellite field, she had received a good deal of help from Western countries and planned to get more. In all space applications, she had made use of the considerable assistance in various areas of electronics obtained from the United States, France, Germany, and Japan, including purchases of computers. The initial program was designed to strengthen her surveillance capacities and her ability to obtain geodetic data, as well as communications. Between 1970 and the start of 1978, China launched eight satellites, with payload capacity increasing from some one hundred seventy kilograms in 1970 to seven hundred kilograms by 1976.[27] It was estimated in the West that at least three of the eight were for photo-reconnaissance purposes, with the ability to eject film capsules, and there were some suggestions that China might, by 1978, have a small but operational photo-intelligence capability.[28] The more recent satellite launches appear to have been achieved with the same vehicle, or the same caliber vehicle, as that used for tests of the CSS-X-4. And by the end of 1977, China had opened her first domestically developed satellite communications ground station, based on a digital computer system.[29] Details of the first eight satellite launches are as follows:[30]

Satellite	Launch date	Apogee (km)	Perigee (km)	Inclination (degrees)	Period (min.)
1	24 April 1970	2,348	439	68.5	114.0
2	3 March 1971	1,900	270	69.9	106.0
3	26 July 1975	464	186	69.0	91.0
4	26 November 1975	483	173	63.0	91.0
5	16 December 1975	447	183	69.0	90.2
6	30 August 1976	2,145	195	69.2	108.8
7	7 December 1976	492	169	59.4	91.1
8	26 January 1978	513	186	57.0	91.3

China also paid a good deal of attention to civil defense. The reasons may have had something to do with creating a public awareness of danger and mobilizing the population to meet it. Chairman Mao's injunction to "dig tunnels deep, store grain everywhere, and never seek hegemony" had, like most of his sayings, multiple aims. But it would be wrong to regard the motivation as exclusively political or propagandistic. There had been some effort to disperse industries. The shelter digging program in most major cities was remarkable and extensive and represented an important allocation of resources.[31] In some places, the shelters seemed designed to enable the population to survive an attack, even a nuclear one. In others, they formed conduits through which the population could escape to the countryside or through which tunnel warfare against an invading army might be attempted. Not only people but factories and stores were put underground. Foreign visitors were told that the tunnels were intended not so much for bomb shelters as for communications and logistic support for a "people's war."[32] The effectiveness of these preparations might be a matter for debate. Certainly, much of the equipment was out of date. In most areas of China, for example, warning of air attack had to come over the ordinary telephone system. On the other hand, Chinese civil defense preparations were likely to impose at least some doubts upon the attacker and reduce casualties for the defense.

Strategies

Given such force capabilities, what strategies could China adopt for their deployment? Any strategy for the defense of China has to take account of a number of unusual features. China was, and is, the only lesser nuclear power to have a long land frontier in common with one of the superpowers. She has much the most serious difficulties among lesser nuclear powers in the matter of size, topography, and internal communications. She is the least developed and least industrialized of the nuclear powers (with the possible exception of India), and the one with the most dispersed population. By the end of the 1960s, her urban population remained less than 3 percent of the total. On the other hand, a population density map suggested that by the mid-1970s around 70 percent of the population was in the more densely populated areas, leaving vast stretches of land relatively empty, especially in the Northwest and West. In some of these same areas, there are stretches of flat country, often without ground cover. These factors tended to make China less vulnerable than most other nuclear powers to counter-city strikes, but more vulnerable than some to certain other forms of attack. At the same time, China was the only nuclear power whose longer-term plans had to envisage at least the possibility of conflict with either the United States or the Soviet Union. And she had unusually unfavorable combinations of long coastlines, coastal population centers, and adjacent seas dominated by superior navies in the hands of actually or potentially hostile powers. In addition, there were vulnerabilities ranging from the difficulty of exercising close control over China's nuclear weapons in the absence of sophisticated command and control or fail-safe systems, to problems of regional or provincial self-assertion or minority nationalities in border areas and political difficulties which might arise not just from internal disputes about the interpretation of prevailing ideological tenets but from any major challenge to the ideology and, with it, the domestic legitimacy of the regime.

These facts created for China a set of political, military, and technological requirements of particular complexity, both as to force structure and internal and external political and strategic relationships which might be difficult to manage. Chinese strategic thought had to contemplate, for example, the possibility that both the United States and the USSR might design their strategic forces so as to have some fraction available against China. They would probably wish to retain some qualitative lead over her. Even in a superpower conflict in which she was not a party principal, they might be jointly or severally unwilling to allow her to escape unscathed and therefore politically strengthened. At the same time, the existence of a Chinese threat to the USSR, including a capacity to strike at Moscow, had utilities for Washington just as any future Chinese threat to the continental United States, following the deployment of a full-range Chinese ICBM, might be useful for Moscow. Some forms of Chinese coastal defense might cause uneasiness in Japan, while greater defense cooperation with Tokyo could help to offset the superiority of one or both superpowers for at least some purposes. China's size and topography create certain strategic assets, the chief of which are space and manpower, but make it impossible to plan for a defense of China solely at or beyond China's borders.

In formulating their approach to security problems, Chinese leaders have usually proceeded in ways somewhat different from those recently customary in the West, and particularly in the United States. The Chinese have regarded the usual Western attempts to divide the political and military elements of these problems, to separate strategy from its necessary internal and external political context, as an exercise in self-defeating formalism. As the Party must command the military in internal political arrangements, so questions of political context are always prior to ones of military strategy or tactics. It is, of course, a classic view and one by no means confined to Maoist thought. In China herself, emphasis on the political basis and context of conflict and of military action dates back to Sun Tzu and beyond. In the Western tradition, the principles are equally ancient and the most detailed and sophisticated modern analysis of them may be contained in the writings of Clausewitz.[33] For Peking, since 1949, they have meant that the response to military or security problems has been through careful orchestration of political, military, economic, and psychological factors. Underlying that orchestration have been views, often of great force and subtlety, about the central role of man in conflict situations, rather than of means and methods, and the advantages of ambiguity and uncertainty in conducting politico-military disputes.

Until his death, Chairman Mao seems to have maintained the view that the masses are, in the end, irresistible and that whether in nation-building or social arrangements it is men who are decisive, not technologies or means. As he put it in a well-known passage as early as 1938: "objective factors make change possible, but it requires correct directives and efforts on the subjective side to turn this possibility into actuality. . . .

It is man, not material, that counts."[34] Accordingly, Chinese policy has been devised within the framework of a certain moral fundamentalism whose manifestations in the military field have tended to emphasize the virtues of morale, training, discipline, and political and social enthusiasm rather than reliance, certainly sole or principal reliance, upon weapons. The development and maintenance of this view has been more than a tactical exercise to disguise China's material weakness. It has been closely related to the chief operating principles of the CCP in the internal realm. It has reflected important objective political insights. It also has had important practical advantages. The denial of individual or national helplessness when faced with an apparently more powerful enemy has been good for morale. It has strengthened the role of the CCP in its relations with the military and the technocrats, and it has consolidated the rationale for discipline and authority. Without pressing the parallels too far, it is fair to say that the overriding importance of morale has been well recognized in the Western tradition also, exemplified by Napoleon's tag about the moral being to the material as three to one. And the history of war has a number of instances of armies inspired to victory by a combination of discipline and religious enthusiasm. Oliver Cromwell, in recruiting his Ironsides, looked for "men of religion" and asked of a soldier "that he knows what he fights for and loves what he knows."[35]

This emphasis on the primary role of unity, discipline, energy, and determination at home has been coupled with an attempt to cause maximum division and uncertainty among competitors and opponents. In the case of the Soviet Union, the Chinese leadership has sought to constrain Moscow by making or encouraging countervailing political arrangements and unsettling the Soviet leaders by constant attacks, both rhetorical and diplomatic, in terms which, inter alia, question the entire domestic legitimacy of the Soviet regime as well as its global pretensions. Peking has sought to deprive the Soviet leaders of internal support as well as of sympathy within the Communist world and outside it. It has stressed, even exaggerated, Chinese fears of the Soviet Union, partly to help underline an international posture as the victim of the stronger power's aggression and partly to help mobilization and discipline at home.[36] It has stressed China's own pacific intentions, underlined as these have been by a lack of means for prolonged forward action. The whole has been designed so as to add to the uncertainties and dangers of any military or other aggressive action by the Soviet leadership.

Within this framework, the nature of threat perceptions and the analysis of China's defense needs changed dramatically during the two decades from the mid-1950s to the mid-1970s. One of the major elements in the deterioration of the Sino-Soviet alliance was the difference in attitudes to the developing global situation and in prescriptions for action. Peking, encouraged by the launching of Sputnik in late 1957 and the possibilities arising from the decolonization of Western empires, desired a harder Soviet line vis-á-vis the United States together with fuller support of wars of national liberation. Soviet leaders, conscious of the risks of nuclear war, especially in a period of overall U.S. strategic superiority, and unwilling to play adventurist games, opted for a strategy of "peaceful coexistence" or continuing ideological and political competition with the West, while avoiding military confrontations. Between 1958 and 1961, it became amply clear that Peking could not rely on Soviet military backing to attain China's national objectives, whether over Taiwan or relations with India. As the politics and strategies of the two sides diverged, Soviet military help was formally withdrawn. The effort to create a Chinese nuclear weapons system had been under way since the Korean War. By 1959 the Soviet leadership, apparently going back on a 1957 promise to help China develop and acquire nuclear weapons, was no longer prepared to help develop the strategic capacities of a China whose international strategy was increasingly at variance with Soviet interests. In 1960/61 the supply of Soviet conventional equipment for China was also cut off. The result was to transform the wish to create independent and self-reliant military capacities into a necessity. But it also made that necessity more difficult to achieve.

Given China's resource limitations, there was no possibility of a swift simultaneous development of the sectors that would

be vital for such capacities. A strengthening of the economic
and technical base was an obvious precondition for the
attainment of substantial defense capacities later on. But
security problems would not wait. They grew more urgent with
the involvement of the United States in Vietnam during the
early and middle 1960s, and with the sharpening of the Sino-
Soviet dispute. The Cultural Revolution was accompanied and
followed by an especially acute period of danger. The Soviet
Union was declared to be China's principal enemy. The Soviet
invasion of Czechoslovakia in 1968, and the Brezhnev doctrine
used to justify it, caused particular alarm in Peking as an
obvious precedent for a Soviet assault on China. The very fact
that China was on the brink of a nuclear weapon capability was
bound to create pressures in Moscow for preemption. And
though border difficulties had occurred during the earlier
1960s, the scale of the Sino-Soviet border clashes of March 1969
and further incidents in Sinkiang in July, together with the
political and propaganda reactions on both sides, suggested
that the danger had indeed become urgent. So did indications
that the Soviet leaders were sounding out Washington about its
tacit acquiescence in a possible Soviet elimination of China's
embryonic strategic capabilities.

Between 1969 and 1972, the number of Soviet divisions on the
Chinese frontier tripled to approximately forty-five, with
substantial artillery and armored forces, much tactical air
support, and a force of shorter-range nuclear missiles. Though
the number of divisions remained about static after 1972, they
continued to improve in equipment, firepower, support
structure, and general combat readiness. By 1978, Soviet forces
on the Chinese frontier were variously estimated at between
forty-three and forty-six divisions, with substantial tank and
motorized rifle components.[37] Japanese estimates suggested
that the Russians were faced by seventy-two Chinese divisions
totaling 1.3 million men; but the Soviet force enjoyed a 3:1
superiority in tanks and 10:1 in armored personnel carriers.
New airfields were under construction in the Vladivostok
region, and new bases for the Soviet navy were being
constructed on the Pacific coast, all facilities likely to permit a
more rapid reinforcement of Far Eastern forces from Europe or

central Asia. In 1978 the Soviet Pacific fleet had some seventy submarines and sixty-five major surface-combat vessels.[38] Soviet intelligence ships were freely roaming in Chinese and Japanese waters, and the fleet was supported by twenty-six floating docks, including a new Japanese-built eighty-thousand-tonner capable of servicing a Kiev-class carrier.[39] There were substantial air capabilities, and once the new Soviet Backfire bomber was deployed in the region, the Soviet fleet could expect to get air cover anywhere between Vladivostok, Hawaii, and Guam.

In the matter of nuclear weapons, the Soviet 1969 inventory probably included no more than 250-300 ICBM warheads with the accuracy and other attributes to permit their use in a pre-emptive counterforce role. Clearly, these could not all be made available for a strike against China. Nor were any of the M/IRBMs in the SS-4 and SS-5 force accurate enough for such a role. By 1977/78 the situation had markedly changed. The number of tactical warheads available to Soviet forces on the Chinese border had increased, and delivery vehicles included advanced MiG-27s and SU-24s as well as SS-1 and SS-12 mobile missiles with ranges of 180 and 500 nautical miles, respectively. Nearly 200 M/IRBMs had been deployed along the Trans-Siberian Railway, including some of the new SS-20 IRBMs with their three MIRVd warheads and a CEP of one-tenth of a mile. In addition, the Russians had over 400 ICBMs in the Far East, as well as over 260 SLBMs. Though Soviet IRBMs could reach all significant Chinese targets, no doubt a good many ICBM missiles, targeted against the United States, were also capable of being quickly reprogramed for use against the PRC.[40] Official U.S. estimates suggested that the Soviet Union was devoting some 20 percent of its defense expenditure and effort to confronting China.[41]

Nor were numbers the only issue. The economic development of Siberia, due to be speeded up by the construction of the new Baikal-Amur Railway which would bring new factories and urban settlements to the region, as well as swifter transit for military equipment, would lead to a tighter Soviet grip on Far Eastern territories and even pressures for expansion. As if to underline Moscow's increased interest in the region, Mr. Brezhnev and Defense Minister Ustinov visited the region and the border in March/April 1978. At the same time, the Soviet alliance with Vietnam might lead to Soviet facilities to China's south.[42] The 1978 coup in Afghanistan changed the central Asian balance and could herald new pressures on Chinese territory. Such forces and positions seemed to give the Soviet leadership a gradually increasing variety of options as the 1970s wore on, from nonmilitary pressures or small-scale conventional probes to a full-scale nuclear assault. Whatever the Chinese leadership's estimate of probabilities, or its methods for avoiding or deterring such contingencies, it could not ignore the possibility that such events could occur.

If the Soviet Union was the principal strategic opponent of the 1970s, conflict with whom might involve any part of the spectrum of violence from small-scale border skirmishes to nuclear exchanges, it was by no means the only object of concern. Though China did not appear to face many other urgent or immediate threats, her planners, like their counterparts elsewhere, were presumably obliged to hedge against a great variety of possibilities as they contemplated the future. These might be near or far in time and space, concerned with future crises or the lead times for the development of systems usable in future circumstances. Even at the nuclear level, the Soviet Union was not the only source of possible danger. The constellation of power, which made the partial entente with the United States and Japan possible and desirable, could alter. The domestic constraints on America's willingness to act, for example in China's support, might change.[43] Or American attitudes might even at some stage revert to renewed hostility. Then there were questions about the military role of Japan during the 1980s. In the middle and later 1970s, the Chinese government repeatedly made it clear that it regarded the maintenance of existing Japanese-American security arrangements as desirable. The Sino-Japanese and Sino-U.S. agreements of 1978 suggested entente rather than confrontation. Yet it was not clear that every kind of Japanese rearmament would be welcome in Peking. Military, including nuclear, questions could arise in the relationship with India and with other segments of a global community in which nuclear capacities were proliferating. Taiwan also posed difficulties. Both Peking and Washington had for some years been concerned about Taiwanese moves toward a nuclear capability. The acquisition of nuclear power plants by the nationalists[44] was bound to reduce the lead times for any military application.[45] If these capacities were developed, they could be a major hindrance to any growing together of China and Taiwan; yet, in other circumstances, they could be a very welcome addition to the capabilities of a united China.

Conventional military action might also become necessary in a number of areas ranging from the Sino-Soviet border or Korea to Southeast Asia and the Indian frontier. This might range from large-scale actions, for example, in any Sino-Vietnamese clash, to limited or paramilitary engagements, as in any effort to maintain Chinese claims in island groups in the South China Sea or in suppressing subversion or dissidence in Tibet. China's existing military capabilities gave her only very limited possibilities for projecting power beyond her own borders. Peking lacked the logistic capacities for, as well as the apparent intention of, operating on a substantial scale or for long periods outside China. On the other hand, the government had acted forcibly at various times to repel threats or chasten neighbors, as in Korea in 1950, India in 1962, and Vietnam in 1979. Peking wished to help friendly revolutionary and national liberation movements and governments engaged in resisting Soviet influence, for example, in Cambodia and Africa. There was bound to be the question how far China could, even if she would, go beyond diplomatic and propaganda support for her friends and protégés, and whether she could do more than provide some training, advisers, and minor quantities of military supplies.[46] It was part of the larger question whether, in different political circumstances than those of 1977/78, China might not become more actively involved in supporting allied and Communist powers and movements.

In considering China's responses to such possibilities, Mao and the dominant schools of thought on politico-strategic matters agreed on two propositions. If a nuclear strike came, it would destroy China's industrial centers and many of her cities.

But it could not destroy rural China or most of the country's massive population. Furthermore, in almost all circumstances, a long-range strike would have to be followed up by an attempt to impose the attacker's will through occupation or the threat of it. Whether or not nuclear weapons were used, the political success of an attack on China therefore depended upon the credibility of an invasion by conventional forces. And against a ground invasion China was, or might be made to be, unconquerable. Three instruments were available to a Chinese leadership trying to achieve this. The first and principle one was the doctrine of "people's war." It had been the basic military doctrine of the revolutionary armies before 1949. At the end of the 1950s, it was resurrected, refined, and adapted to the new requirements. It was a doctrine that could take full advantage of China's vast and often difficult terrain, of the possibilities afforded by massive mobilized manpower, and of the enthusiasm and determination inculcated by the CCP. It could not prevent the invasion of Chinese territory. But it could help Chinese forces wage a war of attrition and annihilation against an invader after he had arrived. Border areas and perhaps cities would be abandoned, with the army withdrawing some way into the interior. The enemy would therefore be forced to fight on Chinese soil, in unfamiliar surroundings, his troops and lines of communication harassed by Chinese forces. In fighting the "people's war," the entire population would support the PLA. There would be a nationwide organization of millions of trained people and tens of millions of partly trained ones. (Most of this manpower was regarded as expendable for tactical planning purposes.) Regions and counties and the forces fighting in them would be relatively self-sufficient. On their own ground, local Chinese forces would have all the advantages of mobility, deception, and surprise in guerilla operations. The enemy's strength would be gradually worn down, and, in spite of his technological superiority, he would be "drowned in a sea of people" or driven out by an eventual PLA counteroffensive. It was the way to victory over a materially superior enemy, even one armed with nuclear weapons.

There is no doubt that the doctrine provided a powerful and

plausible basis for China's defense against many kinds of danger. It was likely to be especially useful against an attempt to impose a system of territorial control, either by the enemy or by his local allies. And, not least important, it provided a focus for mobilization and effort. But the strategy also had important weaknesses. It was likely to be of limited use against an enemy who avoided the attempt to control population centers. It might not be very useful against, say, a swift and temporary Soviet armored incursion designed to destroy particular industrial or military facilities and humiliate the Chinese leadership. It was an inappropriate response to many forms of diplomatic and other coercion and other levels of threat. It was, therefore, not surprising that the primacy of "people's war" should be subject to challenge, especially from PLA professionals who argued that it left too many possibilities uncovered, that it tended to overstress political considerations at the expense of modern weapons, technical competence, and military discipline. They did not ask that the concept be abandoned. But they wanted more emphasis on the second instrument of defense, military professionalism and improvements in weapons.

Arguments of this sort surfaced at the end of the 1950s. They reappeared during the mid-1960s, before the fall of Lo Jui-ching and the onset of the Cultural Revolution. Naturally, the balance in these debates depended partly on the shifts of domestic politics. Though the Cultural Revolution slowed down military modernization, by the time it ended in 1969 the PLA had emerged as the sole remaining administrative organization capable of filling the power vacuum in many key sectors of Chinese life. The head of the PLA, Lin Piao, became Mao's designated successor. PLA representation in political and decision-making organs, both at the center and in the provinces, increased. The result was to politicize the PLA's leadership further and to complicate its internal relationships. But the central leadership saw to it that there were demands for force modernization and a sharp rise in the military budget.[47] Nuclear weapons were deployed until, by 1971/72, China had a small M/IRBM force large enough and dispersed enough to give a high probability of sufficient survival in the event of a Soviet attempt at preemption. At the same time, China declared that she would never be the first to use nuclear weapons. The result was to increase the diplomatic inhibitions on the first use of nuclear weapons against her, while herself bringing nuclear deterrence to complement reliance on "people's war." In the meantime, Chou En-lai was deploying the third instrument for China's protection, a foreign policy designed to draw allies to China's aid, isolate the Soviet Union, and increase the uncertainties and risks of any Soviet military move against China.

After 1971, the balance between these elements changed. Lin's fall, together with that of a number of other senior officers, must have weakened both the arguments with which they had been associated and the position of the PLA in the resource-allocation debates in Peking. At the same time, the deployment of Chinese nuclear weapons and the leveling off of Soviet force improvements on the Chinese frontier suggested that the danger of Soviet attack had subsided. The gradual U.S. withdrawal from Vietnam was simultaneously removing another major source of military danger, the possibility that China would become involved in a war in the South. This easing of China's strategic situation, at a time when the government was attempting to deal with the economic damage left behind by the Cultural Revolution, may well have concentrated the administration's mind on the need for economic recovery rather than quick military improvements. At any rate, the evidence suggests that military allocations declined for some time after Lin's fall, presumably making any early move away from "people's war" strategies impractical.

The argument was, however, postponed rather than resolved. The reasons were four. First, the strategic threat became more complex as the 1970s wore on, and in some ways more difficult to meet. The increasing size and the technical improvements of Soviet strategic forces created two kinds of problem. One was the renewed possibility of a Soviet preemptive attack, this time with more accurate strike methods. This raised afresh the problems of maintaining the viability of the Chinese strategic arm. The other was the possibility of Soviet deterrence of any Chinese use of nuclear weapons, even in the midst of a Soviet conventional incursion into China.

Given the disproportion between the damage which a Chinese first use of nuclears could inflict and that which she would suffer from a Soviet response, the question of the credibility of China's deterrence mechanisms was becoming more acute. The second reason was the increasing evidence in large and small wars around the world of the continuing utility of conventional weapons and conventional war in all situations where nuclears were for one reason or another not usable. And this at a time when the field of conventional weapons was undergoing technical changes at least as remarkable as those in the strategic realm. The Middle Eastern war of 1973 and the nature of North Vietnam's victory in the South, confirmed by General Giap's "third phase" in 1975, seems to have concentrated Peking's attention on the utility of conventional forces and the desirability of more sophisticated equipment and greater mechanization to deal with a variety of threats, including ones from Soviet armies. The gradual rehabilitation of senior officers who had been disgraced during the Cultural Revolution seems to have strengthened this line of thought. So did staff studies reanalyzing the German victories in World War II and the Soviet 1945 invasion of Manchuria, all of which involved fast armored sweeps against armies whose chief strength lay in nonmechanized infantry. The third reason was that the very modernization drive to which the post-Mao leadership committed itself was liable to increase the incentives for Soviet leaders to consider action against China. In periods when the government in Peking was in the hands of groups unable or unwilling to attend to the growing adverse gap in military capacity between the Soviet Union and China, a postponement of military action was obviously to Moscow's advantage. Any evidence of real Chinese progress toward modernization was liable to increase the pressures to use Soviet forces.

Finally, the logic of the situation suggested that there were a number of possibilities for Soviet action to which China had no full or adequate response. Soviet armed strength was sufficient to prevent any forceful alteration by China of the disputed Sino-Soviet frontier line. In spite of China's ability to interdict the Trans-Siberian Railway (a capability which will greatly diminish once the new Baikal-Amur Railway comes into operation around 1985), the increased Soviet forces represented a much firmer garrisoning of Soviet Far Eastern territories. Third parties could be offered support against Peking, as in the case of Vietnam. Moscow could consider offering support to national minorities in border areas or giving aid to one side or another in an internal Chinese dispute. For all Peking's stress on "people's war," in some areas, like Sinkiang, the local minorities of Uighurs, Uzbeks, Khazaks, and Khirgiz could not be relied upon to be sympathetic to the Han and Peking rather than to their brothers across the northern border. Soviet conventional forces could threaten a conventional attack against some portion of China while relying on the presence of Soviet nuclear weapons to deter a Chinese nuclear response. The more peripheral and sparsely populated areas, for example, in China's Northwest, would be especially difficult to defend. Segments of it had terrain that would facilitate a swift armored incursion supported by adequate tactical air power, and nowhere were natural obstacles likely to be a serious barrier to a Soviet advance unless they were defended by well-equipped modern forces. The Northwest was remote from China's population centers not only in distance but in communication time. The Chinese authorities would face formidable difficulties in trying to mass forces there against an invasion. Yet guerillas and infantry antitank weapons (once China possessed them) were not likely to be effective against modern combinations of tanks, self-propelled artillery, and motorized infantry, least of all in fairly open country. Manchuria, China's industrial heartland, was vulnerable to attack from three sides and gave no opportunity of trading space for time. Peking itself was close enough to the Mongolian border to require special defenses. And the level of any Soviet nuclear attack could range from the use of tactical nuclear weapons in support of an invasion to limited strikes, for example, against China's nuclear forces and facilities, or full-scale attacks upon Chinese industrial and population centers.

There were very different, and broader, considerations. Some had to do with the general diplomatic balance, which would set the framework within which more narrowly defined security problems would be considered, both by China and by any opponent. From this point of view, China's security was weakened by events in Afghanistan, mainland Southeast Asia, and perhaps by Soviet successes in Africa. But it was strengthened by the new relations with Japan, the United States and Western Europe. Though none of these could be counted upon to participate directly in repelling any attack on China, their postures could increase the doubts and difficulties of the Soviet leadership. Moreover, under modern conditions the distinction between some kinds of domestic and foreign operations was in any case changing its meaning. If China were to accept stronger economic ties with the outside world, it was bound to be a corollary of such a policy that Chinese influence upon markets and suppliers could be increased. If China were to encourage foreigners and overseas Chinese to organize productive activities on Chinese soil, as she did by 1978, the domestic policies regulating such activities would be bound to have economic and political effects abroad. Political consequences would also flow from an expansion of Chinese cultural influences, ranging from the encouragement given to foreign tourists to visit China to a gradual expansion of ethnic Chinese influences or dominance in border areas and beyond.[48] At quite different levels, if China wished in the future to safeguard her observation satellite systems, let alone to be able to affect any Soviet satellite system operating over China, that might well require arrangements with states beyond her borders. If China wished to constrain Soviet capacities for naval and other operations in the Bay of Bengal or the seas off Southeast Asia, or to counter Soviet influence in Africa or the Middle East, this could equally mean methods for projecting Chinese defense concerns in ways that were not available to Peking in 1978.

New Developments

The post-Mao regime devoted fresh attention to these matters. The key position of the PLA leaders in the new power grouping ensured that their claims would be heard at the same time as the disappearance of the Gang of Four removed some of the most serious obstacles to putting their wishes into effect. The desire for rationality, professionalism, and modernization was in any case likely to be well received in a Politburo committed to rationality, professionalism, and modernization in the economy and the nation at large. Moreover, China was demonstrably falling further behind the technical and military developments of her competitors and potential opponents and existing shortcomings could conveniently be blamed on the Gang. "The Gang of Four," it was now said, "slandered efforts to develop the most advanced national defense technology, saying that when the 'satellites go up into the sky,' the red flag would inevitably 'trail in the dust.' "[49] And again, "According to its [i.e., the Gang's] reactionary logic, we should not have atomic bombs, make new weapons, or equip our PLA units and militia forces with new weapons. The only thing that can be done is to do what our ancestors did: use sharp arrows to cope with an enemy armed to the teeth."[50] Past official rhetoric had clearly diverted attention from serious gaps in national preparedness. The need for defense modernization and for a scientific, technical, and economic effort to underpin this became one of the more persistent themes of the new government.[51]

Modernization, and all other measures to achieve greater force effectiveness, depended in the first place upon a restoration of PLA discipline and morale. Teng remarked on the need for discipline.[52] The *Liberation Army Daily* called for an elimination of "overstaffing, lethargy, arrogance, extravagance and the signs of softness, laxity and neglect in the leading groups of some units."[53] The PLA's organization must be simplified. Orders must be obeyed. The periods of military service were restored to their pre–Cultural Revolution levels, presumably to give time to train troops properly in the use of newer and more complicated weapons. Altogether, there was considerable emphasis on the need to step up training, both at the level of troop training and in giving officers and staffs the most up-to-date knowledge of military affairs and tactics.[54] In the customary way, some of these lessons were driven home by simple homilies, for example, the praise showered on a hardworking little army unit named the Hardbone 6th

Company.[55] The new line was strengthened by the rehabilitation of former senior officers, included Lo Jui-ching who, disgraced in the mid-1960s, now returned to a seat on the Military Affairs Commission.

In addition to discipline and training, however, the government wanted the PLA to continue and even intensify its political training. In the words of Chairman Hua, politics "is the commander, the soul in everything."[56] Both Yeh Chien-ying and Teng argued that political and military discipline were interrelated, that the leadership role of the CCP was more and not less necessary. In the words of Yeh, "A modern war will be more ruthless and more intense than past wars and this requires a higher level of political consciousness . . . more proficient technique and tactics . . . tighter unity, stricter discipline and a higher degree of centralism."[57] Without a system of politics in command, China would not be able to use modern weapons effectively, even where she had them.[58] An article by the Defense Ministry in *Red Flag*[59] made it clear that what the new doctrines amounted to was not a replacement of "people's war" but a grafting on to it of modern weapons and tactics.

Materially, the overriding need was for better weapons, equipment, and logistic and support systems. There would have to be improvements in a wide range of equipment from the provision of new battle tanks and APCs to the deployment of more effective antitank and antiaircraft weapons, from radar and communications systems to the upgrading of the strategic force. The demands from at least some sections of the officers corps were far-reaching. "We must have not only more aircraft and cannon but also atomic bombs; we must have not only what other countries have, but also what other countries do not have."[60] Though such demands were clearly unrealistic, they stressed the urgency of the material needs and China's existing relative weaknesses. By 1978, efforts were being made in selected areas such as improvements in infantry weapons, in logistics,[61] and in air defense. It was also clear that force upgrading would require efforts that were massive, difficult, and expensive. It would require, as *Red Flag* pointed out, an entire new defense industry technology.[62] It would not be enough to develop new tanks without laser range finders and modern communications equipment, stabilizing gear and tank ammunition. Air defense would require ECM-resistant surveillance radars, data-processing backup, modern ground-to-air missiles, and protected control centers. Antitank preparations had to include more than the antitank missiles available, even in the West, in 1977/78. By the 1980s, antitank defenses might have to cope with laser counter-missile systems.

The requirement for survivability and upgrading of the nation's strategic and retaliatory forces imposed especially severe demands upon China's leaders. During the 1970s, a wave of technical changes was under way in fields as diverse as guidance systems, communications, strike methods, command and control, electronic countermeasures, and space-based attack, defense, surveillance, and other methods. New weapons systems were in the process of development and deployment by the United States and the Soviet Union, ranging from cruise missiles of great accuracy but equipped with nonnuclear warheads to laser-guided weapons delivery or, in time, the prospect of weapons based on high-energy laser beams. No less important were the implications of increasingly close real-time observation, of electronic monitoring, or of automated battlefield control systems. These developments not only implied the appearance of a whole generation of postnuclear strategic systems but involved increasing complexities and major changes in the whole topography of strategic and other military relationships.[63] For the Chinese government, what was at issue was nothing less than the adequacy, even relevance, of its present strategic and conventional methodologies in circumstances a decade hence. Chinese planners would continue to confront the complex and expensive problems of strategic force upgrading under conditions of long lead times, imperfect information about probable opposing systems, the emergence of new political circumstances, and the discovery of new scientific or engineering phenomena.

Maintaining viability seemed likely, at minimum, to require an increase in survivability through some combination of hardening, concealment, increased mobility, and quick reaction. It did not, to judge by the deployment figures during the

1970s, mean safety in numbers, or at any rate not numbers of China's first-generation missiles. It also seemed likely that Chinese leaders would wish to give their force increased reliability in all phases of operation, a minimal rate of malfunction, greater accuracy, and much tighter and more reliable command and control methods. Yet problems in all these fields were formidable. Some solutions in the matter of quick reaction, mobility, and reliability would depend on electronic capacities that China still lacked. Others would have to do with solid fuels, which would create logistic difficulties. Land mobility was likely to be more expensive than silo basing, presented some additional command and control difficulties, and would depend on general improvements in support capabilities, especially in road and rail transport. In addition, the missiles would have to be sophisticated in order to function with adequate reliability under the stress of frequent movement.

Another option China's planners obviously found attractive was that of putting strategic forces to sea. Preliminary work toward the deployment of an SSBN force had proceeded steadily through the middle 1970s. Before such a force could become effective, further development would have to take place in submerged launch techniques, long-distance command and communications systems, ocean mapping, navigation equipment and training, silent-running methods, and counter-ASW systems. There were additional questions. Some concerned the safety of Chinese boats during transit through the island chain off East Asia, or even on the high seas. These were environments dominated, both technologically and numerically, by the greatly superior Soviet and American navies. It would be difficult to assign responsibility in a plausible, let alone conclusive, way in the event of an "accident" to a Chinese boat. There was also the question of targets. If Chinese boats were to operate within easy reach of Chinese harbors and areas where Chinese shore-based aircraft could be effective, they would either have to confine their targets to the rim of the Pacific or else be equipped with four-thousand-mile range missiles. These latter would be equivalent to the new SLBM deployed by the Soviet Union and the United States during the concluding years of the 1970s and were most unlikely to be

deployable by China during the 1980s. Or else China could
develop Polaris-equivalent missiles with ranges up to two
thousand to twenty-five hundred miles, in which case, any
attempt to reach targets in the Atlantic region or European
Russia would require long transit times to reach appropriate
firing positions. That would increase the number of submarines required and their period of vulnerability to hostile
antisubmarine warfare. Something like six boats might
be required to guarantee that two could be fairly constantly on
station in such conditions. There would be a range of ancillary
requirements such as inertial positioning devices. If China
wished to develop higher-accuracy, point-target capable
systems, there would be more stringent requirements still. The
force would need an investment of several billion dollars. And
once it was deployed, it would be relevant only to a limited
sector of the threat or deterrence spectrum. By 1978 the
indications were that the Chinese leadership had discounted
such problems. A whaling ship, capable of conversion to a
submarine tender, was being purchased from Japan. Estimates
in Tokyo were that solid fuels for SLBM would be available by
around 1981 and that, by 1981 or 1982, China would have built
five or six Han-class submarines, each with six missile tubes
capable of accommodating a Polaris-type missile. The boats
would later be converted to take twelve tubes and probably be
destined for deployment in Arctic waters to strengthen the
deterrent system against the Soviet Union.

There was also evidence of a considerable effort in the field of
command, control, and communications, as well as surveillance. China notified the International Telecommunications
Union (a message that reached member nations in March 1977)
of its intention to launch two experimental geosynchronous
communications satellites. The planned date of operation was
1980/81. Some Western estimates suggested that China's
launching equipment would be capable of placing four hundred kilograms into such a geosynchronous orbit. Though
the satellites were planned for civilian application, the military
potential of such capabilities was obvious. On the other
hand, for Chinese planners the problems of surveillance and
communication involved not just the acquisition of satellites

and ground facilities but the question how the effectiveness and survival of Chinese satellites could be safeguarded once the United States and the USSR developed effective satellite deception and attack devices. This, in turn, seemed bound to involve China, like her competitors, in problems of system reliability, system duplication and redundancy, and questions of satellite defense or replacement. Solutions to such problems would require command of a wide range of technologies.

It must have been evident that these problems were not soluble without outside help, least of all in the short or medium term. Much of the equipment, and the know-how for its production or use, would in the first instance have to come from abroad, and particularly from the "second world." China's resources of military and technical knowledge had to be augmented by drawing on foreign knowledge and experience. And China would have to attract not merely diplomatic and political support but, if possible, complementary military efforts by others in order to minimize her own security problems and to diminish domestic pressures for "quick fix" military expenditures. Peking therefore emphasized the areas of common interest in strategic attitudes and interests between China and the West. Teng suggested that the United States should expand its naval strength in the Pacific to cope with Soviet naval expansion there and spoke of the need for greater Japanese defense efforts.[64] The government indicated to President Marcos that China would be happy to see U.S. bases in the Philippines maintained and for U.S. power to remain in the region in order to block the Soviet Union. There was also China's unofficial agreement to the maintenance of Taiwan's own security forces: Taiwan would not have to disarm for reunification of China to be achieved.[65] There was the general Chinese interest in indirect military cooperation with Japan and the United States, in the maintenance of regular contacts, and in planning discussions.

All this was complementary to improvements in China's own defense posture. In 1976/77, the new administration seems to have decided that some of the more urgent improvements required a program to import foreign military-related technology. Such a program would not merely enhance China's military capabilities and raise troop skills and morale, it would strengthen the domestic technical-information base and it would increase China's capacities for further design and development at home. And acknowledging China's existing weaknesses would at one and the same time strengthen the reform groups at home and rally external diplomatic and political support, at least to the point of making the West more willing to sell military-related equipment. At any rate, the new line was emphasized to a series of foreign visitors including the French and British chiefs of staff, General Guy Méry and Sir Neil Cameron, as well as U.S. and Japanese officers. Some of the visitors, including the former U.S. Secretary of Defense James Schlesinger, told their hosts what they expected to hear: that while PLA morale and organization were satisfactory, weapons and equipment were inadequate to meet a Soviet thrust. Senior Chinese officers, including the deputy chief of staff, expressed themselves frankly on the inadequacies of their equipment, blaming it on the backward state of Chinese industry due largely to the influence of the Gang of Four.[66] In May 1977, the defense minister suggested that China was in a race against time and had decided to step up the manufacture of modern weapons.

What China wanted from the industrialized West was information, aid, and sales. The West was prepared to respond. Some improvement in China's military capabilities could diminish the danger of a Sino-Soviet clash by increasing the risks for any Soviet military adventures. It might make it harder for the Soviet leadership to transfer troops and resources from the Far East to Europe. It might even lead to a diversion of resources away from Europe and hence to an easing of pressures on NATO. And Chinese help would be useful in stemming any increase in Soviet influence in central or Southeast Asia or Africa. In any event, political authorities from the White House to the Western Consultative Committee were willing to relax previous restrictions on the sale of military related goods to China. As long ago as the late 1960s, China had obtained uranium samples from West Germany, together with a private offer from the West German government to supply another twenty tons. Toward the end of 1976, President Ford overrode Pentagon objections to allow China to buy two large computers. Other computer sales were made by Japan. Though the Japanese machines were said to be for meteorological purposes and the American ones for oil exploration and earthquake detection, it was clear that they could be adapted for at least some kinds of military uses, including air defense.

Following a study by the U.S. administration during the first half of 1977 of likely Soviet reactions to a further relaxation on the sale of strategic materials to China,[67] signals about an easing of weapons sales were sent to Peking. In September they were publicly confirmed by an instruction from Defense Secretary Harold Brown to his officials.[68] At the start of 1978, European Community officials stressed that the new trade agreement with China did not envisage any restrictions on strategic goods sales to the PRC. By mid-1978, the Pentagon decided to let China have some infrared scanning equipment for geophysical use, but with some possible military applications. It was now generally understood that the United States, while not about to engage in major arms sales to China itself, would not raise objections to such sales and transfers by U.S. allies. A great deal of dual-use technology would also be made available. Nevertheless, some restraints still operated. One Peking order with a U.S. firm for advanced airborne scanning equipment was blocked for fear that the equipment could be adapted to intercept U.S. military signals.[69] France was persuaded not to sell China the new Mirage-2000 interceptor. And, in general, it seemed that attempts were being made to limit weapons and equipment sales so as not unduly to alarm the West's allies, especially in Asia; not to give Chinese forces substantial naval or airborne reach; and not to fit them out with equipment that was genuinely competitive with the West's most advanced systems.

Such policies left a good deal of room for maneuver in designing China's acquisition policies. Her appetite for information seemed omnivorous. In part, it came from enquiries by a steady stream of Chinese delegations to countries that might be able to supply equipment, as well as from return visits by foreign groups. In September 1977, a Chinese military delegation led by Yang Cheng-wu, one of the deputy chiefs of staff, visited military installations in France, and the purchase of modern arms may have been discussed.[70] At the end of that month, Teng Hsiao-ping received the head of the European Center of Atomic Research and showed some German visitors round Chinese military installations.[71] Shortly afterward the Ministry of Defense received the commander in chief of the Swedish armed forces,[72] while a Chinese air force delegation visited Switzerland. The issue of military information and equipment was raised during a visit by the French prime minister to Peking at the start of 1978,[73] it was discussed with Japanese industrial groups visiting Peking, and it was the subject of the visit to Britain by several Chinese leaders. Foreign Minister Huang Hua went to London in October, and he was followed, a month later, by the vice-premier in charge of China's arms industry, Wang Chen.[74] They were only some of the delegations that scoured Western capitals.[75] Information and know-how of a less immediately applicable and commercial kind, but of arguably even greater importance for the longer term, was made available through scientific and technical cooperation agreements. That with West Germany, for example, concluded on 10 October 1978, provided, inter alia, for cooperation in information technology, civil aviation, and space research.

Another facet of the drive for information was the dispatch of Chinese technological personnel for training abroad. In 1978 there were reports, for example, of Chinese scientists and technologists working in the United States learning to use airborne and other scanning equipment and making themselves familiar with a range of Western sensing technologies.[76] The Chinese wanted to know about neutron bomb technology and cruise missiles, about satellite communication and naval engines, about guidance systems and transistor manufacture.

The potential or actual purchasing program was equally varied. The Chinese displayed an interest in battlefield electronics, lightweight rifles, and small-caliber ammunition. They agreed to the purchase of the Franco-German HOT antitank missile and related technology.[77] By the end of 1978, agreement seemed imminent on a $350 million purchase of French antitank and antiaircraft missiles, including the hand-held MILAN and the surface-to-air CROTALE as well as the European ROLAND.[78] Purchasing missions displayed an interest in artillery, several kinds of vehicles, and bridging equipment. There were even discussions about possible construction of quantities of Chinese-designed armored vehicles by Western manufacturers. In June 1976, the Chinese agreed to buy four West German BO-105 Messerschmidt helicopters, and, at the start of 1978, Peking hinted that it might buy thirty. The BO-105 was configured to carry six anti-tank missiles.[79] In the naval area, the Chinese were interested in buying French EXOCET ship-to-ship missiles,[80] diesel engines for submarines, and a range of ASW equipment including airborne dunking sonars, homing torpedoes, and shipborne sonars, as well as satellite surveillance and fast-acceleration turbine engines for ASW vessels. In the air, in communications, and in space, they displayed a catholic interest in ECM equipment, computers,[81] U.S. C-141 cargo aircraft, Itek satellite cameras, British jet aircraft technology and Harrier VTOL aircraft,[82] American RCA global communications radar and other equipment, French transport and other aircraft,[83] detection and missile-tracking equipment, air-to-air missiles such as the British Red Top or Sparrow, and air-to-surface missiles, possibly with terminal guidance.

In addition, there was China's continuing interest in satellite operations. In April 1978, China signed an agreement on the use of Franco-German satellites.[84] Later in the year, it became clear that the West was prepared to offer general help with reconnaissance satellite development, and by October it was confirmed that Sino-American negotiations were under way for the sale and launching of a U.S.-built internal communications satellite for China.[85] Orthodox acquisition policies were, moreover, supplemented by more original methods where this seemed useful. China at various times offered substantial rewards to any Nationalist defector from Taiwan, especially one who brought a ship or aircraft with him.[86] And China was able to obtain not only specimens of Soviet MiG-23 aircraft, but perhaps of Soviet surface-to-air and antitank missiles, even some T-62 tanks, from Egypt.[87]

In spite of the Chinese government's clear interest in such

arms purchases, its ability to modernize the PLA by this route seemed likely to be subject to servere constraints. Some were technical. Though the very scale of China's total new import program gave her some leverage in pressing for Western sales of advanced and not merely second-line equipment, the government could not expect to close the entire military technology gap in this fashion. By the end of 1978, there was no sign that the West was willing to transfer military technologies in the quantity, or of the sophistication, required to meet the longer-term needs of China. The Chinese themselves, for all their interest, signed contracts sparingly. The main thrust seemed to be the selective purchase of advanced technology, of prototypes and technical assistance with a view to further manufacture in China, including that of selected items under license, rather than the large-scale importing of finished weapons. The arms import program could not in any case relieve China of the need to construct a substantial domestic armaments industry or R and D sector. For an adequate R and D base in both the military and nonmilitary sectors would be required alike for hardware development and for purposes of technological information and prediction.[88]

There were other constraints. Many of China's more immediate needs had to do with simpler forms of equipment rather than high-technology items. A good deal of effort needed to be devoted to such things as infantry weapons or perhaps an examination of Yugoslav methods of deploying men on motorcycles and carrying antitank weapons. More importantly, it would be strategically imprudent as well as politically unacceptable to allow any major segment of the Chinese defense effort to depend unduly upon foreign sources of information or supply. The Chinese authorities were naturally determined to minimize the extent and duration of their reliance upon foreign supplies and expertise. They would also not allow any single supplier or group of suppliers to dominate any important segment of the supply process, let alone accord any outsider substantial influence upon China's military structure or thought. The behavior of the USSR in 1959/60 no doubt served as an unforgettable warning. No less important was the shortage of trained manpower—in the military, in industry, and in the administration—with which to manage the import program and to use the imported material. The PLA clearly had a long period of training ahead if it was to use the modern equipment effectively.

But the most important single constraint was economic. Most Western estimates seem to agree that China's defense expenditures in 1975-78 hovered around 10 percent of the GNP.[89] That GNP was estimated to have been around $300 billion in 1975/76 (expressed in 1976 U.S. dollars). A 1978 British estimate for 1976 was $350 billion, and other U.S. estimates for 1977 and 1978 were in the region of $370-$390 billion.[90] Since the proportion of the GNP devoted to defense may also have slightly decreased during 1977, these figures would suggest annual defense expenditures of approximately $30-$35 billion during 1976/77. It is true that such aggregate totals tell us very little about China's defense structure, the relationship between quality and quantity of defense production, or the way in which defense costs can be dovetailed with other economic needs or possible methods for modernizing both the armed forces and the economy at large. Defense cannot be considered a simple minus in the balance sheet of the national economy or of national development. The defense budget may imply elements of general demand creation and the stimulation of production, with positive overall economic consequences.[91] The convertibility of some defense resources to nondefense use may be high.

In any case, the PLA has been of more direct use to the civilian economy. It plays a role in the provision of technical training. Its units have taken a regular part in harvesting and some production activities, in construction and maintenance of roads, railways, and communications of general and not just military utility.[92] In times of political trouble, troops have played a role of even greater importance. During the Cultural Revolution, for example, the PLA took over transport and communications, railways, postal and telegraph services, and even civil aviation and broadcasting stations.[93] At least some similar functions seem to have been carried out during the disorders of 1976/77. The PLA also played a major role in relief activities after the 1976 Tangshan earthquake. It was a role that the government, no doubt for a variety of reasons, wanted the PLA to go on playing. Teng, for example, thought that it was important for the army to develop a better relationship with the people and to help the collective economy.[94]

Yet from a broader point of view, defense claims presented economic problems of a kind that were, at least in the short term, insoluble. Given China's resource base, no practicable increase in overall defense allocations would allow the effort to approximate that of the United States or the USSR, or to permit a closing of the defense technology gap between China and the two superpowers. Indeed, for the PLA to be able to face the Soviet Union on something like equal terms would require expenditures so vast as to be clearly not worth discussion. A modern air-defense interceptor force, with its supporting command and communications systems, would require a multi-billion dollar investment. Taking the U.S. Mk60-A3 tank as a guide, a force of one thousand tanks would cost something like $700-$800 million, and its logistic and other support systems would run the cost of the force into several billions, even though one thousand tanks would scarcely constitute an adequate counter to Soviet armored power. Even if such a tank force could be deployed, moreover, there was the possibility that, by the time it appeared, it would have been made technically obsolescent by Soviet or U.S. developments. Imports, on the other hand, were unlikely to be available on such a scale, and, even if they were, they would create a force with special resupply problems if and when the policies of supplier nations changed.

The realities were that modernization had to be planned within a resource framework markedly more slender than that of China's competitors and potential opponents. That fact was bound to render interservice competition for resources even more acute. And the PLA as a whole was clearly a major competitor within the national allocation process for such goods as steel and cement, for machinery and trained manpower. It was in competition for investment resources,[95] in the form both of capital and of technology. A more rapid rate of military modernization was bound to mean a lower, or less rapidly rising, standard of living or rate of investment. But, arguably, the most important pressures that the PLA created for the economy did not have to do with demand management or overall investment decisions. They had to do with the need to modernize. It is this which was, and is, at once the most difficult demand to resist and the hardest to fulfill, for its implications go deep into the problems of industrial and economic structure as well as those of socio-political internal and external objectives. Nor can such defense claims and pressures be easily switched on and off. Once a decision to fulfill them has been taken and appropriate research and development and other technological programs begun, to switch them off may be even more costly than to continue and reinforce them.

Even if one agreed that the PLA needed to be modernized, that did nothing to resolve the choice between remedying immediate shortcomings or waiting for the appearance of new generations of equipment, or the choice between direct military allocations and a strengthening of the general industrial and scientific base as a condition for future development, or the difficulties about the proper relationship between imports and domestic production. The scanty evidence suggests that, while military allocations in general and procurement in particular fluctuated during the 1970s,[96] in general the leadership was repeatedly forced to accept the twin propositions that investment in infrastructure was a necessary precondition for creating greater military capabilities and that it would not be wise to devote additional resources to the immediate domestic production of equipment which might soon be out of date.

A start was made even before 1976 to import advanced technology from the West in military-related areas.[97] But the general tone was one of restraint. In his republication of Mao's "Ten Major Relationships," Hua was also republishing a call for a reduction in both military and administrative spending because "only with the fast growth of economic construction can there be more progress in defense construction." The administrative and other activities of the leadership followed these broad hints. At the beginning of 1977, for example, Peking held four conferences dealing with military production and planning. One was on air defense, one on the work of defense plants under the Third Ministry of Machine Building, one on defense planning, and one on research and development.[98] But the indications were that the armed forces had been told to expect no quick fixes or infusions of money. The *Liberation Army Daily* spoke editorially of the imperative need "to adhere to the principle of practising economy in army building . . . to do our utmost to save and reduce military expenditure and step up our country's economic construction." Or, as a Peking broadcast put it more pointedly, "Stepping up economic construction means strengthening the material foundation of national defense construction. . . . Our principle is that . . . we should strengthen national defense construction on the basis of the development of economic construction."[99] And Chairman Hua emphasized, "We must take steel as the key link, strengthen the basic industries, and exert a special effort to step up the development of power, fuel and raw and semi-finished materials industries and transport and communications. Only thus can we give strong support to agriculture, rapidly expand light industry and substantially strengthen the national defense industries."[100] In other words, the leadership was not insensitive to urgent defense needs or arguments about the Soviet threat. But it did seem willing to adopt a policy of limited modernization for the time being, strengthened by the political principles of "people's war," and in the meantime give general priority to strengthening the industrial base. Improvements in defense capability would depend crucially on progress in the other three of Chou's modernizations, those of agriculture, industry, and science and technology.

3

The Economy

Analyzing the Chinese economy is a notoriously difficult exercise. The Chinese authorities stopped issuing aggregate economic data or budget figures around 1960. They also stopped publishing newspaper and journal articles in which the data were discussed and analyzed. For the period 1960-78, foreign observers have had to make do with micro-data on various aspects of output and other economic activities which have appeared from time to time, for example, in provincial newspapers and broadcasts, and with aggregate claims or assertions couched in percentage terms. Some of this material is unreliable and some actually misleading. It is therefore not surprising that there should be marked differences not only between the observations of different foreign analysts but between the observations of individual analysts at different times.[1] There is some evidence of similar differences between various segments of the Chinese bureaucracy.

These uncertainties extend to such basic matters as the size of the Chinese population and its rates of growth. The Chinese leaders themselves have made no secret of their uncertainties over the size, and rate of growth, of the population. Li Hsien-nien has admitted that "unfortunately there are no accurate statistics" and said in 1972 that different ministries used different population figures.[2] Chou En-lai told foreign visitors that the authorities did not publish their population data because they were unreliable. At least some authorities appear to have maintained two sets of population figures, one "nominal" and one a "planning" figure.[3] In 1974, the vice-minister of public health gave his government's estimate of China's population as just short of 800 million. At the same period American estimates ranged from just under 840 to 920 million. In late 1976, some Chinese figures suggested a population of little over 850 million while the U.S. Central Intelligence Agency was using a figure of 951 million. In August 1977, it was reported that some Chinese officials were changing, suddenly and without explanation, from a figure of 800 million to one of 900 million.[4] In 1978, though official references to the 900 million figure became more frequent, vice-premiers Yu Chiu-li and Li Hsien-nien, as well as the new defense minister, Hsu Hsiang-chien, were still using the 800 million total.[5] The World Bank gave a figure of 826 million[6] while the U.S. Bureau of the Census was crediting China with a population of one billion.[7]

Whatever the precise total, it was clear that the government was concerned to bring down the rate of population increase. But the results of the official family limitation programs were equally uncertain. They were also uneven, with more successful limitation in the cities than in the countryside.[8] Data derived from provincial population figures suggest an uneven decline from 2.0-2.3 percent growth toward the end of the 1950s to 1.6-1.7 percent in the mid-1970s,[9] with an intervening rise to 2.0-2.5 percent at the end of the Cultural Revolution. Other U.S. estimates suggest that population growth was still over 2 percent in 1978 and might not decline to 1.5 percent until the early 1980s.[10] If these estimates were sound, Chairman Hua's target of national population growth reduced to 1 percent by 1980[11] may have been decidedly ambitious. In any event, it seems likely that such major uncertainties about population levels and growth rates created difficulties not only for general economic planning but for particular policy areas such as demand management and investment allocation. The reasons for uncertainty were various and complex.[12] The population investigations of the Chinese authorities during the period 1949-1978 were occasional, frequently uncoordinated, and probably defective. Improvements in the data base would have required considerable effort. The problems were therefore, a fortiori, greater for foreign observers. There may have been

additional handicaps, including possible foreign underestimates of the demographic consequences of various upheavals
and periods of great hunger.

In general, however, it can be said that Chinese economic
development after 1949 saw marked cyclical swings against a
general growth trend which, though substantial, had not, by
1978, proved outstanding by East Asian standards. The early
period of post–civil war rehabilitation and the first five-year
plan (1953-57) saw especially high growth rates, starting from a
small base and including substantial once-for-all gains in
putting to work unemployed or underused labor and capital. It
was a period when, with the help of Soviet imports and
technical assistance, the government emphasized the buildup
of heavy industry. Later experiences, including the failure of
the Great Leap Forward and the vagaries of the weather during
the early 1960s[13] as well as the withdrawal of Soviet economic
aid, underlined the need to shift industrial equipment imports
to Western sources and to make greater investment allocations
to agriculture. This contributed to a growth rate for the two
decades 1957-77 of approximately 2 percent for agriculture and
9-10 percent for industry, yielding a total average growth
figure of approximately 6 percent or 3-4 percent per capita.[14] At
the same time, investment may have been as high as 20-25
percent of the domestic product, with relatively high figures
during the 1950s and, after a drop during the period 1958-69, a
rise during the early and middle 1970s.[15] Substantial gains
appear to have been made in many areas, such as health care.
Inflationary pressures, though real, were contained.[16] On the
other hand, labor productivity suffered during the 1960s and
middle 1970s. And in basic commodities as well as in consumer
durables there had to be strict rationing. In these staple
commodities, per-capita gains seem to have been quite limited,
no doubt largely because of the sheer scale of the problem.[17] In
foodstuffs, production increases were enough to keep up with
population increases, but with little or nothing to spare[18] and
no assurance that hunger could not reappear in some places
from time to time depending upon weather, harvest, and
transport difficulties, or civil unrest.

Debates about general economic policy have inevitably taken

place against the background of China's larger social and
political intentions and difficulties. Economic growth was
given considerable priority after the end of the Korean War. But
its precise modalities, the rate of growth which was desirable,
the political and social costs of alternative growth curves, and
the appropriate mix of effort to construct producer industries
with emphasis on consumer goods were the subject of constant
and often bitter debate. Closely related to this debate were
differences of opinion about the desirable patterns and
distribution of income and wealth, the role of incentives, and
the proper relationship between technical expertise and
political enlightenment. Some schools of thought naturally
argued the need for higher growth rates, whether for reasons of
domestic development and an improvement in the standard of
living of the average man, or to consolidate China's position
vis-à-vis external rivals and competitors. Such views tended to
be associated with a tolerance of material incentives and wider
income differences, as well as encouragement of technical and
other expertise even at the cost of some blurring of political
positions. It does not matter, in Teng Hsiao-p'ing's famous bon
mot, whether a cat is black or white as long as it catches mice.
On the other hand, there were schools of thought, with Mao
himself especially sensitive to their arguments, that stressed the
primacy of revolutionary beliefs and conduct, distrusted
material incentives as the thin end of the wedge of bourgeois
habits, and were willing to argue, in words attributed to
Chiang Ch'ing, that "we would rather have a low socialist [rate
of growth] than a high capitalist one."[19] During the 1960s, the
latter group was especially influential. Since capital is merely
embodied labor and not a separate factor of production, it was
widely held to be improper even to think of a rate of return on
capital. If, during the 1960s and 1970s, budget figures were not
announced and if economic goals were often stated in vague
and general terms, this may have been at least in part because of
the inability of the leadership to agree on detailed and
quantified goals, and the need to blur factional disputes.

Throughout 1975 and 1976, during the period of contention
over the shaping of post-Mao China, the struggle between these
alternative lines and approaches continued. Indeed, around

mid-1976 the official campaign against "capitalist roaders" like Teng, with their emphasis on production, efficiency, and other undesirable economic and social views, became more intense. Yet the discrepancy between this rhetoric and the real economic conditions of the country could not last, especially in a year when increasing mismanagement and disorder were compounded by natural disasters. Already, two days before Chairman Mao's death, the *People's Daily* had called for a greater drive for construction and production. When the new leadership took over a few weeks later, it lost no time in declaring its firm support for Chou's "Four Modernizations" and in emphasizing economic development based on a series of new principles of economic management. In blaming China's economic ills on the Gang of Four, and calling for the elimination of their ideas, the government, perhaps not incidentally, managed at one and the same time to discredit a good deal of what had hitherto passed for Maoist economics and to finesse a number of issues of detail.

The new line was conveyed in a series of both general and sectoral conferences. In 1977 alone there were over forty major economic conferences designed to convey the administration's commitment to modernization and managerial rationality. The two most important of the early conferences were probably the second "Learning from Tachai" and the "Learning from Taching" conferences. The first, which lasted for eighteen days in December 1976, was attended by five thousand delegates, and the second, lasting for twenty-four days in April and May 1977, was attended by seven thousand. These audiences included not merely agricultural and industrial managers but CCP and PLA delegates and civil servants. To them, Chairman Hua presented the outlines of the new administration's program. The conference format may have had a number of functions. It may have helped in the reformulation of the fifth five-year plan which followed the consolidation of the new regime. It may also have helped to stress the role of the central government without directly affronting either provincial sensitivities or other local and populist sentiments.[20] It may have served not only to disseminate directly the larger economic goals and the operating principles of the new government but to disseminate

technical information and to help improve efficiency, especially in outlying areas, without the intervention of a
bureaucratic apparatus. It may also have helped to combine
stress on the leadership, planning, and education functions of
the center with localism, or self-reliance, in detailed resource
allocation and policy execution.[21]

The restoration of effective planning control by the center
was not sufficient to ensure economic development, or even the
conduct of any coherent fiscal and financial policies.
Following the political and administrative dislocation of 1975-
76, the government had to try to gather reliable information as
to what the economic situation in the country actually was.
There also had to be a better distribution of functions. Some
ministries needed reform, and others needed to be regrouped.
Planning Minister Yu Chiu-li, in speaking to the Taching
Conference in May 1977, revived the pre–Cultural Revolution
system of six great administrative regions, each to operate with
some measure of self-reliance. The role of planning and
management was further underlined by Teng's return, in July,
to all his old official posts. In 1978, a State Economic
Commission was created to monitor the implementation of the
national economic plan. Where the State Planning Commission's task was to produce overall economic plans, the task of
the new body appeared to be coordination and, especially,
implementation.

There were signs of increasing government impatience with
the tangle of difficulties which hampered progress toward
growth and modernization. Chairman Hua observed that large
segments of China's industry were working well below
capacity, that managerial skills were low, production costs too
high, profits too low, and turnover too slow. Problems of
embezzlement, theft, and speculation had not been adequately
dealt with.[22] By late 1978, one or two wall posters in Peking
even asked, with some daring, why China was unable to
emulate capitalist growth rates. There was a marked swing
toward decentralization of executive authority to localities and
units[23] and, within units, away from the management of plants
by revolutionary committees of the kind set up during the
Cultural Revolution, and toward a return to professional

management and managerial authority. Financial controls were strengthened. The government insisted that financial discipline be enforced on production units and that financial institutions, including banks, should play a closer supervisory and advisory role. Individual production units would have to bear responsibility for the balance of profits and losses (a principle which was, perhaps not incidentally, likely to lead to the production of goods for which there was a demand). A unit that overfulfilled its profit target would be allowed to keep part of the extra profits to improve the well-being of the work force by improved earnings or working conditions or both. As 1978 rolled by, more radical ideas were aired. The president of the new Chinese Academy of Social Sciences, Hu Chiao-mu, elaborated on the need to obey "objective economic laws." He emphasized the role of prices and of personal and group responsibility for failure or success. He advocated contractual relationships between enterprises and between enterprises and the state, as well as greater specialization of functions among enterprises, reward for work, and individual and collective property rights.[24] One of the worst crimes of the Gang of Four, it was now said, was to give the impression that profits were criminal and losses were justified. As a result, many enterprises had not accumulated funds for the state, but rather relied upon the state to subsidize their losses.[25] Yet "socialist profits are the source of socialist accumulation" and hence a condition for socialist construction.[26] Similarly, there had to be more honest and accurate bookkeeping and financial discipline. The very fact that these elementary points had to be made may show how far the rot had gone during 1975/76.

The quality of production was also too low. September 1978 was declared "quality month" as part of a nationwide campaign to improve quality.[27] Ministries apologized at public rallies for substandard or overpriced work. New factory regulations on quality control were introduced providing, among other things, for factories to repair, exchange, or give refunds for faulty goods. Technical work was to be strengthened by introducing annual examinations for technicians, with salaries and titles adjusted to the examination results.

Underlying many of these proposed changes were issues of

labor discipline and the need to raise labor productivity from levels dismally below those of the advanced countries.[28] To begin with, the government allowed wages to rise. On 1 October 1977, close to 46 percent of the urban work force, those on the lowest wage levels, found their wages raised by something like 15-20 percent,[29] and altogether about 60 percent of all workers received some raise.[30] At the same time, the government took a decided line on the politically sensitive issues of competition, differential material incentives, work related bonuses, and the general widening of an income distribution system which had arguably become too narrow. Equalitarianism was condemned,[31] and the notion (attributed to Lenin) stressed that "under socialism those who do not work will have no food."[32] Accordingly, there was official intolerance of sloth, gossip, absenteeism, and inefficiency under the banner of "making revolution." But it was combined with a strong interest in cooperative self-management, for example, on the Yugoslav model,[33] and suggestions for the direct accountability of management to the work force. There were policies to improve working conditions and work safety and to create systems for the legal protection of ownership by production teams and communes in the countryside.[34] In consequence of all this, numbers of factory workers found themselves earning substantial tax-free incomes, on top of their fixed wages, under the system of profits and bonuses. Not surprisingly, sharp rises in productivity were reported in several areas.

In trying to promote such reforms, the administration was faced by a number of difficulties. Some were short-term, like the 1976 earthquakes, including the one at Tangshan. There were unusually low temperatures in some parts of the year and flooding and drought in others, including the early parts of 1977. Production therefore suffered in all areas, not least in agriculture. Losses in this sector compelled China to purchase food and especially grain abroad and led to shortages which contributed to the widespread civil disturbances of that year. Information which filtered out later suggested that in many places there were virtual mini–civil wars. The *People's Daily* itself made it clear how far things had got out of hand. Early in

1977 it urged its readers to "direct major blows at active counter-revolutionaries and those saboteurs, embezzlers, speculators, murderers, arsonists, grafters, swindlers, criminal gangs and those other bad elements who disrupt social order, stir up incidents, incite work stoppages and loot."[35]

These disturbances reflected a variety of difficulties. Some had to do with mundane concerns about wages and conditions. In spite of rises in production and productivity, the October 1977 wage rises were the first since the early 1960s. Wage structures and relativities seem to have remained equally frozen. They were not even greatly changed by the Cultural Revolution.[36] Then there were the consequences of the denunciation of rules, incentives, and technical expertise by the radical conservatives later labeled the Gang of Four. These were to encourage indiscipline and either apathy or rebelliousness in the labor force. In some places, workers' factions attacked the management and many plants had to be closed down. All this went together with contempt for technical competence, and foreign technology, to the point of disregard for the very design characteristics of machines. These attitudes tapped the xenophobia which is not far below the surface of Chinese life. Yet the reforms of the new administration could not immediately resolve either the political or the law-and-order problems. On the contrary, some of its policies caused fresh resentments among those who were disadvantaged by them, and there were reports of harsh measures against malcontents, including some executions.[37]

Of even greater importance than shop-floor indiscipline may have been the extent to which Chinese management had become unwilling to accept risks or even responsibility. The political upheavals of 1966-69 and 1974-76 had clearly encouraged safety-first, low-profile attitudes and an unwillingness to enforce even elementary standards of management and accounting. According to one later comment about this period, "On the Industrial front there were at one time ten things which no one dared to talk about: production, technology, management, concentration, quality and quantity, economic accounting, rules and regulations, concern for the masses' daily life and importing foreign technology."[38]

There was also the question of the extent to which the central
government could effectively control industry or cities or the
outlying parts of the country, or even centrally plan the
economy. As late as the mid-1970s, only about half of China's
villages had adequate road connections with the outside
world.[39] Control over the countryside seems to have been
weakened by the Great Leap and the Cultural Revolution, and
there is some question about whether, by the mid-1970s, the
control mechanisms had fully recovered. In any case, the
Chinese peasant displayed a constant tendency to revert to
small-holding, market-economy habits.[40] Rural industries and
communes could and did engage in barter with one another,[41]
were susceptible to local and family influences, and, in general,
represented a layer of economic and social activity that not only
was not subject to close central control but about which the
center could not even be sure of getting adequate information.
There were the elements of corruption and black marketeering
endemic in any large-scale command system. They ranged
from great inequalities of real wealth and privilege as between
elites and ordinary urban workers, let alone peasants, to the
shadowy lives led by the unemployed urban young or the
bribery in practice required of those who needed favors in the
matter of housing or traveling or merely the turning of an
official blind eye to some intrafamily arrangements.[42] Even in
large-scale industry there was evidence of indiscipline and
activity which, though frequently productive or creative, was
quite contrary to the intentions or plans of the center. In 1976,
for example, the oil industry at Taching built an entire oil field
quite outside the plan.[43]

Indeed, there is little doubt that during the 1960s and the first
half of the 1970s there were some serious challenges not only to
particular aspects of individual plans but to the entire central
planning mechanism. These were of at least three kinds. There
were the populist and antibureaucratic attitudes systematically
sponsored during the Cultural Revolution and later by the
Gang of Four. The second was of greater long-term importance. On the political level, the relationship between the
center and the provinces and localities usually had been to
some degree a matter of give-and-take and of bargaining rather

than of simple command and obedience. In economic matters, too, the planning and control structure seems to have developed in a relatively decentralized way. The central administration did not find it easy to decide how far centralization could be promoted without discouraging provincial self-assertion, or necessary local initiatives, or running into problems of overbureaucratization. Political sensitivities of this sort had important economic effects. Part of China's overseas food purchasing, for example, may have been due from time to time to a desire to avoid the administrative and political costs of enforcing deliveries, or interprovincial transfers, and to seek alternative supplies for some of the great coastal cities. The third serious challenge was, of course, the problem of implementing a policy once it had been formulated, proclaimed, and publicized. In all large and complex social systems, this is a principal problem for governments. In China, too, there was ample evidence that governmental pronouncements were one thing, but grass-roots action was another. In mid-1978, an Australian industrial mission reported that lack of discipline, overstaffing, low productivity, and poor maintenance persisted, and that some of the Cultural Revolution and post–Cultural Revolution managerial malpractices of politicized planning were continuing.[44]

But in attempting these reforms, the government also had certain important assets. China had an impressive basis for potential economic development, in the form of land, people, and industrial assets. In the words of Chairman Hua, "We have a large population and abundant natural resources and after 20-odd years of construction we have established a fairly solid material base and accumulated a rich store of experience . . . we have all the preconditions for speeding up economic growth." At least some of the problems of 1976-78, being short term, might be capable of swift remedy. Among these were the effects of droughts and earthquakes. Even a modicum of industrial discipline and improved management was likely, in the short term, to yield substantial catch-up benefits. During 1975-77 very considerable gains were, in fact, made in areas like consumer durables—including bicycles, radios, and sewing machines—and in raising personal savings. If the rise in industrial production slumped from some 10 percent in 1975 to zero in 1976, it rose again to 13-14 percent in 1977. Chairman Hua took care to explain that China was in a catch-up phase and that the progress of 1977-78 must not be taken to mean that more fundamental problems had been solved.[45]

Yet the capital development programs of the previous twenty years, fitful and controversial as they had been, were coming on stream. In spite of evident difficulties in absorbing the plants and their products into the Chinese economy, the foreign-supplied fertilizer complexes were entering production. So were some iron and steel and petrochemical units and telecommunication equipment. More could be expected to begin operations by 1980. In sum, China's production capacity had expanded and would continue to expand, irrespective of short-term political fluctuations. These had, in any case, never affected the whole of industry. Sections of the military-industrial complex, for example, though in some cases working as far below capacity as most of general industry (usually for reasons to do with technical and managerial difficulties), had always remained relatively insulated from general political turmoil. Not only was productive capacity going up, but the quality of production was also rising. Chinese industry, and certainly its export-oriented sectors, were beginning to produce higher-quality goods, capable of commanding higher prices.

Most important of all was the support the new administration could command in the community at large. It could, and did, profit from a certain weariness with overblown political rhetoric and a willingness to accept a clear and pragmatically plausible sense of direction, evidence of a new sense of reality. Even then the new reforms were, in many instances, not quite as new as they seemed. Bonus schemes and piecework had been used in some areas, including coal mining and dock work, for years.[46] Even to the extent that the reforms were indeed innovations, they were in no small measure a response to demands from the shop floor. A wish to relate work and reward more closely was likely to be popular both among those who had grown increasingly impatient with recently prevailing equal rewards for the lazy and the efficient, and among the younger and stronger workers who could expect to do well under such a new regime.

In one matter at least the Hua administration agreed with its predecessor. If the Chinese economy could be said to have a key problem, it was that of agriculture.[47] Where some 88 percent of the population lived in rural areas at the beginning of the 1950s, by the mid-1970s the figure was still a trifle over 80 percent. Though the usual experience of industrializing countries is an increasing population concentration in the towns, the Chinese government sought to avoid this development.[48] The rate of growth of agricultural productivity was, and remains, the most important single factor not only in raising the standard of living of most Chinese but in the growth of the nonfarm economy. From the beginning, the government recognized that agriculture was the foundation of China's economy. Yet the growth of that agricultural productivity ran into major structural difficulties around the middle of the century. Dwight Perkins has argued that before the mid-1950s most of the rise in Chinese agricultural output can be accounted for by increasing inputs of land, labor, and capital, with technical changes responsible for only a minor contribution.[49] The difficulty, according to this view, is that by the twentieth century most of the good agricultural land had been put to use and larger inputs were running into diminishing returns. The ratio of people (and hence of available labor, but also of consumers) to land is high, with only some 11-12 percent of China's total land area under cultivation.[50] Increasing the areas of cultivated land became increasingly expensive and difficult.[51] Chinese agriculture has therefore tended to concentrate on high-energy-yielding products and production increases through more intensive land use, including in more recent periods double and triple cropping.[52]

In the quarter century after the Korean War, the government sought remedies to the problems of agricultural production and productivity in a variety of ways. In the 1950s there were attempts to increase the areas under cultivation. The costs of the program were high, productivity on the marginal new land was low,[53] and while new lands were being cultivated other areas were swallowed up by industrial, urban, and transport developments. The result seems to have been that the total area under cultivation in 1975 was much the same as it had been in the early 1950s. The government also devoted much effort to irrigation, water conservancy, and flood control. After 1949 rural labor was mobilized for such purposes during off-seasons, with the result that between 1952 and 1977 the percentage of China's farmlands under irrigation more than doubled from 20 percent to 40-50 percent.[54] Inputs of feed, insecticides, and, above all, fertilizer, rose markedly. Between the start of the 1960s and the mid-1970s, the supply of chemical fertilizers multiplied by ten or eleven. This was made possible by a substantial fertilizer import policy, culminating in the early 1970s in the purchase from Western firms of thirteen large urea complexes which were scheduled more than to double China's output of nitrogen fertilizers. And yet, given the vast scale of China's agricultural problem, as late as the mid-1970s about three-quarters of the nutrients per hectare probably were still in the form of organic fertilizers.

The government also emphasized mechanization and a great variety of farmland construction projects. Small-scale industries were developed throughout the rural areas and, in conjunction with them, electricity developments, often based on hydro-power, were largely built by the off-season rural labor force at low real cost. According to Western estimates, in the ten years from the mid-1960s to the mid-1970s the share of China's energy supply consumed by the agricultural sector rose from 3 to 6 percent. These efforts were supported by a number of necessary inputs from the modern industrial sector, from iron and steel or fertilizers to the construction of agricultural machinery. At the same time the general demand pressures on that industrial sector, together with the high costs of distributing urban manufactures throughout the countryside, appear to have reinforced the tendency for the agricultural modernization effort to be based largely upon the efforts of the rural sector itself, rather than on transfers from the urban or industrial sectors.

Over the quarter century following Mao's assumption of power, Chinese agriculture achieved some remarkable improvements. Grain output, for example, rose from 111 million tons in 1949 to 285 million tons in 1977.[55] But an unchanged area of cultivated land had to support a rural population which may have increased by about half. Much of the investment in such things as irrigation schemes was again in the form of labor at very low real cost. And there is much evidence of a decline in the rate of return on rural investment, in the shape of more labor and other inputs required per unit of output during the 1960s and 1970s. In general, it does not seem that food supplies in calorific value per head of the population improved in the twenty-five years or so after 1950 or, indeed, between the 1930s and 1970s, though quality, and equality of distribution, may have become somewhat better.[56] At times of poor harvests or other natural disasters, there was real hunger in places.[57] Occasionally, as in the period 1959-62, there was substantial starvation. There is evidence that "free markets" in such things as meat and cooking oil survived in many localities, markets that were either overlooked by the authorities or passed off as "human kindness and mutual help between friends."[58] Nor was food cheap. Werner Klatt has suggested[59] that, in terms of working time expended, one kilo of rice in Peking cost, by the mid-1970s, as much as the average wage for one hour, compared with the half-hour's work that a Tokyo worker paid for one kilo of rice or a Muscovite for one kilo of bread. In this view, the average urban family in China paid three-fifths of the average urban family income for its food, compared with one-half in the USSR and one-third in Japan. Alexander Eckstein, on the basis of somewhat different calculations, suggests that the ratio of the Chinese to the U.S. purchasing power of one hour's average wage at this period was 1:7 for rice and for food generally.[60] There are, of course, enormous difficulties not only with the official figures but in trying to estimate the effects of the running battle of wits between peasants and tax collectors, or communes and higher authorities. Any underreporting of crops or overstatement of the number of inhabitants, for example, would tend to lower obligations or increase the supplies of the commune concerned. Still, it would be overly optimistic to suggest that China had solved its food problems. This fact had important implications for many areas of the economy. For example, there was an erosion of China's

traditional agricultural-export capacity, with resulting constraints upon China's capacity to import and problems for her
balance of payments.

The argument so far suggests that China's main difficulties
in expanding agricultural production and productivity were
structural, to do with the availability of cultivable land and
declining rates of return on additional technical and capital
inputs. It can, however, be argued that many of the difficulties
were aggravated, if not created, by the prevailing political and
social arrangements. The arguments in support of such a
proposition tend to be of two kinds. On one side is the kind of
view advanced, for example, by Ramon H. Myers.[61] This holds
that while the government of the People's Republic has been
unable to stimulate agricultural growth at rates that would
have exceeded population growth and, therefore, permitted
substantial development, such high growth rates have been
achieved in areas of China not under that government's
control. Myers suggests that in the Japanese-occupied Liao-
tung peninsula before the Second World War, on Japanese-
occupied Taiwan during the same period, and on Nationalist-
controlled Taiwan since 1949 the growth of farm production
was substantially higher than population growth or than the
growth of farm production in the People's Republic. On the
other side, there is the suggestive fact that, according to
Peking, about one-quarter of all agricultural and subsidiary
products purchased by the state has come from household
sideline production.[62] Since only about 5 percent of the land
has been devoted to private production, the implication
appears to be that substantial production gains might be
feasible under somewhat different conditions and incentives.

The new government was encouraged to focus on agriculture
by the poor showing of this sector and the reduced harvests of
1976/77. In those two years, the output of grain barely
remained steady at around 285 million tons in 1976 and 1977.
The performance of other crops was also disappointing, with a
decline in the production of oilseed and, probably, cotton.[63]
The result was a sharp increase in the import of wheat, cotton,
and soybeans and decreased exports of rice. Though the
propensity to import may have been encouraged by the politics

of a year of changes, the impact upon China's balance of trade was significant and must have driven home lessons about the need to grow more food at home, not only in aggregate terms but within each province. The government was also acutely aware how closely its hopes for growth in other parts of the economy depended on an improvement in the country's agricultural performance. The rural sector was accorded primacy in economic pronouncements. Teng complained that the productivity of Chinese agriculture was quite inadequate. Even the design for China's scientific advancement must have as the first of its priorities the modernization of agriculture.[64] According to Chairman Hua, between 1977 and 1985 China's grain output would rise by some 40 percent to 400 million tons (a rate of growth which implied an annual increase of some 4-5 percent, or over twice that achieved in previous periods) and by the end of the century output per unit of major agricultural products was expected to reach or surpass advanced world levels.[65]

Given that the supply of additional suitable land was limited,[66] the government concentrated upon the other major inputs: labor productivity, mechanization, farm construction, and higher technology. It was explained that labor productivity in Chinese agriculture was a mere 2 percent of the U.S. figure.[67] Encouragement was given to the steady, often unobtrusive, accretion of skills within the rural population. The government furthered, as its predecessors had done, the utilization of underemployed rural labor for the purpose of rural modernization and improvement.[68] The aim of 70 percent farm mechanization by 1980, originally announced by Hua as spokesman for agriculture in 1975, was reiterated by him as chairman. During the opening months of the post-Mao regime, farm mechanization became a major propaganda theme. Some attempt to spell out details was made during the Third National Conference on Agricultural Mechanization in Peking in January 1978 and the Fifth NPC two months later. At the first of these gatherings, Yu Chiu-li echoed Hua and spoke of the "basic mechanization" of agriculture by 1980. The government intended that 70 percent of the major agricultural, forestry, animal husbandry, sideline production, and fishery operations should be mechanized by that date. In addition, a 70 percent increase in large and medium tractors was promised, and so was a 58 percent increase in the production of chemical fertilizer.[69] At the Fifth NPC, the nation was told that by 1985 all major farm processes were to be mechanized. There were indications that this program faced formidable difficulties. These had to do not merely with the country's production and distribution capacity for more sophisticated items of machinery, or the pool of skills for running and maintaining them, but with structural problems such as standardization. Given the way in which Chinese agricultural units had obtained their tools from factories and shops on a variety of administrative levels with different design and work habits, it was inevitable that both the stock of available tools and machinery and the facilities for producing them should display great variety. By July 1978, Li Hsien-nien was denouncing the practice of "letting a hundred flowers bloom" in farm machinery production and calling for the imposition of standardization by the central authorities. In any event, even if the aim of "basic mechanization" by 1980 were to be achieved, it was clear in 1978 that this would mean a level of mechanization well below that of more advanced agricultural economies.[70]

The government also continued and strengthened the farmland capital-construction program. The vagaries of the weather, in the ever-present possibilities of flood or drought in both southern and northern China, and the availability of rural labor at low marginal cost combined to persuade the authorities to emphasize water-control and river-harnessing programs, as well as improvements in soil fertility, afforestation, road building, and expansion of the available supply of land by expanding croplands and bringing mountainous areas under cultivation.[71] Possibly of even greater importance was the evident determination of the authorities to increase the scientific and technological inputs into agriculture. Perhaps the most obvious aspect of this was the continued emphasis on chemical (as well as organic) fertilizers. But this was complemented by an official stress on various developments in the field of agricultural science, from domestic crop-improvement efforts, including successes in the production of hybrid rice, to a substantial agricultural-science exchange program with other countries. During 1976 and 1977, the PRC received almost fifty agricultural delegations and sent some twenty Chinese delegations abroad. Though these Chinese delegations may also have had political purposes,[72] their principal function was clearly the gathering of technologically useful information. This information gathering process was both general and specific. China used her membership in the UN Food and Agriculture Organization in this sense and showed particular interest in certain areas such as food processing and storage, ways of minimizing losses during transport, citrus and corn growing, and soil conservancy. The dispatch of a delegation to Peru in 1977 to study wheat production may well have had to do with China's own need to expand grain growing into higher and generally less-favorable areas. There were also signs of a Chinese interest in the opportunities that space science might afford to agriculture, for example, in remote sensing techniques of the kind developed by the United States.

But the most important element in the government's program had to do with changing peasant attitudes from relatively passive, even sullen, acquiescence to active and willing cooperation with the Party and the state. The evidence that all was not well in this vital area was clear, ranging as it did from marked discrepancies in production between communal land and private plots to the increasingly frank and critical remarks of China's leaders. According to Li Hsien-nien, the basic aim of government policy had to be to "arouse the masses' enthusiasm and get the peasants to take the socialist road." There had to be more pay for more work: egalitarianism must be stopped. The "unreasonable burdens imposed on the peasants" must be reduced, and their "share of distribution and cash income increased" as production increased. At the same time, the "commandism" of some cadres must be curbed: there should be more consultation and less ordering people about.[73] Accordingly, government policies encouraged profits, incentives, and a reduction in the tax burdens on the farming population.[74] A policy of raising prices to encourage production increases was not, of course, new.[75] But the policies now formed part of an attempt not just to grow more food but to keep the income differentials between town and country within tolerable limits. At the end of 1978, it was decided to raise the price levels in both tiers of the grain purchasing system[76] as well as for cotton, sugar, and other products. At the same time the prices of farm machinery and fertilizer were scheduled to be cut by 10-15 percent to reduce costs.[77] There were also more state loans for agriculture.

If raising peasant incomes was one side of the new policies, stress on local responsibility was the other. China had some fifty thousand rural communes, and, on average, each had a population of approximately fifteen thousand. The commune was composed of several brigades, and each brigade of several production teams composed in turn of perhaps twenty-five to thirty families. The team was the basic accounting unit. It was responsible for day-to-day management, and the team's income depended upon its production. Individuals and families received income in accordance with work points. It could be argued that this constituted a piecework system, in which the brigade played a role akin to that of the Western corporation, and that the relationship between the peasant family and the cadre who had to sanction the award of work points was not entirely dissimilar to that which used to obtain between landlord and tenant. Moreover, it has been strongly argued that the commune could be seen as the natural successor to the old market town with its satellite villages.[78] It was clear, at any rate, that the new organization had important links with China's rural traditions and that the elements of competition, market forces, and reward in accord with work done remained strong. They were elements that the new administration wished to strengthen. It encouraged private plots. It restored the system of rural trade fairs, at which peasants were allowed to buy and sell their privately produced foodstuffs at market prices.[79] It promised to strengthen the legal protection of ownership and power of decision by communes, production brigades, and teams.[80]

Yet policies of this kind were likely to create difficulties. How, for example, could one under these new conditions prevent a restoration of capitalism in the countryside? The answer seemed to lie in a change of emphasis away from close, direct administrative control to the maintenance of a political atmosphere that would discourage an overemphasis on private profit, make efforts to fix state prices so as to make private trading less attractive, and maintain limited supervision of the "free market" sector to avoid visible profiteering. Or again, could the new line lead to greater differences between provinces or counties with different resource endowments and different modes of leadership and hence to a greater measure of specialization and interprovincial transfer? On the contrary. The government made it clear that agriculture could not look for any substantial program of resource diversion from other sectors or even for a continued program of interprovincial transfer of food stocks. The State Planning Commission, in an important statement on 11 September 1977, explained that "in developing agriculture, we rely mainly on the Tachai spirit." In other words, the theme, repeated ad nauseam by ministers and other officials, was the need for peasant self-help. And Chairman Hua explained that the aim must be for all provinces and autonomous regions to achieve self-sufficiency in grains and foodstuffs. In fact, all prefectures, cities, and counties which had the potential for self-sufficiency were expected to achieve it in the next few years. Provincial or county self-sufficiency should extend from staple foods to some nonstaples and to the most essential manufactures.[81] It was an aim clearly designed not merely to improve food production and the diet of the average man and woman, but to ease both the political strains of interprovincial transfers and the claims on relatively slender transport facilities.

By 1978 there was no evidence that the basic problem of increasing food production at a faster rate than population growth had been satisfactorily resolved. China was still importing grain from abroad each year, in particular to help feed northern cities. Chairman Hua's aim of 400 million tons by 1985 seemed to Western observers to be very much at the upper limit of the feasible, assuming that all went well and that all available means were fully used.[82] It was more likely that the aim would not be achieved. Farming investment, though large, continued to encounter decreasing rates of return. In any case, farming modernization as it did proceed looked like raising even larger problems. In October, the *People's Daily* mused that, of the 300 million adults in the countryside, perhaps no more than 100 million would be needed for farming in the future, making the rest available for rural and other local industries. The social problems agricultural modernization would bring in its train were clearly enormous. For food production as for employment, therefore, China urgently needed technological advance. If China's grain and rice yields were to approximate those of the United States in the one case and Japan or Italy or South Korea in the other, there would have to be much greater investment still in agricultural technology.[83]

In the field of industrial development, China experienced substantial growth after 1949. Western estimates are that for most of the period 1949 to 1978 industrial growth ran at some 13 percent per annum. But that growth was interrupted, at the start of the 1960s, by the legacy of the Great Leap Forward and the results of the Sino-Soviet dispute and, at the end of that decade, by the Cultural Revolution. The result was to bring the overall growth rate down to some 10 percent over the entire twenty-five to thirty year period. Growth, partly fueled by substantial investment, was accompanied by changes in industrial structure. The impetus given to heavy industry and machine building was even greater than that given to industry as a whole. During the 1950s growth also relied greatly upon Soviet inputs. But following the break, need and inclination alike dictated to China a policy of self-reliance and alternative methods for strengthening China's industrial base. These methods proved to be a stimulation of both advanced and large-scale industry and of small- and medium-sized, labor-intensive industries and plants including rural industries. The growth of this second category had certain advantages.[84] It brought industry to the peasants rather than bringing labor into the cities. It played an important role in servicing agriculture, in producing goods for local consumption, as well as in absorbing and training labor. And by the beginning of the 1970s, it was probably responsible for 60 percent of China's production of chemical fertilizers, two-thirds of the production of agricultural machinery, one-third of all coal, and half of building materials. It tended, perhaps inevitably, to employ somewhat out-of-date techniques, to put out inferior products, and to be somewhat more labor intensive, with lower labor productivity, than would be the case in modern industries. Moreover, the emphasis on local self-sufficiency necessarily ran counter to any nationwide program of specialization and comparative efficiency. Stimulating the development of these local industries may therefore have created positive hindrances to the development of more sophisticated and higher technology production. At the same time, these units appear to have been much less responsive to, or reliant on, higher authority than larger industrial plants.

Steady progress was made in a number of fields. Steel production, after some fluctuations in the middle 1970s, recovered to approximately 28 million tons in 1978.[85] Transport was much improved. Between 1970 and 1976, the country's highway network, for example, is estimated to have increased from 640,000 to 820,000 kilometers. In addition to the new construction, the engineering and surfacing of existing stretches was improved.[86] The railway network increased from 41,300 to 50,000 kilometers during 1970-76, and further construction was reported, as were increased double tracking, electrification, and expansion of yards. Most engines remained steam driven, though the number and proportion of diesel engines was rising. Major airport improvements and airway expansion plans were under way.[87] Port facilities were being expanded, and China's merchant navy increased in numbers as well as size of ships. There were substantial advances in energy production. Estimates of China's coal reserves varied widely, but the best 1978 Western estimates seemed to be that recoverable reserves were not less than 100 billion tons with total resources around 1,500-2,000 billion.[88] Coal production appears to have doubled between 1970 and 1976 to approximately 460 million tons, though the increase was less if allowances are made for the low heating value of some of the coal.[89] There was progress in electricity production, and by 1977 oil production was estimated to have reached over 90 million tons.[90] Oil, with total Chinese reserves of crude (excluding shale oil) probably between 3 billion and 10 billion tons,[91] was clearly destined to be an especially important commodity. It would play a major role not just in fueling China's increasingly energy-intensive industrial development and her military programs, but in relation to her external trade.

Yet by the time the Hua administration formulated its own industrial program, it was clear that there were shortages, output lags, and bottlenecks in most major areas of the economy. The political tensions and upheavals of the previous years had made matters worse by creating or accentuating errors in resource and investment allocations which contributed to serious imbalances within and between sectors. Confronted by these weaknesses, and the internal and external difficulties which they created, the government announced a series of most ambitious industrial aims. By A.D. 2000, Chairman Hua declared, China's output of major industrial products should approach, equal, or outstrip that of the most-developed capitalist countries. During the key years of 1978-85, he said, industrial production would grow by over 10 percent.[92] By 1985 steel production would have almost tripled to 60 million tons. During the same period some one hundred twenty large-scale industrial projects would be developed, including ten iron and steel complexes, nine nonferrous metal complexes, ten oil and gas fields, eight coal mines, and thirty new power stations. Priority would be given to the development of power, fuels, raw and semifinished materials, transport, and communications. There would be administrative changes ranging from Yu Chiu-li's wish for an improved distribution of functions, to the organization of industry into fourteen clusters which would, in turn, form part of the proposed six economic regions of China.[93] The chairman also promised a drop in population growth to 1 percent per annum but did not say how this was to be achieved. Some aspects of this plan were not particularly novel. Seven of the ten iron and steel complexes, for example, were already in various stages of planning, and some aspects of the scheme seemed to resurrect elements of development programs harking back as far as the 1930s. But in sum, the aims were bold enough to create immediate doubts about their feasibility, as distinct from their utility for the purposes of general planning and domestic mobilization. The *People's Daily* itself remarked cautiously that it might be possible to develop the ten new oil fields before the end of the century—a very different timetable from Chairman Hua's seven years.[94]

It was clear that such a program depended on simultaneous advances in a number of adjacent areas. Its implementation required a rapid growth in steel production. It required a massive import program for advanced equipment and technology in many areas, including such key ones as machine-tool production.[95] And it required a rapid rate of development for China's minerals and energy industries. In the area of steel production, Chairman Hua's objectives implied an average rate of growth of 5 million tons, or over 14 percent per annum. Yet much of the ore available in China was of low grade; reserves of coking coal were not large;[96] and raw-material processing, finishing capacity for steel products, general technology capacity, and transport were not adequate. In the words of an Australian team, "Unless new high-grade discoveries are made, production from existing mines will need to expand greatly to achieve the national steel target by 1985. Huge capital investment in mining equipment, beneficiation and pelletisation facilities would also be required. There must be serious doubts whether China could marshal the necessary finance and technical expertise/management in the available time."[97] In the minerals field, though China is one of the world's richer minerals areas, there were questions about the time it would take to develop her great potential.[98] By 1978 the resources remained underdeveloped. They were not, in many areas, even adequately explored.[99]

In the transport field, still more effort was devoted to extending air services and purchasing aircraft, to building roads, railways, and ports. The Chinese authorities expanded their merchant shipping fleet, both for international trading and for coastal transport. They purchased ships, in considerable quantities and at rock-bottom prices during the world shipping slump.[100] The purchases included several second-hand ships in the 75,000-100,000 ton class from Europe and Japan, including some tankers from Norway. A number of ports were expanded to handle these ships, though by late 1978 only Lu-ta was able to accommodate 100,000-ton tankers and only Chan-chiang and Huang-tao could take 70,000-ton vessels.[101] Other reports suggested the Dairen, Shanghai, and Wuhan could only berth 30,000-tonners.[102] But Dairen, Tsingtao, and other ports were being expanded; a new port at Shanghai, associated with the proposed new steel mill there, was scheduled to take 100,000-ton vessels, and no doubt something could be done in the meantime, with some kinds of goods, by means of lighters.

A key role would have to be played by the energy industries, which would have to fuel China's industrialization as well as provide export earnings. Domestic requirements were sure to grow quickly. Western experience suggests that the ratio of growth of energy consumption to the growth of the GNP is approximately 1-2:1. In aggregate terms, by 1978 China was already the world's third largest energy consumer.[103] Future requirements were likely to grow rapidly if the government's plans were to be fulfilled or even approached.[104] Yet the new administration inherited an electric-power production system that was inadequate.[105] Chairman Hua referred to it as a "weak link." Chronic shortages were caused by rapid increases in consumer demand, including the construction of new industrial facilities, especially ones in remote areas, and by shortages of inputs like coal. But maintenance was also poor, and many plants did not work at full capacity. As part of the government's electric power program, therefore, special emphasis was placed upon the development of hydro-power.[106] While some 38 percent of China's installed capacity was believed to be in the form of hydro-stations, this was less than 2.5 percent of China's hydro-power potential. By 1978, planned developments included some major hydroelectric developments on the Yangtse and elsewhere, making use of imported technology and plant. Other steps which seemed required were more investment in coal production to fuel electric generation, better transport, larger thermal stations, better transmission lines, and a start to the acquisition of nuclear power technology.[107]

There were similarly urgent problems in coal production. Between the mid-1960s and the mid-1970s, investment in the coal industry had lagged,[108] with production shortfalls being made up by intensive working of old mines and even some coal imports. The lag was especially serious in view of the fact that coal supplied two-thirds of China's primary energy. Moreover, coal shortages may have had a ripple effect; for example, in the steel industry which, partly because of its reliance on relatively backward technologies, required large supplies of coking coal. According to official claims, production rose by 10.2 percent during 1977, which would mean gross production of approximately 510 million tons. Even so, according to the government, growth would have to be speeded up,[109] especially if coal production were to reach levels that would free additional oil supplies for export. That would mean a major program to modernize existing mines and build new ones. Indeed, according to the minister for coal, the 1977 production level was to be doubled within ten years and doubled again by A.D. 2000. There would be more intensive use of existing mines; a systematic development of small mines in rural areas; the opening up of major new mines in southern China, partly with the aim of eliminating the South's traditional dependence on northern fuel; more intensive use of low-quality fuels; and a major effort to mechanize the working of all mines, partly with the aid of imported technology. Whether this program was feasible and, if so, at what cost to other sectors, remained to be seen. By mid-1978, for example, China had agreed on a deal with West Germany by which the Germans would construct and modernize six deep mines with a total capacity of 22 million tons and build two opencast lignite mines with a capacity of 20 million tons a year each. The mines were scheduled to be mechanized to the best European standards, and the projects, together with the plant to build the necessary machinery, were expected to cost China around $4 billion. Yet when completed, all these mines would only raise China's production capacity by a little over 60 million tons,[110] not a large proportion of the 500 million tons of additional production capacity which, if government statements were to be taken at face value, would be added within a mere decade.

In the area of oil, similarly, the government plans implied a very greatly accelerated exploration and exploitation program.

Though reserves were large and the expansion of production and exports during the mid-1970s was substantial, the Chinese authorities confronted severe problems in trying to increase the rate of extraction. Some were technical. Chinese oil technology, originally based on Soviet models, was backward. There was a shortage of equipment, inadequate drilling, piping, and pumping equipment, and the legacy of some doubtful extraction methods. Though China had, by the mid-1970s, developed a substantial equipment-producing capacity, much more, it was clear, would have to come from abroad.[111] Though Chinese refining technologies were adequate,[112] there was a persistent shortage of refining capacity.[113] Other problems had to do with the shortage of trained oil technicians. Others again were geographic. The northern and northeastern onshore regions which provided some 80 percent of China's oil during the first half of the 1970s seemed likely, at 1976-78 rates of production, to be nearing exhaustion by the end of the 1980s. The development of less-favorably situated resources was certain to require both time and substantial capital and technical investment.[114] The early exploitation of offshore deposits, in particular, was bound to depend on the acquisition of foreign technology and know-how even if all jurisdictional difficulties in relation to Japan and other states proved soluble. Up to 1978, China succeeded in raising rates of oil production, albeit at declining rates of increase. Whether China would be able to maintain the capital investment required for continued or even increased rates of production growth, at internationally competitive prices, and to do so in a way that satisfied other major planning objectives, remained to be seen.

The foreign trade implied by such patterns of national development was a matter of considerable political as well as economic sensitivity. China's recent experience with foreign trade had been mixed. The foreign connections during the century before 1949, as well as the result of the decade of dependence on the USSR during the 1950s, left a memory of economic difficulties and political humiliation. The abrupt termination of Soviet economic assistance around 1960, the mixed quality of Soviet industrial supplies, and the difficulties of repaying the Soviet debts at times of acute economic difficulty all carried the lesson of the potential dangers of foreign economic ties. The People's Republic therefore stressed the importance of trading in a balanced way (albeit by the 1960s through multilateral balancing) and the need to avoid international credit arrangements. Foreign loans were regarded as unacceptable, and import policy was designed in terms of the goal of balanced trade.

Within such a framework, foreign trade was used to achieve several kinds of economic aims. It was used to obtain technology and know-how from abroad. It was used, for example, in the chemical fertilizer field, to increase the volume of investment and development to otherwise unobtainable levels. It was used to help stabilize the economy by importing food and textiles to make good particular shortfalls, oil to supply particular markets close to large ports, and machinery and equipment for selected industries. Inevitably, its scope and development were subject to the more general debates about the forms of China's social and political development. In particular, the debates between those who distrusted foreign entanglements and any undermining of the revolution, and those who thought the success of the Chinese experiment depended on the speed with which the country's economic potential could be developed, were reflected in trading matters also. In practice, however, industrial development in particular had been tied to technological imports since the earliest days of the People's Republic, and, given the importance the Hua administration attached to economic growth, it was not surprising that it should stress the need to increase trade.[115] If China were to develop as the government hoped, it was mandatory that she learn from the advanced science and technology of other countries and increase the volume of imports.[116] China must "develop economic and technical exchanges with other countries in accordance with our national needs and the principles of equality and mutual benefit and supplying each others needs, provided these activities do not infringe on China's sovereignty or hamper her economic independence and provided they conform to chairman Mao's line in foreign affairs."[117] Or, as Li Hsien-nien put it, China must maintain her independence and keep the initiative in her own hands.[118] They were clearly principles that left a great deal of room for maneuver.

Some aspects of the new policies, notably the emphasis on machinery and plant imports, revived or continued trends which had been apparent since the 1950s. During that decade, the Soviet Union made a major input into Chinese economic development, supplying capital goods, raw materials, blueprints, and technicians. Between 1950 and 1959, the Soviet Union completed some 130 industrial projects and delivered large quantities of equipment.[119] During the first half of the 1960s, the trading emphasis changed. In the early 1960s China found it necessary to import grains and fertilizer, and by 1963 she was turning to Western Europe and Japan as suppliers of plant and technology. During 1963 to 1966, contracts were signed for over fifty plants, at a cost of some $200 million and involving medium-term credits and the services of Western technicians. Machinery and equipment imports may, in fact, have increased faster than either total imports or total domestic investment in machinery and equipment. The Great Leap Forward slogan of "walking on two legs" was revived, implying a policy of more careful balance between imported industrial plant and equipment and domestically developed growth and improvement. At the same time, the stress on large-scale heavy industry that had marked the period of reliance on the Soviet Union was replaced by a policy of more careful balance among heavy industry, low and intermediate technology of special relevance to small and medium labor-intensive industries, and encouragement of essentially self-reliant commune and county-based efforts based on traditional and local techniques. This was followed by the drive for complete self-sufficiency that formed part of the chauvinism of the Cultural Revolution. The result was to overemphasize local, small-scale industry.

The importation of advanced technology and whole plants resumed in 1972. The fading out of the Cultural Revolution saw a reassertion of greater political pragmatism and, with it, fresh emphasis on the modern industrial sector of the economy. At the same time, the Soviet equipment acquired during the 1950s was becoming obsolete and, its value further lessened by poor maintenance, was clearly inadequate for the next period of economic growth. Greater stress on industrial growth, modern weapons, and military production, therefore, was bound to mean higher levels of industrial and technical imports.[120] The details of the import drive were probably designed by Chou En-lai and his associates. Total trade rose between 1970 and 1973, in real terms, by some 80 percent. Capital imports were complemented by purchases of industrial supplies, from steel and other metals to rubber. But the main thrust of the import program concentrated on producer goods and especially on equipment for the capital-intensive, advanced industrial sectors ranging from the chemical industry and machinery and equipment to equipment for road, rail, and air transport. The whole plant purchasing program began in 1972 with the acquisition of two thermal electric power stations and a chemical plant, all from Japan. These purchases, totaling some $27 million, were dwarfed in 1973 when China bought thirty-two chemical plants and five electric power ones, together worth $1.2 billion. By 1973/74, the program was being vigorously supported by Teng Hsiao-ping. In 1974, China extended her range of purchases from chemical and electric plants to steel-making facilities, all to a total value of $900 million. Roughly the same volume of purchases continued into 1975. In that year, capital-goods imports as a whole totaled $2.2 billion, though this figure dropped to $1.8 billion in the following year.

During the middle of the decade, imports, including plant and technology imports, declined. There were political attacks of a xenophobic kind on reliance upon foreign technology and the export of Chinese raw materials. Perhaps more importantly, China suffered a severe imbalance of trade, caused by a combination of heavy deliveries of previously ordered goods; inflation in the West, leading to rising prices for Chinese imports; and a Western recession, leading to diminished demand for Chinese export goods. In 1974 China experienced a $1.2 billion deficit in its trade with the nonsocialist world. The major reaction was a sharp downturn in imports. Delivery orders were canceled or postponed, and not only plant but agricultural imports reduced from the record $2 billion imported in 1974. In 1975, the deficit was halved to approximately $580 million. By 1976, the combination of reduced imports and sharply increased oil revenues ($910 million in 1976) led to a record $1.2 billion surplus. In 1976/77, after the new regime came to power, machinery and capital imports dropped further—by around one-third—as the deliveries of whole plants contracted for during 1973-75 were completed.[121]

But there were many indicators that the government was preparing for a new and much more intensive round of plant and equipment purchases abroad. The new trading program can be said to have had a number of general characteristics, most of them an extension of previous policies. China was attempting to exchange labor for capital to increase China's export base and the quantity, quality, value, and attractiveness of Chinese goods in foreign markets; to encourage imports likely to develop her industrial capacity while stimulating and supporting the export drive; and to trade raw materials, especially oil, for technology and plant. The two novel characteristics were the unprecedented scale of the program and a new willingness to depart from principles of balanced trade and accept more far-reaching forms of indebtedness and involvement with international financial markets.

The import program displayed considerable variety. The government was sensitive to consumer needs and increased its agricultural purchases abroad, especially in grains, sugar, and soybeans. Over 11 million tons of grain were ordered for delivery in 1977 and 1978,[122] and actual 1977 imports were estimated at around 7 million tons, the second largest import total since China had begun to import grain in 1961. Grain deliveries were well over three times, and sugar deliveries just under three times, those for 1976. And in 1978 the pace of the purchase program showed little sign of slackening. Other consumer goods were purchased, including watches and television sets,[123] as well as plants to make them. There were purchases of chemical fertilizers and of industrial goods like steel. But the bulk of the program was devoted to imports of capital goods, plant machinery, and equipment. Throughout 1978 there were signs that this was being pressed with determination and at an accelerating pace. Early in the year China signed its $20 billion trade agreement with Japan.[124] But subsequent negotiations with a number of Western countries suggested that this was merely the beginning. Western business observers suggested that the volume of plant, machinery, and equipment purchases during 1978-85 might be in the range of $45-60 billion. These totals might even be exceeded, perhaps before 1985 and certainly in subsequent years. At the start of 1979 there were Japanese estimates that Chinese orders concluded or under negotiation with Japanese industry amounted to $79 billion.[125] These included a number of massive projects, among them Japanese equipment for Yangtse and Yellow river hydro-power projects, a Japanese steel mill near Shanghai, and Japanese participation in oil exploration and exploitation and petrochemical developments. In addition there were American hotel developments in Peking and elsewhere, German coal mine development, and large deals with Britain and France. The normalization of diplomatic relations with the United States seemed bound to increase the available flow of plant and technology further and, by strengthening competition among Western suppliers, to bring down prices or improve terms.

On the export side, traditional Chinese exports like agricultural goods showed a gently rising trend through the 1970s. Its basis, however, was not a growing surplus of production over demand. It was rather the way in which a command economy was able to free quantities of produce to take advantage of particular opportunities in particular markets at particular times. Rice, for example, was sold in some quantities to Indonesia and, in competition with Thailand, in Malaysia.[126] Other markets were found from time to time in Southeast Asia and even Europe. But if export earnings were to be increased, it was clear that the increase would have to come in other areas. Given China's relative resource endowments, the translation of labor, with which the country was so plentifully supplied, into capital was the most obvious strategy of all. It was an aim pursued in a variety of ways. One was through an emphasis on labor-intensive exports such as textiles. During the decade from the mid-1960s to the mid-

1970s, while there was no increase in the cloth ration for the average citizen, annual net imports of cotton rose and so did exports of fabric, yarn, and clothing.[127] This must have reflected a policy of importing fibers and exporting manufactured fabrics and clothes. The possibilities in this area were likely to grow. Though Chinese textiles were likely to encounter quantitative difficulties, in the form of quotas in some markets, gains could be made through exporting higher quality and higher-priced goods. Once the petrochemical and fiber plants purchased in 1974 and 1975 came on stream, it became easier to diversify production and exports into synthetics, mixed fibers, and higher quality garments. In 1978, the value of textile exports seems to have risen by some 10 percent, partly for such reasons.

Parallel efforts were made to improve the marketing of China's goods and to widen her export base. There were official warnings about the need to improve quality, packaging, and labeling.[128] Peking began to accept foreign trademarks and to register her own abroad.[129] Market surveys were undertaken, and trading bodies were encouraged to take part in foreign trade fairs.[130] The Chinese authorities paid closer attention to guaranteed delivery dates, foreign specifications, assured supplies for foreign customers, and production for market requirements. China's chief economic planner, Yu Chiu-li, also made it clear in mid-1978 that special factories and areas would be set aside to deal in export goods. Some major import deals were arranged so that the purchase price for the equipment and technology was to be repaid from the end output (compensation agreements). China's customers reported a new willingness to import, process, and reexport a variety of goods such as coffee beans from Africa, jade from Burma, ivory from Tanzania, and undyed cloth from Japan.[131] Senior Chinese officials spoke of a willingness to process foreign materials to foreign specifications.[132] Some foreigners encountered suggestions that if they were prepared to set up factories to produce goods for export, the government would provide sites, facilities, and labor. The Chinese authorities found that the proprietary technologies of international manufacturers could be made available either through foreign participation in investment or through licensing operations. Tourism began to receive active encouragement.[133] Foreign operators, such as airlines, found they were able to organize tours with the explicit blessing of the administration. In 1978, the Bank of China began to offer traveler's checks for sale.[134] Within China, the transport infrastructure required for trade and tourism received attention, from road construction and hotels to improvements in port efficiency. Perhaps most important of all, the government tried to make individual provinces and prefectures aware of their own increased responsibility for the new export drive.[135]

Yet the export base remained narrow. To widen it meant importing more equipment and technology to strengthen the export program. It was therefore not surprising that one of the major elements of the 1977/78 industrial import program should have been the strengthening of China's export capacity. It was Teng Hsiao-ping who, as early as August 1975, spoke of the need to import foreign coal-mining equipment for the purpose of increasing coal exports. In 1977/78, there were major purchases in the areas of steel and electronics which would serve, among other things, such purposes. Machinery and equipment were bought to develop China's nonferrous metal potential.[136] And the fertilizer, pesticide, crop-seed, and breeding-stock import programs suggested a similarly dual purpose. There were, however, limiting factors. They had to do with limits on China's capacity to produce exports, including the competing domestic claims on resources which might be directed to, or derived from, foreign trade. And there were questions about China's absorptive and innovative capacities in technical areas. Some categories of exports, including textiles and some manufactures, were likely to encounter local protectionism in some of China's most important potential markets, including Japan and the United States. Sales, even under compensation agreements, were subject to the vagaries of the international marketplace. And though the Chinese authorities clearly placed great hopes on an increase of oil exports, some caution about these prospects also seemed to be in order. This is not to deny that by the end of 1978 substantial and promising developments had taken place. The drive for oil had helped to intensify cooperation with the advanced industrial world. Substantial contracts for exploration, processing, and sales had been negotiated or were under discussion, especially with Japan[137] but also with France and the United States.[138] Under the trade agreement with Tokyo, China undertook to sell Japan 7 million tons of oil in 1978, rising to 15 million tons in 1982, plus totals of over 5 million tons of coking coal and 3.3-3.9 million tons of steam coal for power stations.[139] China's tanker facilities seemed adequate, and her large tankers were being used on the Japan-China run and to import Algerian oil to southern China.[140] Refinery and petrochemical facilities were being substantially expanded.[141] On the other hand, by the mid-1970s China was consuming some 90 percent of her own oil output, and domestic demand was increasing at a rapid clip. The government suggested to the Japanese estimates suggested that Chinese consumption would rise faster than production, with crude-oil export capacity Japan from some 137,000 barrels per day in 1978 to 1 million barrels per day in 1983 or 1984 representing, at 1978 prices, export earnings of some $5 billion per annum.[142] Yet some Japanese estimates suggested that Chinese comsumption would rise faster than production, its crude-oil export capacity dropping to zero sometime during the mid-1980s.[143] Even kinder U.S. estimates did not suggest that China's oil exports would, by the earlier 1980s, exceed some 20 million tons per annum.[144] And, even if those assessments proved to be unduly pessimistic, some questions were likely to persist.

Moreover, Chinese oil was not cheap and would not become cheaper in real terms, because hitherto untapped reserves were likely to be more expensive to recover, partly because of the more difficult location of new deposits, involving higher extraction and transport costs including, in some areas, the heating of oil in transit. The quality of Chinese oil on offer was also questionable. It had a high admixture of water and wax and a high nitrogen content. In 1976, Japanese estimates suggested that Chinese oil might cost an additional $2-$3 per barrel to dewax.[145] The nitrogen meant that Chinese oil, if used as fuel, would produce quantities of nitrogen oxide as an air pollutant, an especially sensitive political issue in Japan. In any case, the Taching crude which China was selling was not suitable for the lighter distillates Japan most urgently needed, 70 percent of the barrel being heavy oils. Such problems might not be insuperable. Refineries might be persuaded to vary their input mixes so as to accommodate some oils with a high paraffin content. Or Peking could try to persuade a large customer like Japan to build new cracking plants to deal with the particular properties of Chinese crude, if necessary accepting a somewhat lower selling price for the oil. Or some of China's lighter crudes might be allocated for export. And in any case, oil sales could be, and were, diversified, with some oil being sold to customers like the Philippines and Thailand.[146]

Yet, from the point of view of the customers, difficulties remained. Cracking plants and other facilities built to deal with Taching crude could become unsuitable if the oil from new Chinese fields, which would have to supply China's export needs during the later 1980s, turned out to have different properties. Potential customers in Europe and the eastern United States were confronted by substantial transport costs while the western United States had ample Alaskan oil. The slowing down of economic growth in the advanced industrial democracies, together with policies to slow down the growth of energy demand and diversify energy sources, meant a more slowly rising demand for China's oil. Doubts of this kind may have been reinforced by political considerations. Certainly there were signs of Japanese resistance to increasing reliance upon Chinese oil.[147] In all, it seemed unlikely that, at least in the nearer future, Japan (or any other major customer) would allow herself to become unduly reliant on Chinese supplies. Without an energy crunch in the advanced industrial democracies, Chinese oil supplies probably would not become a major factor in the international marketplace and a major source of political leverage during the 1980s.

Other trading difficulties could arise. The prices of Chinese imports might rise faster than the prices of her exports. Much would depend, therefore, on the policies of OPEC and Western energy prices and their impact on the prices of Western products. Much would equally depend on Western inflation rates in general and especially on the success of the Carter

administration in stabilizing the U.S. economy. Some problems of this kind had already appeared by 1978. The rise of the
Yen vis-à-vis the dollar was tending to make Japanese goods
less desirable.[148] On the other hand, at least some part of the
surge in Chinese imports in 1977/78 may have been in
anticipation both of further Western price rises and of
increasing pressure on China's price levels, caused by such
things as the inflationary pressures of domestic wage rises and
of some categories of imports. Or again, China might be
constrained by competition between herself and the Soviet
Union for Western goods (such as military equipment) whose
supply was limited and whose increase in output would
require time, a good deal of capital, and continuing political
goodwill. Similarly, as the recovery of the West's economy got
under way, it was not certain whether Western firms and
institutions would wish to continue to rely heavily on the
China trade or to supply credits on easy terms in what might
become a tighter money market. Such hesitations were liable to
be strengthened, in the medium term, as Western technology
exports (for example, in the petrochemical field) began to
encounter competition from the underpriced products of the
Chinese factories which the West had originally helped to
build. Such competition might occur in third markets or else
within the Western countries themselves, as Chinese goods
contracted for under compensation agreements began to
appear on the market.

No less were the difficulties caused by competing claims on
Chinese resources. The most important were probably the
pressures of rising demand as a result of population increase
and rising consumer expectations. Whatever the differences in
estimates of the precise rate of growth of China's population, it
was clear that the resources required to feed, clothe, and house
the additional numbers, even at comparatively modest levels of
comfort, would seriously reduce the resources that might
otherwise be available to increase China's exports. At the same
time, the process of China's industrialization and farm
modernization was further increasing domestic demand levels
in a number of important areas including energy and
transport. And the growth of output was tending to increase

still further the demand for imports at the same time as consumer demand was tending to divert resources away from investment and from the export drive. Insofar as the government emphasized material incentives and wage rises in urban areas, moreover, it was creating possible further difficulties: if wage differentials between city and country increased, there might be rising pressures for higher consumption in rural areas.

The claims of the military inevitably had an impact on China's export/import balance. It was not just the direct claim on import capacity, or the obvious fact that resources allocated to the military sector did not directly contribute to growth and economic expansion, but that the claims of the defense community were bound to become more urgent in an era when China's rivals were developing novel systems likely to have serious consequences for China's relative military standing. Other competing claims came from various areas of foreign policy; for example, the requirements of the competition with the Soviet union in the Third World and the need to design a foreign trade policy that would be minimally constrained by the requirements of COCOM.

Difficulties were bound to arise, too, in relation to the domestic politics of the trading program, and hence also its consequences for overall investment. To begin with, there were the administrative strains which so large a program, so suddenly imposed, was sure to create for the administrative apparatus, manned by too few technically competent personnel. There was also the problem of the domestic investment required to support imported plant and technology. Though the ratio of imports to supporting investment is to some extent a matter of guesswork, Japanese estimates in 1978 were that the usual ratio was 2:1 or 3:1, with China (given her policy of minimizing import costs) at the high end of the span. In general, then, one would expect that a plant and equipment import program of $50 billion between 1978 and 1985 would require a supporting domestic investment of $100-$150 billion, bringing the total of import-related investment to approximately $150-$200 billion at 1978 prices, or $21-$28.5 billion per annum. Assuming an average GNP of $450 billion during the period, that would yield an investment total of roughly 5 to 6 percent of the GNP or, assuming a total domestic-investment program of 20 to 25 percent of the GNP, roughly one-quarter of a very high level of domestic investment.[149] Such a scale of investment appeared feasible but bold, liable to place considerable strains upon the domestic political and economic system, the more so if some of the external trends developed unfavorably. Such developments would make more acute the differences that, in any case, seemed bound to arise within the governmental coalition. They could make any general tensions between the Hua and Teng segments of the government more severe. These would include regional differences, personality disputes, and the tensions that the evident downgrading of the economic—and hence many of the political—aspects of Mao's inheritance was sure to create. Such developments also could revive fundamental disputes about political priorities and organizational forms. If any major aspect of the program went awry, Teng might find himself once more under fire for promoting the dubious expedient of reliance on foreign technology and management practices.

And yet, while the trading policies of the new regime meant much more intensive and extensive activity, they do not seem to have involved—or at least not in the short term—a major redirection among markets and sources of supply. Ever since 1960, China's trade had been dominated by exchanges with the West, with Hong Kong and the Third World countries, especially Southeast Asia, serving as sources of foreign exchange with which to pay for imports from the advanced industrial democracies.[150] In 1976, for example, almost two-thirds of China's imports came from Western Europe and Japan, areas with which she had a total trading deficit of approximately $1.1 billion. But half her total exports went to Hong Kong and the LDCs, areas with which she had a surplus of some $2.5 billion. China's Hong Kong earnings were especially significant. Visible trade with Hong Kong consisted largely of the export of agriculture-based Chinese products, and these rose even during 1975/76, when China's foreign trade as a whole declined. It rose further in 1977 and 1978 and may, between 1976 and 1978, have gone up from approximately $1.5

to $2.5 billion. But Hong Kong was useful in more ways than those implied by gross figures of visible earnings. It was a source of invisible income and, no less importantly, a convenient place in which to engage in a number of international trading and financial activities. At times, these activities included trading at arms length with politically unacceptable regimes, including that of South Korea.

China made serious attempts to expand her European trade, apparently for both economic and political reasons. The economic considerations appeared to be several. One was to reduce the unfavorable trade-and-payments balance with Western Europe. A second may have been, by securing access to West European technology, to intensify trade rivalry among the EEC, Japan, and the United States for China's benefit. At the same time, Europe provided a convenient and politically acceptable channel for the acquisition of Western money and advanced technologies, both civil and military. The increase in the value of the yen, following the currency movements of 1977/78, may also have helped to make European goods more attractive in relation to Japanese ones. These economic considerations clearly dovetailed neatly with China's interest in strengthening Europe as a counterweight to the Soviet Union and maintaining and increasing the pressures on the Western borders of the Soviet empire. The interest in stronger ties with the EEC did not originate with the Hua regime. Diplomatic relations with the Community were opened in September 1975. Discussions on a trade agreement were begun in 1976 and resumed, following the change of government in Peking, in 1977 and 1978. A five-year agreement was signed in April 1978, providing for most-favored-nation treatment for China and a general liberalization of China's access to European markets.[151] The agreement provided a legal framework for relations between China and the Community, and though the accord had little to say directly about increased Chinese imports from Europe, China moved strongly in that direction. Agreements were concluded with several Community states, notably in the seven-year trade agreement with France, signed in December and providing for $13.6 billion worth of trade.[152] There was to be cooperation in a variety of fields including agriculture, energy resources, mining, and steel. And China agreed to buy French equipment for two nuclear power stations.

China's most important single trading partner was undoubtedly Japan. The new leadership in Peking sought with some energy to expand that partnership. From 1976, Chinese trade with Japan expanded at a somewhat quicker rate than Chinese trade generally. The February 1978 trade agreement,[153] with its $20 billion of trade, did not provide for a trading volume significantly larger than the $18 billion of trade exchanged by the two countries in the previous eight years. Nor was all the trade it provided for strictly speaking "new" trade. The Chinese agreement of 24 June 1978 with Nippon Steel to build a $2 billion steelworks at Shanghai, for example, had already been under negotiation when the general agreement was signed. Yet the February arrangements were important for a number of reasons. They formalized the trading relationship and provided a basis for further trade expansion. By October, Teng was speaking of quadrupling the trade provided for by the agreement,[154] and by January the figures seemed to bear him out.[155] The agreement assured China of a steady and steadily expanding market for its crude oil while, possessed of such a stable market, she became an even more attractive focus for sellers of equipment and technology. China was assured of a steady supply of up-to-date technology and equipment from a supplier with low transport costs. Even more important were the political dimensions. The agreement strengthened a bilateral relationship encouraged by the United States. It prepared the way for the signature of the treaty of peace and friendship a few months later and hence also for subsequent normalization of relations with the United States. At the same time these links might tend, most helpfully from Peking's point of view, to weaken the relationship between Japan and the Soviet Union. Expansion of trade with Japan was also the precursor of, rather than a substitute for, a policy of diversification of sources of supply. There were deals with a variety of countries, for example, with Brazil on the supply of iron ore.[156] Above all, there were signs of a Chinese desire to do more business with the United States in fields as various as wheat supplies and agricultural technology acquisition, mining, steel, and aircraft.[157]

Up to 1977/78, the impact of these trading activities on the Chinese economy were in some respects limited. Though trade expanded rapidly during the 1970s, it was never more than equivalent to some 5 percent of China's GNP. The total volume rose from $4 to $14 billion between 1970 and 1977.[158] Yet capital-goods imports, the most significant component of trade from the point of view of China's industrial development, do not seem to have exceeded 30 percent or so of imports even in peak import years such as those from 1974 to 1976. And there is Robert Dernberger's suggestion that machinery and equipment may, for most of the 1960s and 1970s, have accounted for about one-third of total imports and one-tenth of the total domestic supply of new machinery and equipment.[159] Even if, as seems likely, the proportion were higher in some later years, the volume of industrial imports may not have made a large difference to aggregate capital formation. In this area of trade, and the associated financing, Chinese policies had long been conservative and declaratory policies more conservative still. China's leaders were deeply impressed by the "debt trap" which had snared pre-1949 Chinese administrations and the devastating political consequences of this for the Chiang Kai-shek government. After 1949, and even in the period of more flexible international-finance policies of 1977/78, the government was adamant that China's financial fate must remain in her own hands and that large foreign indebtedness was impermissible. As late as 1977, senior political figures insisted that China would not take foreign loans.[160] In fact, the official claims were never quite true. China had for some time accepted short- and medium-term credits (up to five years) in the form of supplier credits arranged in ways that did not contravene the political inhibitions against the word "debt." Similarly, she had aimed at balanced trade, but latterly accepted multilateral balancing.

The constraints imposed by this conservatism became more burdensome in the mid-1970s. In the years 1973-75 the accumulated deficit on visible trade may have been as much as $1.2 billion and, with the nonsocialist countries alone, as much as $2.2 billion.[161] The trading difficulties of 1974/75 were compounded by China's increased import requirements for cotton and grain during part of the period. The trading balance was back in surplus by 1977, but largely through a cutting down on imports. There was no adequate basis for rapid export expansion.

China's newly voracious appetite for industrial and technical imports in 1976-78 made fresh arrangements necessary. Japanese estimates of the total cost of Chairman Hua's 1977-85 modernization proposals ranged from $437 to $600 billion.[162] The financing requirements for such a program would clearly be substantial. The new government's assessments coincided with ample evidence that there was no shortage of cash on international money markets.[163] Its rhetoric about self-reliance was maintained. But if it could congratulate itself on installing and adapting foreign petrochemical plants as evidence of the spirit of self-reliance, then, as Christopher Howe has said, "clearly there are no technical limits to what is politically acceptable in foreign trade."[164] The first senior Chinese banking delegation went abroad in the spring of 1977 and visited Belgium, Britain, Switzerland, and West Germany. There were some lower-level soundings in Japan and the United States, as well as in Europe, about credits for longer than five years, and perhaps even loans. By 1978 Western bankers were beating a path to Peking doors, and the Chinese authorities were beginning to be extremely well informed about the detailed operations of Western financial and money markets. In financial terms, too, the room for flexibility was considerable.

By 1978 China's reserves were estimated to be around $5.5 billion, with $2.5 billion in hard currencies and another $3 billion in gold.[165] Some of these reserves could be, and no doubt were, deposited at interest in various places. Such a reserve level seemed adequate in the light of the Chinese government's tight control of economic and financial affairs and the nature of its trade management. These funds could give the authorities some freedom of movement. They could use the reserves, at least in part, for direct payment of imports. Given China's excellent credit status in the West and the general political circumstances of the time, there was little reason why her financial managers should not run down these funds to quite low levels if this seemed desirable for a brief period. Or the reserves could be used to finance the interest payments on foreign loans or credits. In comparison with this level of reserves, mid-1978 Western estimates suggested that China's annual commitments under existing payments provisions of various kinds were approximately $2.5 billion.[166]

Naturally, the government also tried to maximize foreign earnings, not only through exports but through other methods. In 1977 the foreign relatives of Chinese citizens were urged to send cash rather than packages to China, and at the beginning of 1978 a more comprehensive policy was announced for tapping the wealth and skills of the 22 million overseas Chinese.[167] Tourism was further encouraged. The U.S. International Hotel chain was brought in to help build and manage five to seven hotels, beginning with a one-thousand-bed structure in Peking, and to help train staff.[168] In the first half of 1978 there seem to have been almost ten times as many foreign visitors in China as in the whole of the previous year. As well, the Chinese authorities invested in Western markets, with a sharp eye for growth potential.[169] Trading and financial operations through Hong Kong were encouraged, and the government appeared to envisage the possibility that something similar might happen in Taiwan.

Such cushions of earnings and reserves meant that China was in no hurry to sign loan agreements. The lead times inherent in organizing and financing major industrial projects gave Peking further leeway. Li Hsien-nien made it clear that there was nothing very urgent about securing foreign credits, and similar messages were consistently conveyed by the officials of the Bank of China.[170] In the meantime, a variety of financing methods could be and were pursued. One that remained was deferred payments. The standard procedure seemed to be for China to pay 15 percent of the price of the imports as down payment and perhaps 20 to 25 percent for down payment plus first payment at the time of initial delivery, with the remainder paid in installments over five years, probably at the minimum OECD rates of 7-1/4 percent. Inevitably this procedure, which usually involved the exporter obtaining a loan from his own export-import bank, amounted to supplier credits and, from China's point of view, to the acceptance of short-term debt. Teng admitted as much in a foreign interview.[171] Various extensions of this principle were beginning to be put into practice or were under consideration by the latter part of 1978. One was Chinese willingness to accept import financing directly from Western banks, tied to imports from the same Western country. Another was the willingness of some Chinese customers, notably in Japan, to pay in advance for deliveries, especially of coal and oil, with understandings linking this method of finance to Chinese purchases in Japan. More importantly, China began to extend the term-of-payments arrangements beyond five years. Several seven-year agreements were recorded, and the government approached Japan with suggestions about ten-year pay-back schedules.[172] On the other hand, there were signs as 1978 wore on that Chinese trading authorities were becoming dissatisfied with the margins suppliers were claiming for such credits, which increasingly tended to incorporate an element over and above the cost of the credit to the suppliers themselves.[173]

Another financing method China found convenient was the maintenance of reciprocal accounts between the Bank of China and banks in the Western world. The method was for foreign banks to make hard-currency deposits with the Bank of China with China, in turn, depositing an equivalent sum in Renminbi with the foreign bank concerned. The nonconvertible Renminbi played the role of security for the loan of the hard-currency deposits which China could use to finance imports. In 1977 China was estimated to have received some $500 million worth of foreign hard-currency deposits, effectively interest-free. A third method, akin to this, was for the Bank of China and Western banks to deposit third currencies with one another. In such an exchange, if a foreign bank deposited more, China was in effect receiving a loan. Following the conclusion of the Japan-China trade agreement, Japanese banks arranged yen deposits with the Bank of China. Li Hsien-nien suggested that the method would continue to be used. In 1980, he told a delegation from Japan, when Chinese development projects were in full swing, that China would ask for deposits to be made with the Bank of China.[174] A fourth method, and another variant on these themes, was for the Bank of China to borrow in a Western interbank market, for example in London. In 1974 Peking was reported to have borrowed in this way for periods up to a year;[175] and in 1978 there was speculation that China might, in somewhat similar fashion, move into the Eurodollar market. Another method again for financing China's foreign operations was for the Bank of China (as well as Chinese-owned banks in centers like Hong Kong) to accept time deposits from individual or corporate depositors.[176] These deposits, for periods of up to seven years or more, were in effect loans extended to China by the depositor. More far-reaching arrangements were under discussion.

These policies amounted to an attempt to increase the variety and volume of the credit lines available to China, together with a shifting of responsibility for credits and, hence, also of risks, from the Chinese customer to the foreign supplier. At the same time, there was an attempt to decrease the volume of financing required. The two most notable methods employed were compensation agreements with foreign suppliers and Chinese encouragement of foreign equity financing and joint ventures on Chinese soil. In the first type of arrangement, the foreign supplier accepted payment in the form of goods from the plant he had helped to build. Both methods, therefore, depended on the ability and willingness of the foreign participants to accept future distribution and marketing risks and responsibilities. They also depended on the degree of security that the foreign participants could be offered. The Chinese authorities recognized the point. By the end of 1978, new laws were being prepared to guarantee foreign partners their share of ownership (up to 49 percent) in joint ventures, not only in property rights but in the ownership of technology and the right to remit profits outside China.[177]

In sum, by the end of 1978 China had accepted, at least in principle, most normal Western methods of finance including, somewhat reluctantly, government-to-government loans.[178] But she seemed to be leaning less toward supplier credits than toward cash purchases, financed through interbank deposits or tightly arranged, syndicated bank lending. The Chinese authorities appeared to prefer fixed-rate financing tied to specific projects and guaranteed by the government of the exporting country. In view of their credit rating, the Chinese were able to accept loans at minimum OECD rates: 7-1/4 percent up to five years and 7-1/2 percent over five years. But the effectiveness of Western banking guidelines was bound to depend on the demand for capital within the Western world as well as on general political desiderata. So Li Hsien-nien may have been speaking to a receptive audience when he hinted, through the chairman of Nippon Steel, Yoshihiro Inayama, that China would consider softer credit terms. The Japanese Overseas Economic Cooperation Fund was known to be in a position to lend for terms up to thirty years at 3 percent for foreign aid purposes. And, indeed, by late 1978 there were various rumors and suggestions about possible Chinese access to such financing, either directly or in the form of mixed packages of cheap and commercial loans, bearing an average rate of return of between 4-1/2 and 6 percent.[179]

But there also remained a number of constraints. The Chinese refused to accept loans denominated in hardening currencies, notably yen and deutsche marks. They appear, for example, to have rejected an offer in September 1978 by the Japanese government to lend China some 200 billion yen at 6 percent (or 1-1/4 percent below the OECD guideline level), largely on the grounds that they would not take yen even at such a rate. China also tended to avoid general-purpose loans, as distinct from project financing. She rejected floating-rate finance as a capitalist instrument, not capable of sufficiently close control by her own financial managers. And the Chinese tended to avoid large, and especially international, bank syndicates. They appeared to prefer dealing with smaller national syndicates, or single banks, especially in the field of supplier credits where guarantees and even subsidies from the government of the supplier country were likely to be required.

From the point of view of China's partners and suppliers, a number of larger questions remained. The basic, and most obvious, one was how large China's import program would prove to be and what proportion of it would require debt financing. By the end of 1978, Western estimates on this point varied widely. Citicorp, for example, was reported to be expecting a Chinese debt total of $12 billion by 1983, while the Bank of America was expecting $30 billion by 1985.[180] This raised, in turn, the question of how China could or would pay back large, long-term loans. Many Western observers doubted whether a Chinese export total of around $7 billion in 1977, even if it were to expand at an average annual rate of 10 to 20 percent, would be an adequate basis on which to support massive debt levels. Moreover, both the volume of credits available to China and its terms were likely to be sensitive to larger trends within the Western economies. As long as the Western recession lasted, the wish to stimulate industrial activity at home, as well as the need to employ capital profitably, would create pressures on Western governments and banks to grant softer loans on more favorable terms. But if the major Western economies picked up, these conditions might not last. In addition, there were a number of political risks in lending to China which, though difficult to estimate with precision, were likely to be large.

From Peking's own point of view, what was at issue was not merely a set of political principles and the detailed management of China's relationships with the outside world, but the proper mix between the urgent requirements of financing development and the prudential needs of financial management. This last consideration was concerned with things like the desirable ratio of current earnings to debt servicing and the reaction of foreign lenders to Chinese policies on this vital point. In 1976, the debt-service ratio had risen as high as 17 to 22 percent.[181] Though the increase in exports during the following year had brought the ratio down to some 9.3 percent, the trading and credit policies of 1977/78 were bound to raise questions about its movement in future years. Batsavage and Davie suggest that, if China purchased $3 billion worth of plant each year between 1978 and 1982, then, assuming also a 10 percent annual export increase, 7 percent interest rates, and ten-year credit terms, China's debt-service ratio would range from 4 to 11 percent between 1981 and 1985 and, even including down payments, peak at a safe 15 percent.[182] However, later figures suggested a much larger Chinese purchase program, which might involve average annual import figures of $7 billion rather than $3 billion. In that event, China would presumably be compelled to adopt more complicated policies, perhaps including much longer-term loans. At any rate, her officials indicated that they were anxious not to allow the debt-service ratio to go above 20 percent.[183]

It was, perhaps, significant that the only large-scale debt arrangements actually signed by the Chinese up to the end of 1978—as distinct from those discussed or publicized—remained the $1.2 billion deposit scheme with a ten-bank consortium of British banks providing for 7-1/4 percent over five years. Indeed, though there were some questions in the West about whether China might not be in danger of overextending herself financially, the real problems could turn out to be quite the opposite. If the gap between the expectations which had been created in 1977/78 and the eventual reality was too great, there might even be a political backlash of sorts. For the time being, Western traders and bankers seemed prepared to wait. They were aware that Chinese officials were all but overwhelmed by the flood of Western suggestions and applications of 1978. They were aware also that the Peking government had given its own officials until October 1979 to define China's financial needs and requirements more closely. But when the definitions did emerge, the outside world's assessment of them would carry political as well as economic consequences.

There was one other, very different, category of problem with China's new technology import policy. It concerned her ability to absorb technology imports and to innovate on the basis of them. These were questions about a relatively thin and uneven modern industry sector. As China invited foreign visitors, observers were able to see for themselves the wide variations between some excellent modern factories, for instance in Harbin and the dilapidated facilities elsewhere. It was not merely that, on the showing of the Chinese authorities themselves the level of skills was adequate, indiscipline widespread, and local inertia a basic fact of industrial and political life. There were problems about the fragmentation of the industrial sector, language difficulties between different parts of the country, and problems about using foreign machinery in the face of local xenophobia. The demoralizing effects of cronyism in management and party, the system of personal privileges quite unrelated to economic or innovative performance, and the forces of local politics were bound to hamper the implementation of any planning initiative. In China, as elsewhere, material incentives may not be enough. What may be needed is a general social environment which is welcoming to productivity and quantifiable performance. Though the government was clearly trying to produce this in 1977/78, the creation and maintenance of such an environment is a complex affair, in which the nature of the prevailing political and social beliefs, as well as their relationship to practical habits at grass-roots levels, have an important and possibly decisive role to play. In relation to modernization, therefore, what was at issue was not just, and perhaps not primarily, government policy but rather a social and psychological environment that was hospitable and receptive to innovation and change. Whether that environment existed in China, or could be quickly created, was not clear.

That was only one, though perhaps the most important, of the question marks surrounding the relationship between Chinese industrial performance and the processes of modernization. Some of the other issues were whether the price structure was such as to stimulate the development of new products; whether the rules, incentives, and penalties in industrial management, including the experience of past purges, encouraged risk-taking, experimentation, and high-quality production rather than choices in favor of the known and predictable and of quantity production; whether there was an adequate maintenance and service sector to accompany and sustain production; and to what extent production and product development may have been hampered by the absence of such servicing personnel and what larger economic costs might have been imposed by any lags in this area. Outside observers wishing to judge the effects of the import program and the rate of development of China's technical capacities might, it seemed, do well to distinguish between rises in aggregate quantitative indicators, such as increases in the GNP or total industrial production or transport performance in terms of ton-miles or steel production, and rates of increase in the sophistication of Chinese products or production methods.

4
Technology

In the realm of technology, questions of external acquisition are secondary to problems of its creation, adaptation, absorption, and dissemination at home. The Chinese attitude to these has been ambivalent, as the Chinese attitude to the definition and achievement of modernity has been ambivalent. There has been no recent attempt to deny that Western forms of modernity have meant more powerful economic structures, higher standards of living, and greater military capacity. On the other hand, there has been a reluctance to concede that China's relative lack of economic and technical power could be allowed to diminish, let alone to contradict, her ancient sense of cultural superiority. The way out of the dilemma has been a search, sporadically interrupted by domestic objections, for economic growth and technological innovation on Chinese terms, in pursuit of a Chinese definition of progress, and to sustain a Chinese desire for cultural and national power. During the 1950s, the Soviet model of development and modernity could be used in the pursuit of Chinese development and in ways that rejected the capitalist Western version of modern society. During the 1960s, the Soviet model itself became objectionable as revisionist, and the search for progress had to be based even more firmly on models developed within China. Nor were the new models designed only for narrow Chinese purposes. They would sustain China's independence. But that independence would, in turn, allow her to play a central political role in a revolutionary movement which was in principle global. Modernity was as necessary for revolution as revolution was for the achievement of modernity. While being revolutionary meant transforming the economic base so as to achieve new social forms, this was entirely compatible with assumptions about China's central role in a worldwide revolutionary culture.

That culture meant stressing the continuing importance of class struggle and the consolidation of the dictatorship of the proletariat. The latter, in particular, became more necessary than ever as the search for modernity was pressed, for it would provide the framework within which technical expertise might be allowed to flourish without producing bourgeois thinking of a kind likely to blunt the revolutionary drive. To achieve these aims called for revolutionary activism. In economic and technical matters, as in others, Mao and his disciples stressed the human factors of morale, political consciousness, and determination rather than material factors. The notion of the masses, inspired by appropriate ideas, as an objective political force able to bring about qualitative changes in economic and social development marked many aspects of the chairman's thought. This in turn led him to criticize undue devotion to established hierarchies and routines and undue emphasis on technical equipment rather than on men and human ingenuity. In sum, neither technology acquisition nor diffusion should be allowed to determine, or even strongly to influence, political and social policies and organizations which were in tune with overriding historical needs. Together with this went a profound suspicion, based not so much on revolutionary convictions as on bitter experience during the century before 1949 (and again at the end of the 1950s), of the potentially disruptive effects of foreign techniques and ideas on Chinese ways and the desirability of self-reliance. Insofar as technology meant foreignness, it was to be treated with reserve and only in the context of strengthening China's eventual capacity for self-reliance. Those groups that argued in favor of foreign technology therefore tended, from time to time, to become vulnerable to charges of running after foreigners.

The result of these considerations was not, however, an abandonment of technology acquisition. Over the thirty years of the PRC's existence, its governments generally stressed the need for economic growth. For most of that period, they also recognized that growth required heavy reliance upon imported technology and know-how and that the essential problem was not whether to import it but how to manage the import policy so as to fit most comfortably with China's preferred economic and political arrangements, including the aim of self-reliance. It was a question of selectivity, of neutralizing undesirable side effects and of the domestication of imported technology. As *Red Flag* put it with cold pragmatism, "the point is not whether we need or do not need to learn good things from foreign countries but how to learn them."[1]

The technology base for the 1970s was established, for the most part, during the 1950s when China enjoyed what was probably one of the more massive technology transfers in history in the form of Soviet aid. The reassertion of political moderation and economic rationality in the early 1970s, following on the fluctuations of the previous decade, brought renewed emphasis on modernization. But the new policies were not a simple return to those of the 1950s. The Chinese authorities were careful not to become overly dependent on one supplier or group of suppliers. They attempted to maintain a more careful balance between various industrial and economic sectors and the technologies appropriate to them. And they tried not merely to import machinery and goods but to obtain blueprints, specifications, and laboratory reports,[2] and to dispatch technical delegations abroad. Qualitatively, there was a marked emphasis on the development end of the R and D spectrum. This was understandable. Scarce resources had to be directed to the nation's most urgent needs. When so much needed to be done, the most urgent general need seemed to be for the development of low and middle-level skills and capacities, adaptive skills, manufacturing capacities, and, not least, the exploitation of the potential inherent in the skills, including the traditional handicraft skills, existing in China's population, which might be harnessed to a variety of industrial and developmental purposes. Prevailing patterns of training tended to widen the group of people with some technical grasp, rather than to increase the depth of training. Even the workshops and plants attached to scientific institutes seem to have been used to educate technicians and extend existing practice rather than to diffuse newly created knowledge. Until a large industrial infrastructure had been created, higher-level and research skills would be both expensive[3] and impossible to exploit. There were other considerations. The regional tensions of the Cultural Revolution and its aftermath did not lend themselves to the creation and development of a substantial and centrally directed high-technology sector. The substantial weakening of the Academy of Science's control over research institutes between the mid-1960s and mid-1970s in favor of local control was a significant pointer.[4] And the leadership was determined to avoid creating a new scientific or technocratic elite.

In importing technology, China also concentrated upon fabrication, processing, and adaptation of foreign equipment and know-how to Chinese circumstances. In particular, there was a tendency, observable since the 1950s, to concentrate on the import of prototypes. These were used to strengthen the Chinese manufacturing process by means of "reverse engineering": i.e., taking the imported machinery apart and reconstructing it. Emphasis in the key area of machine building, for example, was on variable-performance machine tools most of which were imported, copied, or adapted from foreign prototypes or designs. The benefits of technology transfer were most marked in such areas as fabrication and processing. At this level of manufacturing skills, Chinese absorption of technology appears to have been quite successful. But the import program also permitted the growth of adaptive skills and of some further development. Indeed, design modification appeared to be the chief element of China's drive during the 1970s to "retain the technological initiative" and encourage a combination of technical advance and self-reliance.[5] In the field of computers, for instance, the first electronic computers, copies of Soviet digital and analog machines, were constructed on an experimental scale during the 1950s.[6] Serial production of small digital computers with vacuum tubes was under way by 1962, and in 1966 there appeared the first transistorized digital computers. The Chinese reached third-generation level in 1973 with the production of an integrated circuit machine,[7] and two years later large-scale integration was under experimental development.[8]

The result of all this, at least in the modern industrial sector, was to give Chinese industry something of the structural and administrative flavor known in other parts of the world, including patterns of work specialization, hierarchical authority, and close control of the work force.[9] In terms of industrial technology, it has been suggested that by the mid-1970s China may have been roughly in the stages of change from mechanized manual production to semiautomated production.[10] Nevertheless, there remained not only a general lag in industrial capacity vis-à-vis the advanced industrial nations but some more specific gaps. Some had to do with industrial organization and incentive systems; others with the political and social difficulties caused by differential development; others again with education and manpower training; and last, but not least, the system appeared to have a number of weaknesses in the fields of science, research, and development.

Within industry, there were indications that managers continued up to the mid-1970s to be under pressure to fulfill preplanned production targets in terms of existing production norms and under conditions where improvements would be likely to lead to changes in norms rather than to tangible benefits for the institution or the workers or the managers themselves. Moreover, one of the principal Western motivations for industrial improvement was conspicuous by its absence: pressures to reduce costs. In a system where costs and output were planned, it was often easy to secure the acceptance of plans which incorporated continuing high costs. At the same time, the rewards for experiment, even successful experiment, could be slender and the penalties for failure huge. Industrial and innovative audacity were not likely to be encouraged in an atmosphere where an initiative might turn out, following the next turn of the political wheel, to be "revisionist." The natural consequence of such pressures was to make managers prefer tried and tested arrangements, including the purchase of tried and tested technology, possibly with some adaptation, to any experiment.[11] In all, there is some evidence for supposing that, at least by Western standards,

Chinese growth emphasized the construction of more of the same plants and the production of more of the same goods from a more efficiently used plant, rather than the construction of new plants or the shift of production to new products. These various factors appear to have combined to restrict industrial innovation in the period up to the mid-1970s in at least three ways. The fact that technological advance was so largely by way of imports tended to confine its impact geographically to the urban, modern, and large-scale industry sector. This may have increased the geographic differentiation of economic habits and patterns. The advanced sector, moreover, was that controlled partly by provincial and municipal governments but mostly by the central government which also controlled and designed trade flows and hence was able to maximize its general economic command by manipulating the growth of this sector. Thirdly, the lag in design capacities helped to restrict the rate of change of the goods that Chinese industry could produce.

There may have been other weaknesses, though the available information does not permit precise comment. It seems probable that the relationship between R and D and consumer demand, as distinct from factory or production demand, was at best tenuous. Even if one were to assume that the shortage of consumer goods was so great that effective demand existed for almost anything that could be produced, the government would probably have been wise to assume that there could be disjunctions between product innovation and end demand as and when per-capita consumption rose. The effort by 1977/78 to produce consumer goods marketable abroad gives similar indications of difficulty. Or again, one does not have the impression that the system reflected the necessary complementarity, or interdependence, between separate but adjacent technical fields or facilities. Western delegations who found appalling roads leading to modern factories could hardly fail to draw unfavorable conclusions about China's comprehensive industrial planning or systems engineering. Most important of all, though details are lacking, it is obvious that the Chinese authorities confronted especially acute manpower-allocation difficulties, especially in scientifically and technically trained personnel. One of the more important questions about China's factory import policy during the mid-1970s, for example, in the petrochemical field, was whether China had the resources of trained manpower to operate and maintain the factories at maximum efficiency.

In the areas of experimentation and innovation, upstream R and D work, and the creation of new inventions, technical products, techniques, and organizations, Chinese progress was at best fitful.[12] During the 1950s China remained very largely dependent upon Soviet technical guidance, and the development of her own research and design capacities was relatively neglected. Though the generally stimulating effects of Soviet technological imports may have lasted in some areas until the 1970s, these effects could not take the place of an indigenous Chinese innovative and developmental system. Here Chinese capacities were slender. By the mid-1970s Chinese machine tools remained twenty years behind those of the West.[13] As late as 1975, her capacity in the field of solid-state electronics was estimated to be a mere 5 percent of that of Japan.[14] And the reliance upon imports meant that capabilities obtained by this route were bound to lag behind the state of the art elsewhere. In the same year an American delegation observed that the technology gap in the field of optical lasers was something like three to five years and that "this is probably the minimum gap that can be achieved under the present system, which does not emphasize original contributions to increase knowledge."[15] Indeed, until the mid-1970s and perhaps beyond, very little research was officially approved unless it was designed to meet specific needs or at least to lead to practical results. Basic research was, in general, strongly discouraged.[16] It was discouraged by official pronouncement as well as by budgetary constraints. Research and innovation appear to have grown out of a national economic planning scheme which made very little allowance for work in basic, or pure, or theoretical fields.[17] And there was no sign that industrial or R and D managers had discretionary budgets to allocate to exploratory research with longer-term or doubtful payoffs.

While pressures to meet immediate needs were understandable, there remained something disturbingly shallow about the official attitude. What Benjamin Schwartz has called

Mao's Baconian-pragmatic view of science, the emphasis on learning by doing and by observing concrete facts is an overly simplistic view of modern scientific processes.[18] And it surely underestimates the costs of eschewing basic research and the creation of a scientific community. Those costs included the wasting of resources in reinventing existing knowledge and technology; the failure to create a new generation of scientists and technological experts to succeed the men, now in their sixties and seventies, who had received their scientific training abroad;[19] and the lack of an adequate science-communications system even within the Chinese scientific community, let alone between it and its scientific colleagues elsewhere. These gaps affected not only the scope and quality of work in the scientific sector but its ability to be of service to the economy and to the government. There was, for example, the lack of adequate feedback from the production and consumption system to research and design, a situation bound to aggravate a variety of design, utilization, and maintenance problems. In the absence of such close links between research and production, and of close evaluation of research in quantitative terms, there were reasons for thinking that in spite of the close declaratory dependence of R and D upon production, the utility of the research sector was not maximized. Even decisions to move into a new scientific or technical area tended to be based on a reading of Western literature and to depend on the import of sophisticated research equipment from abroad,[20] suggesting that the R and D system had not, by the mid-1970s, achieved a level capable of providing an adequate basis for managerial and governmental decisions.

These problems of science and technology were inevitably and intimately related to those of the education system and its ability to provide scientists, technologically trained personnel, administrators, managers, and, not least, a generation of leaders and citizens who would understand the problems of creating an advanced modern society and the urgency of the search for solutions. When the CCP came to power, some 70 to 80 percent of China's population was illiterate. Approximately one out of four school-age children was attending primary school, and less than one in ten of those who graduated went on to secondary school. The total enrollment of China's 180 tertiary educational institutions was some eighty thousand, roughly 0.015 percent of the population. During the next twenty years, primary attention was given to subsequent official educational base. By 1965, according to subsequent official claims, the primary schools contained 85 percent of the school-age children of an increased population.[21] The secondary-school population had increased from approximately one million in 1949 to nearly fifteen million. The improvements were, however, concentrated in urban areas. The most important element in the attempt to combine improvements in mass education with the identification and nurturing of special abilities was especially concentrated in the cities. This was the keypoint system under which the best students from the best primary schools were sent to the best (or keypoint) secondary schools and from there, by way of a standardized entrance examination, to the best tertiary institutions. Keypoint schools and colleges were themselves ranked by academic standing, though admission by examination performance was qualified by consideration of a student's class background and personal political record.[22] At the top of the ladder were national keypoint universities under the direct control of the Education Ministry, followed by provincial universities run by provincial authorities, and then city institutions.

The Cultural Revolution and its aftermath changed the system in several ways. There was an attempt, apparently successful, to extend primary education to all children of the appropriate age-groups. Secondary and tertiary education were expanded in scope but shortened in content and subjected to a variety of stronger outside and especially political pressures. Elite keypoint institutions were abolished, and the education system was made into a major tool for diminishing, and eventually abolishing, the differences between manual and mental work, between city and countryside. The dispatch of secondary-school students and graduates to the countryside served a number of aims, including that of disposing of young people with no further educational opportunities and no satisfactory urban jobs.[23] The assault upon hierarchy and central bureaucracy resulted in greater control by provincial and local authorities and by local revolutionary committees, and considerable local variations within the general guidelines issued by the central authorities. The upshot was that between 1965 and 1977 the primary-school population increased from approximately 116 million to 150 million and the secondary-school population quadrupled during the ten years to 1977 to just over 58 million.[24] There were attempts to play down learning by rote and to emphasize problem-solving as well as political enthusiasm.

University classes, suspended in June 1966, took longer to resume. Some tertiary institutions enrolled their first post-Cultural Revolution classes in 1970, others in subsequent years. Undergraduate courses were reduced from 4-5 years to 1-3. Courses were simplified and emphasis put upon practice. Enrollment procedures and curricula strengthened political and social considerations at the expense of intellectual elitism. During the early 1970s some critics were heard to argue that the reform movement had gone too far, that higher standards should be sought and more stress placed upon teaching theory.[25] By 1973 entrance examinations seem to have been administered in many provinces. These tendencies produced a backlash, both as part of the general anti-Confucius movement of 1973-74 and in the form of particular causes célèbres such as that of the schoolgirl who was praised for "struggling" against her teacher or the Liaoning student who protested against "formalism" in education by submitting a blank examination paper.[26] The result was a tug-of-war between groups that wished to downgrade scholarship and rigor in favor of politically acceptable postures and immediately applicable knowledge, like the Gang of Four which, according to the Hua-Teng administration, suggested that "study is useless" and "hooligans are useful,"[27] and older educational professionals and economic administrators, who were alarmed by the loss of education and skills. In early 1975 a new Education Minister was appointed, the first since the Cultural Revolution. In a series of speeches he complained that students were not studying, that academic standards at universities were far too low, that universities were doing no research, and that it was not possible at one and the same time to use intellectuals and to blackguard them.[28]

There can be little doubt that the damage done by the political disruptions of the period 1966-76 were severe.[29] The closing of educational establishments, or their intermittent treatment as political laboratories, meant that Chinese society lost a whole generation of schooling, or received it in only mutilated form. It is true that some people were able to use or circumvent the system. Some senior universities, like Peking University, were able from the early 1970s to use examination criteria for entry. Some bright youngsters were allowed to go straight from school to university. Others who had been sent to the countryside were classified as "peasants" for the purpose of university entry. The training of some younger people in the laboratories of senior scientists continued. And at lower levels there were some local efforts to remedy matters, for example, in the operation by some large industrial enterprises of their own industrial colleges and schools for workers.[30] Nevertheless, by and large, China reared a whole generation of school-leavers who tended to believe that politics and social action were all and knowledge was secondary. At the tertiary and professional levels, large numbers of potential graduates received no training at all, and many of those who did graduate were deprived of the broad grounding in the appropriate disciplines which is essential to any sustained learning or professional effort.[31] (Among the results of that, in turn, may have been a further reinforcement of the emphasis on low-level development and minor improvements in production, leaving the higher reaches of both technical studies and R and D even more neglected.) It was officially admitted that "the quality of education has declined sharply" and that the development of a whole generation had been retarded. Particular damage was said to have been done in scientific and mathematical fields.[32] When tests were conducted in 1977 among science graduates working in scientific and technical jobs in Shanghai, it was found that few were capable of reaching proper middle-school standards even in their own fields, with 68 percent failing basic mathematics, 70 percent failing physics, and 76 percent failing chemistry.[33]

Nor was it only the products of the educational machinery which were inferior. The machine itself had sustained severe damage. Whether the steady and consistent application of the principles of traditional educators, or of those of the Gang of Four, would have produced useful results may be a matter for debate. But it is hardly open to dispute that the conflict between them, and the continuing political disruption of the social and educational systems, caused severe and possibly lasting damage. The repression of teachers and intellectuals had a long history. The Hundred Flowers campaign included what Liu Shao-chi described as a "revolt of the scholars." It was followed by three to four hundred thousand arrests, the execution of some student leaders, and the taking over of a large number of universities by Party officials. The Cultural Revolution included a sustained and direct assault on teacher authority and legitimacy, and the subsequent uncertainties, including renewed maltreatment by students in 1974 and 1976, can have done little to reassure teachers about what was expected of them. It was not surprising that teaching became a profession to be avoided, that curricula were emptied of content and designed principally to avoid future political objections.[34]

Nowhere was the "reversal of verdicts" by the new government more decided than in these fields of science, technology, and education. If the previous few years were marked by a continuing tug-of-war between technical and economic advancement and the needs of domestic social revolution, or between political education and emphasis on intellectual discipline and quality, the advent of the Hua-Teng regime represented a clear victory by one side over the other. Abroad, the new policies were variously described as a "Great Leap Backwards" or a return to Liu Shao-chi. But whatever the label, they underlined the seriousness with which the government was pursuing larger aims, such as that of catching up with the advanced nations by A.D. 2000, for whose fulfillment rapid and broad-based educational and technical advance was essential.

The new government took a hard look at science and education and came to some sobering conclusions. The situation in these areas was so bad, the vice-president of the Chinese Academy of Sciences declared at the end of 1977, that "virtually everything needs to be done."[35] Inevitably, the blame was sheeted home to the anti-intellectualism of the Gang of

Four, who were charged with telling people "the more knowledge you have, the more reactionary you become" and "science is of no use" and "it is better to have workers without culture." Yet it was clear that research had to precede economic and military modernization. The whole thrust of the new administration's attitudes was to reassert the validity and utility of intellectual excellence and expertise, even at some cost to the stress on political enthusiasm. It was not that politics was to be any less in command. It was rather that intellectuals had as much right as other working people to have honest work respected. They had every right to be regarded as members in good standing of the working class.[36] Their particular contribution was no less valuable for allowing—indeed requiring—a principal concentration upon technical expertise, including its theoretical basis.[37] Scientists, technologists, researchers, and teachers must be allowed to devote no less than five-sixths of their time to professional work rather than to political education, manual labor, or direct involvement with the masses,[38] for the validation of all theory was, and would remain, practice and especially social practice.[39] It was a carefully formulated principle, which might be read as emphasizing the continued primacy of applied versus theoretical knowledge, or else the need to validate all theory (including, by implication, all political theories) by reference to actual social practice, or simply as the need to test by experiment.[40]

By the second half of 1977, the cultivation of science, technology, and research had become a political campaign, with all the consequences which flow from such a status in modern China. There were mass meetings to promote science and technology. Provincial and city Party committees met to promote the campaign. In November, a science week was held in Shanghai, reported to have been attended by two million people.[41] Conferences were held dealing with particular areas of research, which was officially declared reactivated.[42] The formation of a new State Commission on Science and Technology was announced, to be headed by the vice-president of the Academy of Sciences, Fang Yi, who also joined the Politburo. It was part of a number of administrative reorganizations, under which plans for science would in future be drawn up and coordinated by the state planning and science authorities. There would be more resources for science and better working conditions for scientists. They would also have more prestige, and the titles and authority of technical personnel, abolished during the Cultural Revolution, were gradually restored.[43] More important still, scientists were now allowed to say publicly that theory cannot be simply subordinated to practice, but that theory has a rationale of its own which must be mastered if practical benefits are to be derived from science in the longer run. It was recalled that Chou himself had in 1972 issued a call to strengthen research work and the teaching of basic theory. Suggestions were heard that priority must be given to higher education and the construction or revival of major research facilities.

Heralded by a Central Committee statement of September 1977,[44] the first National Science Conference since 1950 was held from 18 to 31 March 1978 in Peking. It heard policy statements by Chairman Hua and Vice-Chairman Teng as well as the Politburo member in charge of the new scientific and research programs, Fang Yi.[45] The conference confirmed the vanguard role of scientists in the modernization of China. The government set out four broad goals for the period 1978-85, for research in twenty-seven particular sectors, including eight to which special priority was to be given, and a twenty-three-year plan for creating a corps of scientific and technological personnel. By 1985 it was intended that China should approach or attain the advanced world's 1970s levels in several important branches of science and technology. In case anyone missed the point, Fang Yi remarked that, even then, China's adverse gap in the selected sectors would be some ten years and in the meantime the advanced countries would, of course, have made further progress. A nationwide system of research was to be created, including a number of modern research centers, while the number of professional research workers would be increased to eight hundred thousand.

The national science plan would be closely geared to the four modernizations, and it was in this context that the eight sectors had been selected for major attention and resource allocation.

The first of them was science and technology in agriculture, including an approach to modern agro-techniques. The second was energy research, including new techniques and processes for oil exploration and exploitation and the mechanization of coal mining, as well as research into solar, tidal, wind, geothermal, and nuclear power-generation methods. The third was materials science, including ore enrichment and the production of new types of building materials. The fourth was computer science, in particular large-scale and ultra-large-scale integrated circuitry and progress on software and in applied mathematics. The fifth was laser science, including laser fusion. The sixth was space science, including the development of remote sensing techniques and uses of satellites, and the development of manufacture and launch capacities for space probes and skylabs. The seventh was high-energy physics, and the eighth was genetic engineering in which basic studies were to be broadened and applications pursued in the pharmaceutical and new high-yield crop areas.

It was made clear that scientific work would be under the leadership of the Party which would also assume administrative responsibility for science and technology. At the same time, Fang Yi reemphasized that political cadres ought not to interfere in scientific work, and Teng reiterated that the main criteria for judging scientists should be their scientific contributions to socialist construction. In consequence, the scientists should be relieved of some of their administrative responsibilities and of most of their obligations to attend political study meetings. In this context of Party leadership, the scientific community was to engage not merely in scientific research but in the education of a new corps of scientists and technicians on the one hand, and of the masses on the other. The aim was to "train an army of scientists" by the end of the century, by modifying university and research-institute entrance requirements to ensure that the highest quality of students was admitted. Teng noted that China had a "great potential" for recruiting talented persons and raising the standards of the existing scientific and technical work force. But Hua added that scientific knowledge must also be disseminated across the nation. "It won't do to have only a small number or section of the people; hundreds of millions of people, the entire Chinese nation, must reach a much higher level." The means for that, according to Fang Yi, were not just schools, universities, and institutes but television and radio courses. It was from such an expanded pool of candidates that the Academy of Sciences could increase its postgraduate enrollment. Not only were these scientists to be given greater leeway in developing modern scientific methods, they were to be encouraged to study foreign achievements and to adapt these to Chinese needs.

The new leadership frankly acknowledged the superiority of Western science and technology and at least some of the difficulties which would face China in any attempt to catch up. In reviving Mao's twenty-year-old statement "On Ten Major Relationships" at the Eleventh Party Congress in August 1977, the government had also accepted its implication that lessons could and should be learned from other countries even if, in the end, the PRC had to rely on its own initiative to generate technical progress. The Central Committee said flatly that China should "keep to the principle of learning from abroad," adding, "In the natural sciences we are comparatively backward. We must strive to learn from other countries. It is necessary to improve the collection of scientific and technical information, promote international academic exchange and introduce necessary advanced techniques." Indeed, the principle of "learning from others" was written into the new state constitution, one of the many signs of official recognition of China's relative backwardness.[46] It was made abundantly clear that the country's key economic problems had no satisfactory solutions that did not involve heavy emphasis on the acquisiton and absorption of modern technology. Even clearer was the connection, in the government's mind and that of military professionals, between the importance of technical and educational modernization and the requirements of national defense.[47] For them, modernization meant very largely the acquisition of military know-how and hardware, including, in time, the know-how associated with advanced nuclear and postnuclear systems.

In sum, though the objective was self-reliance, the way to it still lay through involvement with international scientific and technical developments. These aims were pursued through a variety of means. During 1977 and 1978, there were substantial numbers of international scientific exchanges in areas ranging from cancer research to oceanography and from agricultural science to scientific instrumentation. Scientific and technical exhibitions were exchanged with other countries. Ministerial and subministerial Chinese delegations toured foreign technical centers. Chinese students and scientists were once more allowed to work abroad.[48] And there were a number of technical cooperation agreements with Western nations. At the beginning of 1978 one such agreement was made with France. It provided for cooperation in animal genetics, pharmacology, scientific information and information science, geology, telecommunications, and sensing techniques. Not surprisingly, in view of their interest in the military dimensions of such exchanges, the Chinese attempted to make French willingness to supply sophisticated military equipment, including surveillance equipment, a condition of the entire package of trade and exchanges.[49] It was a tactic that was to be repeated with other partners, including the West Germans.

The difficulty was that these processes gave others an uncomfortably clear picture of China's needs.[50] With involvement in international and transnational exchanges, the possibility of some foreign influence upon segments of Chinese society might grow. For China's partners, on the other hand, though overriding political considerations might suggest a measure of aid and support, the one-sided character of the benefits of the early "exchanges" was not likely to be acceptable for the longer term. The Western perspective on technological exchanges with China was spelled out with reasonable clarity by President Carter's science advisor, Dr. Frank Press, during a visit to Peking in July 1978.[51] Dr. Press made it clear that the United States wished China well and wanted her to grow stronger.

> President Carter believes the People's Republic of China plays a central role in the maintenance of the global equilibrium. He recognizes that a strong and secure China is in America's

interest. He advocates a broadened and deepened scientific and technological relationship with you for our long-term mutual advantage. America's intellectual vitality and creativity benefits greatly from our contact with scientific communities around the world.

Dr. Press thought that China's assessment of her needs was candid and comprehensive, her priorities were realistic, and her programs were reasonable. Cooperation between the scientific communities of the two nations would become more important as problems came increasingly to transcend national boundaries. Knowledge should be shared on the basis of reciprocity. There should be contacts and cooperation on public health and energy questions, on the exploration of space and the oceans, and the exchanges should take place at a variety of levels, from exchanges of data and cooperative research ventures to student exchanges and commercial relationships.

Very similar principles were applied in the field of education. In the view of the government, what was required was nothing less than a reversal of the educational policies associated with the Cultural Revolution.[52] The reforms were to run through the entire system, from primary schools to post-graduate training. The "progressive" movements launched by the Gang of Four during the earlier 1970s were now condemned on a variety of grounds,[53] including the accusation that they were political plots aimed at sabotaging the policies of Chou En-lai. There was a swing back to teacher authority, structured relationships, examinations, and grading. Within schools and universities, the controlling workers' teams were disbanded or downgraded[54] and authority returned to the hands of school principals and university presidents. They key slogan of early 1977 was "respect teachers, love students."

There was renewed stress on learning, including basic knowledge and theory, rather than on political discussion.[55] It was pointed out that socialist consciousness, academic competence, and practice in labor work were inseparable components of socialist throught.[56] In such a context it was logical to give priority to top talent and to engage in unashamed elitism for the best and the brightest. Keypoint schools and universities were reestablished[57] and given first claim on the best teachers and resources and recruitment of the brightest students. Ordinary schools were told to adopt selective procedures, the most common being a threefold division into fast, average, and slow students.[58] It was officially argued that these were methods favored by Mao himself,[59] that keypoint institutions were urgently required to train the talents which the nation needed, and that it was not possible to raise the levels of all schools equally and simultaneously. Some prospective scientists were selected at the ages of fourteen or fifteen for special classes run by the universities of science and technology. Others were allowed to go to university without finishing secondary school. Though the prime emphasis was on scientific and technical programs, or mathematics and languages, that were demonstrably essential for national modernization, the educational reforms were not confined to areas of immediate utility. The social sciences, too, were encouraged, and a new Academy of Social Sciences set up.[60]

In November 1977, Education Minister Liu Hsi-yao announced a series of decisions by the Central Committee which included the renewal of college enrollments, the reopening of graduate schools, the opening of a number of new schools at all levels, the revival of academic titles, and increased emphasis on research.[61] By the middle of 1978 the authorities claimed that China had 460 schools of higher learning, 700,000 middle (secondary) schools, and over a million primary schools.[62] The government announced that by 1985 it was intended to have universal middle-school education in the cities and junior middle-school education in the rural areas. The aim was nationwide ten-year schooling: five years primary and five years secondary. The entry age for primary education was being dropped from seven to six years.[63] Authorities at all levels were instructed to put more effort and money into schooling. New course outlines were developed, theoretical knowledge and traditional disciplines were emphasized. The post–Cultural Revolution pattern of local diversity of academic administration and egalitarian principles, of locally compiled teaching materials and varying lengths and schedules of schooling, gave way to renewed centralization and standardization in the name of higher standards, and to a thorough revision of textbooks and teaching materials. Energetic efforts were made to get back into the schools the old teachers who had been dispersed into other activities during and after the Cultural Revolution,[64] even to the extent of reinstating some teachers, who had been exiled to farms, with full back pay. At the same time, the student rebel heroes of previous years were officially discredited.

The emphasis on combining expanded facilities with more competition, higher standards, and more rigorous streaming was, if anything, even stronger in the university system. Immediately after the fall of the Gang of Four, there were signs that the open-door educational experiments were being curtailed. Chou Pei-yuan, writing in *Red Flag* in September 1977, spelled out principles which had already begun to appear in practice: the need for keypoint institutions, a concentration of resources, and a raising of standards. There was a return to centralized and standardized entrance examinations, in 1977 at the provincial level and by 1978 nationally. Toward the end of 1977, and following some preliminary sifting at local levels, some 5.7 million young Chinese sat for the two-day, highly competitive examinations for entry to tertiary institutions in the spring of 1978. Nearly 280,000 were accepted. In mid-1978 some six million sat for entrance to a somewhat increased number of places in September. There were attempts to diminish the importance of family background as a criterion for entry, though a candidate's personal political record remained important. Some 20 to 30 percent of the 1978 entrants were allowed to come straight from secondary school (instead of spending time on farms), and hopes were expressed that in time it might be possible to increase that percentage. The selection process was clearly being slanted toward those examinees who could display intellectual excellence as well as good health, who had a good grounding in basic knowledge as well as abilities in problem-solving.[65] Not surprisingly, there were a number of signs of dissatisfaction with the new system by those who thought that it disadvantaged them. The authorities took pains to explain that, on the contrary, examinations avoided unfairness and previous "backdoor deals" on university entry.[66] Not surprisingly, either, there were a number of reports of examination cheating.[67] Once admitted, the student found that the emphasis on competition continued. By 1978 China had eighty-eight keypoint universities, as compared with sixty before the Cultural Revolution.[68] Research and specialization were strengthened by means which included something like the American institution of specialized centers within universities. Colleges, it was stressed, were to be places of academic excellence, the previous decline in the academic competence of students had to be reversed, and there had to be more hard work and theoretical study.[69]

Graduate work was also expanded. In November 1977 the Ministry of Education and the Academy of Sciences issued a joint statement announcing that graduate studies (which had been for the most part suspended for twelve years) should be resumed. In the first wave, fifty-seven thousand candidates were given preliminary examinations for admission to 207 universities and colleges and 144 research institutes which proposed to admit graduate students in 1978.[70] The candidates included not merely college graduates but secondary-school students, some cadres, and youths returning from the rural districts. It was expected that about one applicant in six would be admitted. Graduate study was expected to last for three years in most cases, with a good deal of stress on theory, foreign languages, and the capacity for independent research including the ability to establish and maintain contact with the international mainstream of the field concerned.

Altogether, the foreign relations element in advanced studies received particular emphasis. It had at least two components. One was a program to attract, either directly or by way of exchange schemes, foreign or overseas Chinese teachers and scholars to lecture at Chinese institutions. The other was to send Chinese students abroad. As early as the end of 1976 and the beginning of 1977, there were instances of Chinese institutions wishing to attract Western-trained science teachers from Hong Kong or to tap the resources of skill and expertise of the overseas Chinese community. In later years this was expanded, not only through invitations to particular scholars, but by making use of seminars and lectures given by members of visiting foreign delegations. More important still, however, was the program to send Chinese students abroad. Major decisions in this area appear to have been taken toward the end of July or the beginning of August 1978. It was evidently a crash program to help man the R and D system and the advanced economic and technological structures which the government had decided China needed and which could evidently not be adequately manned by other methods. The initial indications were that China was prepared to send five thousand students abroad in 1978 and 1979 if they could be appropriately placed. It was suggested that the program could expand so that, by 1985, at least ten thousand foreign-trained students would be working back in China. There were indications that of the first five thousand some twelve hundred might go to Britain and five hundred each to Japan, West Germany, and the United States. By the end of the year, it seemed likely that, following the exchange of formal recognition between Peking and Washington, the numbers going to the United States might be substantially increased. Most would be graduate students, and most were expected to be competent in the language of the country to which they were assigned. It was also suggested that the Chinese authorities would allow their students to live dispersed among the host population, not concentrated in Chinese houses or dormitories. It was a point of particular interest, given the possible social and political consequences of allowing a new generation of Chinese technocrats and researchers to become closely acquainted with Western mores.

These formal educational arrangements were to be supplemented by a variety of informal or mass adult-education schemes. Workers and peasants colleges, on-the-job training, and vocational training by the use of radio and television all received encouragement. By mid-1977 nearly eight hundred thousand students were enrolled in workers' colleges and one million in agricultural schools.[71] Chinese purchasing missions displayed interest in Western educational technologies, including computer-assisted learning devices and technical equipment. The government expressed the hope that by 1985 it would be possible to raise the level of education of the working population to senior middle-school levels and to enable the workers to master various modern production skills. Here, too, China might be able to rely on some kinds of foreign help. The import program could obviously be structured in such a way as to give Western suppliers a direct interest in the manpower training aspects of the enterprise and the ultimate efficiency of the investment. A number of Chinese arrangements for importing foreign technology clearly had such components.

These were programs of impressive scope and determination. They seemed likely to yield interesting and substantial results. Chinese scholars, scientists, and managers had a variety of possibilities for making rapid advances. They could intensify their exploitation of foreign literature. They could expand exchanges of persons and oral communication with the outside world. Given existing levels of competence and motivation, the Chinese scientific and technical community would be able to absorb what others could teach them, often quickly. In some areas, competent scientists and technologists aware of what had happened abroad could, even if few in number, leapfrog some stages of scientific and technical development. Moreover, a command economy could even in the face of overall shortages of skills or materials give priority to some areas and achieve significant advances in them. The military-industrial complex was clearly one that had obtained some of the best scientists, been shielded from most of the political disruptions of the 1960s and 1970s, and produced some work which was remarkable by international standards. In general, the intellectual resources available from a pool of 900 million of the world's more intelligent and hardworking people, members of a civilization with a notable scientific record, were clearly such that, once the government had decided to reemphasize education and excellence, a considerable rate of progress could be expected.

Yet important qualifications and difficulties remain. Some stem from the general doubts about the new government line and the permanence of its policies. The very abruptness of the policy reversals of 1976-78 could hardly fail to make people wary about the future and cynical about high policy. The breakneck speed of innovation must have created, in education and science as in politics and administration, enormous strains for the administrative apparatus and the trained personnel who were expected to implement them. Haste was sure to mean some weakness in execution. There were tales of thousands of scientists, technicians, and teachers, who had lost their jobs during and after the Cultural Revolution, refusing to return to their jobs for fear of fresh political changes in the future.[72] There were more specific doubts about the implications of the new science and education policies. At various provincial education conferences in mid-1978, doubts were expressed about the number and quality of available teachers, the problems of teacher training, and the shortage of schools and teaching materials. There were complaints, too, about the way in which the new criteria for university entry favored the urban middle class. There was even some evidence of suppression of acceptance letters sent out to candidates and of continuing difficulties made for intellectuals.[73] Nor were hesitations confined to lower levels. In August 1977, *Red Flag* published a sixteen-year-old letter by Mao praising work-study education.[74]

Further problems are likely to be created by the lead times required for the production of an adequate corps of graduates and postgraduates to man the new system. Though they can be trained, they cannot replace the "lost generation" of 1966-76 whose absence is a severe medium-term constraint on the entire body politic and the economy, including agriculture. The production of high-quality personnel, moreover, must be done gradually. It does not lend itself to forced or mass production methods. It will not be until the early 1980s that the first of the new university entrants graduate. It will be even later before postgraduates emerge whose training has not included the period of the Gang of Four and whose studies have been free from political disruption. For such reasons alone, the creation of an adequate corps of high-quality research, development, engineering, or teaching specialists is likely to take many years during which the shortage of trained people will persist. The creation of research teams and of an R and D system must take longer still. No one has shown clearer recognition of these realities than the Chinese authorities themselves. The timetable suggested by the Central Committee indicates that a contingent of first-rate scientists and technicians should be ready by the end of the century, not before.

Nor are numbers and quality of training the only issues. The reassertion of academic and professional criteria seems bound to introduce or accentuate the sociopolitical problems of meritocracy, ranging from problems of status and status-envy to those of access to special luxuries for officially favored groups. There were indications that some of the doubters within China during 1977 and 1978 were concerned with just such problems. They are more delicate in that they have been at the core of the more egalitarian and populist tendencies in Chinese politics during the last quarter century and more. They are not likely to become less sensitive in a period when the "lost generation," lacking professional training in a world where that fact is increasingly important and finding a declining market for its revolutionary skills and enthusiasms, is trying to find an acceptable role. Yet, from the point of view of the authorities, the problems of supervision and control might be no less complex for the new generation of meritocrats, many of them trained abroad and familiar with foreign ways and looking for official support for their own purposes devised in the light of their own standards.

There are other questions. The supply of trained personnel is a necessary but not a sufficient condition for the construction of a modern R and D program, and the construction of such a program is, in turn, a necessary but not a sufficient condition for the creation of an innovative production sector relying on sophisticated technologies. A few high-quality research groups do not necessarily amount to a significant R and D program, let alone a program for industrial innovation. The ability to produce a few hand- or batch-made products in a specialized field is not the same as a broad-based production capacity. And the quantity of new technology says very little about the quality or extent of its modern high-technology components. It is bound to take a good deal of time to create a mature modern industrial sector, to train its work force and establish its support systems, and to operate it at anything like optimal efficiency. In the meantime, the science and education systems can expect neither the support that a fully established, modern industrial sector would be able to offer, nor the considered demand in terms of which the R and D system should largely operate.

There may also be certain difficulties associated with the principle of keeping "politics in command" of research, science, and technology. Before 1976 the leadership consistently set its face against the ivory-tower tendencies of intellectuals, tried to make science relevant to production, and tied the development of science to the Maoist view of China's political and economic progress. By 1976/77 the new leaders were stressing the need not only for science and technology in general but for freer scientific thought. Teng even went so far as to call for open debate on scientific questions. "It is a good thing, not a bad thing, to have contending opinions on academic issues in the natural sciences." Official rhetoric spoke once again of encouraging a hundred flowers to bloom in academic exchanges. Yet flexibility has remained limited. The whole context of the discussion makes it plain that, as on previous occasions, it takes place at a time of major reviews of economic and defense policy and what is at issue is not the development of science per se but the role and contribution of science to specific issues of public policy. Hua and Teng have stressed that the modernization of industry, agriculture, and defense requires the modernization of China's relatively backward science and technology sector. But they have also stressed, no less than their predecessors, that politics must be in ultimate command of vocational work and that scientists should be both red and expert. Scientists are to be recruited into the CCP,[75] and, in case anyone has missed the point, Hua himself has stressed that "raising the scientific and cultural level is not solely a matter of imparting knowledge but is a great class struggle."[76]

It is all very well for Teng to call for debates on academic issues, but scientists are likely to be interested in who will decide on the distinction between academic questions on which contending opinions are permitted and others on which they are not; which questions are reserved for internal Party discussion and which may be freely ventilated within the scientific community; and what happens to people who make mistakes about these distinctions. The government has been aware of these hesitations. It has tried to reassure young intellectuals, for instance, by bringing home some prisoners who had been in camps since the original Hundred Flowers campaign of the late 1950s. It remains to be seen whether scientists and technicians will indeed feel more secure or, on the contrary, more fearful at this fresh reminder of what can happen to political losers.

Other difficulties have to do with the balance between central planning and local responsibilities and with governmental and bureaucratic sponsorship of innovation and change. The pressures for centralized national planning are universal. They rest on a variety of notions about the efficiency of resource allocation in relation to national purposes, the management of relations between classes and groups, and the proposition that unregulated market forces would produce needless inequities and frictions and ignore some of society's "real" needs, as well as circumvent the proper centers of political and social power. In the Chinese case, central planning mechanisms are fortified by a number of considerations from the political need to even out economic conditions, as between provinces or between town and country, to the role of the CCP. The difficulties are also various. Most importantly, perhaps, the world of the central planner tends to be one of relatively abstract macro-considerations, while much of the important activity in relation to technical change occurs in micro-situations, in expectation of a particular opportunity in a particular place at a particular time. The record strongly suggests that even semimodern economic systems are too complex for very detailed central planning of innovation. The multiplicity of economic and technical micro-decisions which are required, and their secondary effects in a complex social system, create problems in trying to move from policy to implementation which are frequently insuperable. Pressman and Wildavsky have put the problem as follows:

> Our assumptions about new public programs are far removed from reality. We assume that the people ostensibly in charge can predict the consequences of their actions, and that is often not

the case. Since a problem exists, we assume that there must be a
solution and that it is embodied in the program.[77]

As less-developed countries, including China, go further on
the road to modernity, they seem bound to find that the
difficulties of centralized administration tend to increase and
not decrease. Modernity and technical change seem to be
ineluctably associated with pluralism, fragmentation, specialization, and increasing emphasis in management on merito-
cratic criteria. Emphasis on technical change is therefore likely
to increase economic complexity within the PRC and the
interdependence of various provinces and sectors. This could,
in turn, increase the need for further technical imports,
whether by way of purchase or aid, to manage the associated
communications, transport, and distribution systems. Micro-
control from the center would, in such conditions, tend to
become even more difficult. The new policies of 1977/78
suggest that the Chinese government understands many of
these problems. The need for decentralization has been
reflected in the encouragement of local managerial initiatives
and the stress on some kinds of planning authority for cities
and provinces. The infrastructure for a regionally based system
permitting considerable competition and local creativity is in
place, even in such matters as provincially controlled research
institutes, presumably able to engage in at least some research
and innovative activities in unfashionable areas and promising
local payoffs.

But there are other aspects of an innovative system that
remain, at best, underdeveloped. Foremost among them is that
key element of any innovative system, an entrepreneurial class
and a satisfactory relationship between it and the civil service.
Western literature and Western experience strongly suggest
that the innovative process is characterized by individual or
small-group initiative, disorder, duplication, the unexpected
use of knowledge, and quick exploitation of unexpected
opportunities, by inspired hunches and a willingness to risk
failure. Novel and risky enterprise in new areas is particularly
liable to come from small or private groups rather than from
larger firms and laboratories. By the end of 1978, there was no

evidence that such processes, and the groups dedicated to them, played a significant role in the Chinese system. For all the verbal encouragement given by the government to local initiative, there were few signs that a willingness to undertake it had spread in a substantial way from the sphere of bureaucratic initiative on the one hand, and the private or semiprivate sector on the other, into the industrial structure. Still less were there signs that the financing and credit system had been adequately geared to the assumption of such commercial-type risks or that the rewards available to industrial innovators really compensated for the political and social risks of taking major initiatives.

Nor is the attitude of the Party bureaucracy toward the encouragement of innovation and entrepreneurship entirely clear. The dynamics of bureaucratic organizations and operations rarely favor enterprise and flexibility of a kind required to optimize the management of technical and social change.[78] The nature of bureaucratic politics and inter-departmental disputes can easily produce uncertainties and instabilities which inhibit enterprise. Moreover, bureaucratic and planning controls tend, often inevitably, to be based on historic knowledge and "safe" extrapolations from past experience, rather than on inspired hunches about what might work in an unknown future. There is also the question of responsibility. The great majority of innovations are failures. Success is exceptional. If a small or private group is responsible for failure, the bulk of society and the social system can remain unconcerned. But if a political authority, and especially a central political authority, confronts possible failure, other factors come into play. Such a body, typically employing minimax strategies of avoiding vulnerabilities and losses, may be tempted to pour good money after bad, or to pretend that the project has not failed, or in some other way to avoid admitting, even to itself, that a failure has occurred. It may be tempted to try to increase the rate of success in the innovative field by tighter controls on performance and closer estimates of likely success, even though such tighter controls can easily become dysfunctional. China, as a relatively poor country, confronts another category of risk: that of concentrating unduly upon high-reliability and low-risk technologies, with the result that the groups and organizations devoted to original and innovative work develop more slowly than they should. Yet the proclaimed aims of the Chinese government, implying a catching up with the advanced nations, require for their fulfillment a greater rate of transformation, more successful risk-taking, and a faster growth of the innovative sector than that achieved by the advanced countries themselves.

There is another reason why close political control of the innovative process might prove to be counterproductive. Even in a very general sense, the notion that technical choices should be made in the light of broad social or political objectives is not easy to put into practice. Many problems do not have a technical solution. Social objectives, if stated at the level of abstract principles, are likely to be irrelevant to decisions of detail. At the level of practical decision making, not only do social objectives change over time but the alternatives cannot be sensibly discussed until after the appearance of the technologies involved has made assessment of them possible. Though it is true that science and technology are not independent variables, it would be equally wrong to regard them as wholly malleable in relation to any social demand which might be put. Some Western suggestions on science policy during the 1970s seemed to imply that, once society defines a problem, science and technology can or should be able to produce a technical solution and to do so, moreover, under conditions entirely molded to the social arrangements which the polity happens to prefer. Nothing in the recent history of science and technology suggests that such expectations can be fulfilled. On the contrary, more often than not scientific and technical advances require for their optimal impact changes not only in administrative structures and habits but in wider social arrangements. The precisely desirable balance between social preferences and technical possibilities has always been a matter for debate. But there seems to be no modern instance of the development of an advanced industrial society with an effective innovative sector without substantial accompanying willingness to accept greater political and social flexibility.

Within the innovative system, research and development

plays a seminal role. But governments sometimes misunderstand its requirements. They provide, or give the lead in providing, its indispensable financial, logistic, and other support. They influence its social environment and help to mold public attitudes toward it. They play a key role in determining the market conditions to which it reacts and the rewards and sanctions for its personnel. But the impression of control is sometimes even greater than the reality. Government policies tend to concentrate on those sectors of R and D that are most easily susceptible of quantification and control. In particular, the downstream elements of R and D—development, modification, and testing—typically account for the great bulk of manpower and expenditure. They are also areas where it is customary to exercise close administrative, including budgetary, supervision and to produce to demand. This can create two kinds of assumption. One is that the production and productivity of R and D are closely responsive to administrative manipulation and changes in its organizational forms. The other is that development and testing are, if not the whole of R and D, at least the major elements through which the whole can be steered. Yet caution is in order. Even in these downstream areas, development often produces its best results when organizational patterns are relatively disorganized, when no one knows or greatly cares who the boss is, when teams of technologists and engineers are given maximum freedom of movement and left largely to their own devices.

There is also the question of the informal R and D sector. Here occur the incremental changes in scientific or production methods or hardware (what Jack Ruina has called "technological drift"), amendments to organizations, the rediscovery of old knowledge hitherto ignored or forgotten. There is the transfer of minor technical knowledge or know-how from one sector to another. This is an area which is neither capital intensive nor highly visible nor dramatic in its results. Yet it is one that has, at times, produced important progress. It is important for other reasons. Not all scientists and researchers are truly original and innovative, the pool of original minds in any society being limited. Insofar as innovations come from outside the highly trained research community, they expand the number of innovations available but do so in ways attuned to real, immediate needs and without great social costs in providing advanced training for additional persons. This is a field in which China's encouragement of mass participation, and the exploitation of lower-level or traditional skills in particular groups or localities, may give her certain assets, though their full development may not be without problems for central planners.

The upstream elements of discovery and invention, though less obvious, less costly, less directly relevant to immediate economic needs, less quantifiable, and more elusive, are also the sources from which, in the end, come some of the major original elements of knowledge-intensive activity and of innovative drive. Here, close control is often not feasible. In the more rarified areas of theory, for example, administrators and controllers may have great difficulty in understanding what scientists are doing. Other difficulties stem from the characteristics and needs of the research community. One is the wish for autonomy. The desire for professional standing and scientific progress typically produces strong preferences for self-selected research projects and the recruitment of researchers by the senior members of the research staff, as opposed to intervention by outside administrators. Governments wanting more emphasis on mission-oriented research or work of immediate social or economic relevance, and in any case greater value per research dollar, must set limits to this desire for independence. But the forms of limitation must be chosen with care. One possibility is to harness the wish for autonomy to the desire for mission fulfillment through competition for funds and support for specified research projects. Quite another is limitation by administrative direction, whether of research topics or recruitment.

A research community can be considered as a social organism which, like other social organisms, has its own internal dynamics. These are much too complex and delicate to be arranged in an orderly way. A good deal of the system has to do with competition and disorder. Moreover, the social dynamics of research tend to be subject- or discipline-oriented rather than biased toward social or ideological ends. And the dynamics can be constrained only at some cost to efficiency and innovative drive. Behind these social problems lies a more mysterious question still. It has to do with the personal creativity of scientists, technologists, and perhaps even administrators. No one knows very much about the causes of personal creativity or the conditions of its encouragement or maintenance. The evidence suggests that, even as a matter of average incidence among large numbers of researchers, it is not directly or easily responsive to official stimulation. The currents which move individuals in such matters appear to run at levels much deeper than those of mere politics or sociology.

The R and D enterprise is, however, dependent on social—including governmental—support and encouragement in a variety of other ways. It depends on the creation and maintenance of a social, economic, and psychological environment that welcomes research and technical change and an intellectual milieu in which creativity and new ideas can be sustained and rewarded. This involves a balance between traditional attitudes and the welcome to innovation which ultimately rests upon a certain adventurousness and social self-confidence. Since it involves broad social attitudes, as well as administrative ones, it requires the participation of the community as a whole, not merely a governmental fiat or even elite-group preferences. Overlapping with this is the crucial question of demand. The R and D community appears to be fairly closely responsive to customer demand as distinct from political manipulation or planning strongly influenced by a priori categories.[79]

Customer demand can, of course, take many forms. It can be feedback from the marketplace. One obvious difficulty here relates to the criteria for choice. The more imperfect and administratively skewed the market-type mechanisms available, the greater the difficulty in accurately assigning values in terms of which competing demands can be assessed. Another problem has to do with the information flow between designers, makers, and users. The scanty evidence from foreign visitors to China suggests that this informational feedback system, in relation to which future R and D emphases might be judged, so far has not been strong.[80] Or the customer can be a government department making requests. Or demand can even be in the form of peer-group pressure for professional performance. But in every case, demand implies that innovations are produced in relation to someone who can pay, whether in money or power or esteem, and produced also in relation to some person or group that can utilize and absorb the innovation. The notion of demand also implies possibilities for demand creation. The demand may rest upon medium- or long-term macro-economic assessments of social need or on micro-analyses of particular economic or other problems and opportunities. But for it to become maximally effective, a number of requirements should be met. One is the preparing of a coherent and technically appropriate demand definition. Another is the ability to attune the demand to the capabilities, past attainments, and existing research objectives of the innovative group concerned. A third is the ability by administrators, entrepreneurs, and managers to recognize that a discovery or innovation has taken place. And the last is that these same groups originating or expressing demand must be able to make the judgment that the innovation can be fruitfully exploited. Many of these judgments, from demand definition to the evaluation of an innovation, depend on a broad command of a number of relevant technologies, not just narrow specialisms, and on knowledge of the state of the art in several fields. This in turn implies an adequate and continuing supply of information on developments in a number of areas and probably in a number of countries.

To the extent that these judgments on innovations and their exploitation relate to the future, they are necessarily somewhat speculative. They have to do with predictions about the likely governmental or public reception of the innovation, in other words, its acceptability. To produce not only acceptability but the prior expectation of acceptability, which might stimulate the emergence of innovation, is an especially complex affair. It involves the norms and expectations of the people whom the innovation is likely to affect, and its compatibility with existing practices ranging from the status given to existing skills to the rate of change of administrative systems. Acceptability relates to the complexity of the innovation and the evidence of its relative advantage over existing or competing ideas or systems and, not least, to the speed with which people can be brought to understand both the innovation and its implications. In the case of existing technologies, the implications and risks of acceptability are usually known, and its establishment and maintenance have created a constituency for it.

Innovation, by contrast, always implies risks which are to some extent unknown, and the constituency for the innovation may be confined to the innovator and supporting segments of the firm or the governmental administration. In that sense, the scales may be weighted against innovation in most normal situations. For that reason, innovation and modernization usually involve elements of pressure and can rarely be a matter of unforced consensus. But the application of such pressures may be especially difficult in relation to the administrative changes that are required to allow innovation to occur, to be recognized, and to become socially useful. As an observer has remarked, "Innovation in general, and institutional innovation in particular, does not generally take place through a transformation of existing organizations, but by the creation of new ones which bypass them."[81] Organizations, as Donald Schon has remarked,[82] display a "dynamic conservatism" in their attempt to remain unchanged. It may well be that for governmental organizations it is often even more difficult than for private ones to accept either internal change or the need for new organizational entities to cope with new tasks.

The various segments of the innovative process do not have the same characteristics or conditions for success, nor do they require precisely similar administrative arrangements. In the area of pure science and research, the classic view is that the community obeys four "institutional imperatives": universalism of source of knowledge, communality of knowledge, disinterestedness of research, and organized skepticism about proposed results. These Mertonian norms[83] imply that interference from outside is likely to impede rather than promote intellectual progress. Kuhn went further and thought that, while science had to do with concepts and problem structures,[84] external factors might affect the timing and direction of developments, the assessment of technical needs, and the cross-fertilization between specialisms.[85] But he thought that scientific activity proper was that which had to do with the establishment of facts that revealed the processes of nature in relation to the proposed research paradigm, with the establishment of facts that could be compared with predictions arising from that paradigm, and with empirical work to articulate the paradigm. The community engaged in these activities proceeds by way of peer approval. Indeed, the definition of a discovery has to do with the recognition by competent colleagues that a discovery has taken place.[86] It follows that one of the principal requirements for successful scientific activity is participation in the relevant scientific communication flows, through which peer ideas, proposals, and opinions are communicated. This communication takes place in a variety of ways, from informal communication within elite networks, personal migration, and organized meetings to participation in the literature of the field concerned. Research areas tend to expand and contract in relation to shifts of opinion within the "invisible college" of any field as to what are the next scientifically interesting and important problems which might prove to be soluble, and also in relation to major discoveries which open up new requirements for elaboration, follow-up, and testing.

The areas of applied science, technology, and engineering appear to display somewhat different characteristics and attitudes. Where pure science tends to value learning for its own sake and success is defined in terms of peer recognition, technological personnel and engineers appear to place greater stress on success within the firm or organization, and on mission fulfillment.[87] Where science proceeds through the communication of results and peer criticism of them, technology publications may be secondary to effective and marketable utilization, the hoarding of information, or its selected release through personal contact within the organization. Where scientists tend to define problems in relation to explanatory power, technological problems are more readily definable in terms of firm or consumer demand.

But the question also arises whether technical progress

depends upon basic science and, if so, to what extent. The traditional view here is that basic research "constitutes the fount of all new knowledge, without which the opportunities for further technical progress must eventually become exhausted."[88] There are, however, difficulties. A number of innovations are not explicable by reference to prior scientific advances,[89] except under conditions of lead times so long as to suggest a general advance in knowledge rather than the cause of a particular innovation. A good deal of technological advance seems to feed upon technology, and involves changed combinations of available ideas or hardware rather than altered views of the physical universe. Moreover, technology is not simply a consumer of scientific results. It often creates a demand for solutions to scientific problems which its own progress has uncovered. It may, therefore, be useful not to regard technology as resting upon scientific advance in any simple and causal way, but to view the two kinds of activity as partly separate and partly engaged in mutual cross-fertilization and action-reaction stimulation.

But the very complexity of this process, and of the scientific and technical communities engaged in it, suggests certain attendant difficulties. To transplant these social practices and organizations from one polity to another, or to create them in a new environment, may prove to be very difficult.[90] Yet without an adequate scientific and technical expertise of its own, a country is likely to find it very difficult to make a useful contribution to the cross-national information flows on these matters. And countries or groups unable to make such a contribution, reduced to being merely consumers of information, are liable to be cut off from participation in the most interesting areas of information exchange. Moreover, the critical discussion of intellectual traditions and myths, which is an essential part of these processes, may not be everywhere acceptable. It might not be easily confined to "safe" academic subjects, for, as Karl Popper has pointed out, science grows by criticizing not only theories but "the language in which our myths and theories are formulated."[91] In a country like China, it might even, at some point, spill over into a critique of political mythologies such as the role of the vanguard Party.

Various methods can, of course, be tried to limit or stop such discussion. One is the official attempt to recruit senior scientists into the CCP, whose organization can provide a sanitizing environment for debate. But the difficulties are unlikely to be trivial.

There are also the problems posed by what may be the most important requirement of all for the creation and maintenance of an innovative science and technology sector, an untrammeled flow of information. It is the lifeblood of the knowledge intensive process. Innovation depends on, is indeed often defined as, the unexpected conjunction of previously unrelated ideas. It is therefore impossible, even in theory, to plan the relevant information flows on behalf of a researcher or perhaps even of a development engineer. There cannot be a need-to-know principle, for no one can be sure in advance who needs to know what. The innovative organization must therefore arrange for a general openness to new ideas. It must multiply its formal and informal information and communication networks. It must try to ensure that the information flow is comprehensive and swift and that the evaluation and exploitation processes are sufficiently quick-reacting and sophisticated. There has to be a rapid circulation of information about modern science and technology across a variety of disciplines and interdisciplinary areas. The information network must not only convey information, but stimulate demand for further information and research and an awareness of alternatives for research as well as for application. It must cover the exploitation of handbooks, the provision of documentation and data storage and retrieval, and processes of personal and oral exchanges. It is not too much to say that, for any society wishing to move into the innovative high-technology field, the first high technology that has to be acquired is that of information management.[92] Nor can that information flow be usefully confined within national boundaries. At the frontiers of some particular disciplines, advanced and especially theoretical work can be done by individuals or small groups in relative isolation. But at those levels of research and innovation where ideas or findings from many disciplines may be relevant, and especially for the development of an R and D sector with broad competence across a wide range of subjects, adequate transnational flows of information appear to be of the essence. Nor is it merely a question of information. It is equally a process of evaluation, in which work done can be subjected to the judgment of the external scientific and research community.

There is no doubt that in these matters of transnational information the Chinese scientific community was, until the middle 1970s, relatively backward. Foreign observers remarked upon the isolation of Chinese scientists from colleagues abroad and even from one another in different parts of the country. Foreign contacts were sparse. There were important language barriers to better communication. Few Chinese went to international scientific conferences, especially before 1976. And there was no developed system by which Chinese scientists tested the value of their work by publication in the international literature or were able to follow it up by critical discussion with foreign colleagues.[93] Though the new policies of 1977/78 were a sharp improvement, it was clear that in this area the Chinese scientific community had a good deal of leeway to make up.

It may be, therefore, that there are reasons even more fundamental than those of industrial structure and trained manpower for suggesting that China could continue to experience difficulties in the areas of technology acquisition and innovation. Some have to do with social difficulties. The results of innovative activities are differential as between groups and localities. Such differentiation is bound to cause political and social tensions. Yet in order to innovate successfully, China, like other countries, needs the active support and participation of substantial segments of the population, not merely the passive acquiescence which a strong central government might enforce. These problems could become more acute. Entrepreneurial groups are likely to display an antihierarchical spirit. Inquisitiveness may spill over from scientific into other questions. The intellectual and psychological milieu required for the conduct of innovative activities, and the acceptance of innovation by the body politic, could easily lead to a much more radical questioning of prevailing verities than had appeared, or been tolerated, by the end of 1978. A number of hallowed traditions might have to be relegated to the dustbin of history.

Ramon Myers has suggested a useful distinction between transformative and accommodative economic policies.[94] The hallmark of Maoism, in this view, has been transformist thinking and action through sudden and far-reaching organizational changes accompanied by mobilization tactics based on normative and coercive principles. But the modernization of China seems to be compelling a shift to accommodative thinking, based on incremental change, gradualistic methods, material incentives, and reward systems. As the modernization of Chinese society proceeds and political and administrative patterns become more complex, the desirability of incremental change and the costs of revolution are likely to increase. The new government and its supporters showed every sign during 1977/78 that they recognized these considerations and that renewed cultural revolution was to be avoided. But, once again, the permanence of the government's policies remained to be established, and the very sweep and thoroughness of the changes which official policy was attempting to introduce were bound to raise questions about a possible domestic reaction once political circumstances changed.

No less at issue was the question of self-reliance. It is not necessary to question the political attitudes and social loyalties of Chinese scientists and innovators. But from the point of view of the Chinese authorities, the creation of a modern apparatus for science, technology, and industrial growth requires the setting up of a social organism whose worth is not measured solely on local scales and whose members will, as a function of their membership, develop a variety of transnational ideas and ties. Indeed, in a broader sense, self-sufficiency and modernization contradict one another. States that wish to modernize their economies must remain open to technical and modernizing influences from abroad. Simon Kuznets has put the point as follows:

No matter where these technological and social innovations (i.e., those innovations which are the source of the high rate of aggregate increase and of the high rate of structural shifts that has characterized modern economies) emerge . . . the economic growth of any nation depends upon their adoption. In that sense, whatever the national affiliation of the resources used, any single nation's economic growth has its base somewhere outside its boundaries.[95]

The Chinese slogan of self-reliance may therefore have to be defined in terms not of self-sufficiency but of the management of international and transnational flows of people, techniques, and information in terms acceptable to the Chinese government. This is not to deny that some problems of this sort have proved to be manageable in the past. The Chinese authorities managed the impact of foreign technology upon Chinese industry during the 1950s and again during the 1970s with care and apparent success. And other societies have succeeded in combining continued and even enhanced central authority with industrial innovation and growth. Nevertheless, the plans announced by the new government of China in 1977/78 have some aspects unmatched in China's recent experience. There have already been attempts to minimize awareness within China of the extent of foreign inputs.[96] Whether the patterns of management which served China up to the mid-1970s will continue to be adequate in a period of more rapid modernization, what alternative patterns of management might be sought, and how such alternatives might dovetail with the aim of catching up with the advanced industrial countries remains to be seen.

5
Conclusions

The first two years of the post-Mao administration of China brought some important political and administrative changes. The new government was compelled, probably by inclination and certainly by circumstances, to give principal attention to economic and technological matters. It did so in a manner markedly different from that of its immediate predecessors. The proclaimed aim of modernization was pursued in an atmosphere that emphasized financial, technical, and managerial rationality and the desire for quick growth. Though in China, as elsewhere, governmental declarations and intentions may be one thing while implementation and accomplishment are another, the changes in attitude were comprehensive, and the official drive in new directions determined. The question was raised whether China might not be destined, in the last two decades of the twentieth century, to enjoy the rapid and sustained economic growth and technical advance which her leaders sought and for which her size and the inherent capacities of her people have always seemed to fit her. The implications of any such development not only internally but for China's position in the world, and hence for the global balance of power, could clearly be very great.

The implications of the new policies seem to have been a fresh drive for the control of population growth together with rapid advances in both industry and agriculture. Though the precise effects of the population limitation program remained unclear, probably even to the Peking authorities themselves, there was no reason to doubt that it was taking effect and that the rate of population increase was declining during the later 1970s. In agriculture, the declared aims of increased production, enhanced scientific inputs, and mechanization would, if implemented, amount to advances unprecedented in the recent history of China. Even if there proved to be some delay in achieving the output targets set for the mid-1980s, the advances achieved by thoroughgoing mobilization and especially by improvements in incentives might be impressive. If so, the government might succeed in largely resolving the country's key economic problem: the achievement of agricultural surpluses which could be translated into a major investment program. Even a lower level of achievement might contain, even reduce, the drain on export earnings and payments capacities stemming from the requirement for food purchases abroad. On the industrial side, it seemed unlikely in 1978 that there would be any marked short-term reduction in the character and extent of China's dependence upon small-scale and rural industries, for whose labor force no alternative form of employment appeared to be available and for whose output there seemed no alternative source of supply. But the government's main intentions were clearly focused on the cultivation of large-scale modern industries, especially in fields like energy production, transport, machinery, chemicals, and steel. In the world marketplace, the indications were that China was devoting principal attention to high-cost, capital-intensive, and relatively high technology. The quantity of such imports for which China had contracted by the end of 1978 exceeded most previous expectations and in the short term, at least, China's propensity to import plant, know-how, equipment, arms, and technical information seemed sure to continue. This was certain to create consequential problems ranging from the encouragement of entrepreneurship and its place within the preferred socioeconomic system to making optimal use of the imported plant, and from problems of the scope and direction of domestic investment to the introduction of an institutional flexibility which would allow the growth and expansion of successfully innovative groups and the decline and disappearance of unsuccessful ones.

The quantity of imports also implied some methodology,

both effective and agreed, for coping with the associated foreign trading and financing problems. For an external observer in 1978, it was not clear how the very large investment and import claims implied by China's industrialization and technology program could be financed in the medium and long term. Even allowing for a combination of increased exports, including oil exports, new policies on accepting foreign loans, and an ability to tap the aid resources of the advanced world in a period when the general strategic and economic interests of the major Western powers seemed to favor a strengthening of China, prospective import totals in the region of $50 billion between 1978 and 1985 seemed likely to press close upon the upper limits of the possible. Competition among potential Western suppliers for initial contracts with the Chinese government might give way to cooler assessments once China's foreign partners began to compare, contrast, and aggregate the various suggested arrangements and to draw conclusions about the limits of the feasible. Concessional rates of interest might not be available to China for long. Nor could the Chinese authorities themselves prudently disregard the general mortgage upon future economic and political freedom of maneuver which large economic obligations to the West could represent. For that matter, while Western technology was efficient, it was also costly. This fact, together with the general expansion of trade, could easily bring with it increasing domestic criticism in the name of national self-reliance and the exclusion of undesirable foreign influences.

Even larger problems could arise in the management of the other element of the government's modernization drive, the development of science, technology, and their educational backup. The government recognized that education is the key to the struggle for development. But it was also clear that a full educational infrastructure would take a long time to build, perhaps decades. It would take equally long to develop an adequate research and development sector. The government itself was probably realistic in supposing that it might take twenty years. It could easily take longer. Its construction was beginning under conditions of grave shortage of trained scientific manpower. There was an inadequate science

communications system within China and between China and
the outside world. Many scientists were wary of shifts in the
political wind and would not easily be reassured. For all the
Maoist and post-Mao rhetoric about initiative, spontaneity,
and boldness, they were aware of the reality of—by Western
standards—tight control. They could easily bury themselves in
overly narrow specialisms in ways that would slow down, or
even prevent, a fruitful conjunction of ideas across disciplinary
boundaries. In the absence of adequate communications, much
of their energies might be spent in reinventing what had
already been developed elsewhere or else the very scale of
science and technology imports could inhibit some kinds of
local innovative drives.

There were additional questions about the time likely to
elapse between the emergence of an idea, even of a technology,
and the time when it would become broadly used and applied.
Many of the ideas of the Maoist period about modern
technology can be traced back to Kuomintang-era reactions
against large-scale capitalism. Mao himself was influenced by
Bukharin's ideas about agriculture as the successful basis for
industrialization. For all the Stalinist emphasis on heavy
industry during the 1950s, there were elements in Mao's
thought that suggested different conclusions. In any case, the
concept of a mass line and group decision making does not lend
itself to the pursuit of unconventional ideas by unconventional
innovators. Nor is bureaucratic control typically a prescription
for risk and the furthering of unusual ideas. The very strength
of the pressures of 1977/78 for change may have created some
obstacles to it, in that pressures for quick solutions seemed
likely to produce ones involving smaller rather than more
adventurous deviations from the known and accustomed or
from the accepted Western model.

There could be further difficulties. Industrial modernization
might cause some labor troubles. The emphasis on scientific,
technical, and managerial improvements involves a tolerance
of enterprise on the one hand and criteria of technical
judgment on the other which it may prove difficult to keep
subordinate to the needs of Party control. The new classes of
specialists and managers and entrepreneurs, if allowed to

flourish, seem likely to press for liberalization of thought and perhaps of life-style. Students and scientists can hardly avoid being influenced by foreign ideas and experiences. Technical and industrial groups will get new ideas from a variety of foreign contacts. There is no reason to doubt that the Chinese authorities, like their predecessors over two centuries, will try to manage these foreign contacts with circumspection and a careful regard for limiting undesirable influences on Chinese ways. Yet in modern industry and even more in science and research, excellence seems likely to depend to a peculiar extent upon exchanges of persons and ideas which cannot be easy to control. Tensions might arise between controllers and researchers, with an assertion of control likely to lead, as often as not, to some reduction in research performance. Altogether, any institutionalization which is not to be stifling will require, in the new circumstances, a flexibility and speed of reaction by economic and political institutions which could be hard to square with past methods of planning and control. Central plans might have to be complemented more fully by local initiatives. Industrial and laboratory managers might need to be given greater authority and encouraged to take risks. If the scientific and technical community is to be optimally effective, it will need greater autonomy in such matters as recruitment and even direction of research. But the problems of the general controllability of the intellectual and professional lives of such research and industrial communities may give pause to a leadership that wishes to emphasize either central authority or the importance of correct belief. Even the co-opting of the scientific and technical elite into the political leadership could at some point be thought to conflict with accepted patterns of Party membership and Party dominance. Yet, as China proceeds up the curve of technological development, the trade-offs between social planning and political attitudes on the one hand, and freedom of movement for the innovator on the other, could become more and not less difficult. Their successful management might require careful preparation and long-term sociopolitical planning of a kind which had not appeared by 1978.

Therefore, it seemed likely that observers would be obliged to distinguish with care between a quantitative expansion of Chinese capacities, whether in the industrial or the military field, and an increase in the sophistication of the methodologies involved. That China's GNP would grow was certain. That her GNP ratio with the United States and Japan would improve was probable.[1] But the rate of improvement in her industrial and technical capacities need not be proportionate. More important than her ability to develop new technologies, for example, could be the speed of the application of the technologies, once they were available, the rate of technological improvement at the R and D level, and the rate at which such improvements were translatable from development and testing to production and deployment. There was no reason to doubt China's ability to expand and improve her general research, industrial, and military capacities. But for closer assessments, it would be useful to try to distinguish between high-quality research, or production limited to some quite specific fields, and developments that had affected, or could affect, the sophistication of the national effort in one or more broad industrial or military sectors. One touchstone for the rate of improvement in industrial and technical performance, and the rate and acceptability of change, might be the freedom with which men and ideas could be exchanged with the outside world. It was not just that autarchy was apt to produce weaknesses in particular fields; it was, in Kuznets's sense, that economic and technical development could not, *ex hypothesi*, be autarchic. In China's case, too, it seemed likely that interdependence, however delicately managed, would prove to be inseparable from technical progress in anything other than the very short term.

A key question is that of political continuity. By the end of 1978, inevitably, it remained unresolved. But it was likely to be a condition of modernization that managers, entrepreneurs, and other risk-takers should come to feel greater assurance about the likely permanence of the political line favoring their activities. High-technology and capital-intensive projects in particular require an orderly and relatively predictable political and economic framework if their huge investments of men and resources are to be justified. More generally, the development and diffusion of technology is not only, or even principally, an economic or technical problem but a social and political and ideological one. The achievement of modernity depends less on hardware than on particular kinds of social processes, resting not only on particular innovative capabilities but on general attitudes to innovation and change. What is required, therefore, is a social systems approach in which all parts contribute to the achievement. A highly educated research sector is not enough. Access to the world community is not enough. A propensity to high investment need not be enough. The various parts of the system must fit together and be managed in an adaptive and flexible way. Certainly, China has shown in the past that it is not a static society, that it can manage change on acceptable terms, and that the CCP can control and assimilate large changes in the political and social landscape. And the simplest explanation for Teng's radical changes in 1977/78 would be that he wanted to establish before his death a fait accompli to which his successors would be compelled to adapt. Once heavy industrial equipment has been imported, it must be installed and people trained to use it and manage its output, irrespective of the preferences of the then ruling group. Once students have been sent abroad, the impressions they have absorbed will stay with them, as was the case with the former students who once founded the infant Communist Party of China. Once a class of technologists and technically minded bureaucrats has been created, it will develop its own dynamism and pursue its own interests within the political system. And once sizable foreign obligations have been incurred, all the forces of pride and nationalism, of maintaining "face" vis-à-vis the foreigner and commercial standing in the international market, can be harnessed to the task of fulfilling them.

But a number of problems remain, and some of them might become more acute. There are traditional difficulties concerning the relationship of the center and the provinces, the cities and the countryside. These have involved, and will presumably continue to involve, not merely explicitly political issues but fiscal management, industrial planning, inter-provincial resource allocation, and the whole spectrum of domestic planning and management. The process of modernization could make at least some of these problems and tensions more acute. It may increase rather than decrease the tensions between the urban bourgeoisie of Peking, Shanghai, and Canton on the one hand and the peasantry on the other, between richer and poorer provinces in a period of some decentralization of responsibility and greater emphasis on competition. Differentials might lead to regional complementarity and cooperation on some issues but to divisiveness and factionalism on others. The solutions of a Teng, of the "moderates," of the Confucians, had to do with modernization essentially from above and control by planners and enlightened civil servants. They allowed for the retention and expansion of private activities, including private plots and rural markets, and more freedom for enterprises. Yet if these developments are to be adequately controlled, this would require highly automated data and information links between decentralized entities—which are not available—or, more probably, the growth of a large and unwieldy mandarin bureaucracy. It might even, especially under great external pressures, lead to an attempt to achieve mobilization and modernization through a new Stalinism, based upon segments of the military, the Party, and the new classes.

There must also be the danger of a political backlash against an overly abrupt attempt to modernize the country. It has been said that one should not try to do more good than people will bear. Whether the administration, and especially Teng, has transgressed that boundary of the acceptable remains unclear. But a backlash might be based upon some form of xenophobia. It might be a reaction to an uprooting of accustomed ways. And it might be part of a revival of ideas too easily discarded by the new administration. For it may be premature to conclude that any scheme for ruling 900 million people, especially people as varied and diverse as the population of China, can be devised without the help of an overarching ideology to mobilize emotions in the service of the collectivity. Such an ideology must be malleable, sensitive to pragmatic needs, and heavily influenced by considerations of national pride. But it would also be bound to imply a certain rigidity of principle and perceptual framework. Indeed, if it did not have some of these characteristics of a secular faith, it would fail in its unifying and mobilizing role. Hence, the pragmatism of a Teng and of his possible successors should be seen as compatible with the ideology and designed to serve its higher purposes, rather than as an alternative to it.

But it may also be premature to conclude that China either can or will wish to do without an elite group dedicated to messianic beliefs and revolutionary values. The populist, participatory, and egalitarian elements of Maoism, in conflict alike with the new classes associated with technical modernization and the totalitarian traditions of Chinese politics, will not be lightly abandoned. Though Chiang Ch'ing and her associates may be beyond political redemption, it is not impossible that some of the causes for which they stood, no doubt shorn of certain excesses, might in time be revived and used against the bureaucratic state. Indeed, it may be arguable that such principles need to be revived and sustained not so much to constrain modernization but to make it possible. If acceptability of innovation, participation, and willingness to change are essential characteristics of the innovative society, mass mobilization may come to be a condition for it, both to rally the general populace to its implications and to mollify the discontended and those whom the managerial revolution has deprived of their inheritance.

On quite general grounds, therefore, and in the absence of major upheavals in China's internal or external relations, it seems unlikely that, even if all were to go well with the government's plans, any major industrial, economic, or even military developments could take place in China before A.D. 2000 whose basic technical components were not visible by 1978. If so, the following propositions appear to be plausible. The new government will continue its rapid progress from the political and economic trough of 1975/76, at least for the time being. Production and productivity will improve. There may be greater freedom for local managers in a complex pattern of managerial decentralization in a framework of central planning and general direction. There will be an expansion, rapid in the immediate future, of all three major elements of foreign trade: general exports, industrial and technological imports, and willingness to accept credits and aid. There will be greater concentration on incentive systems both material and non-material, such as the use of the family as the unit of account within a commune. But questions will remain for some time about China's capacity to produce much new design and development, as distinct from absorption and adaptation. China may be able, by the use of particular skills, to jump a technological generation in some limited areas. But while industrial capacities seem certain to expand, there were no signs in 1978 that industry as a whole, or any major sector of it, would become a high-technology sector in the Western sense, based on a strong and diversified domestic R and D system, before the end of the century. If so, the government's call for parity with the advanced nations of the world within twenty years, for all its utility in mobilizing effort in pursuit of a concretely stated aim, will have been mere propaganda. In 1978, it seemed more probable that, in very broad terms, the technical differentials between China on the one hand and the United States, the Soviet Union, and Japan on the other would be—in the sense of effective lead times for deployment—not so different in A.D. 2000 from what they were twenty-two years earlier.

In the military field, China had become, by the mid-1970s, a major regional power, capable of defeating or devastating almost all the countries around her periphery. She did not, however, pose a strategic threat to the superpowers and was not likely to do so within the foreseeable future. The policies of 1977/78 suggested a much greater emphasis on discipline and professionalism within the PLA and the beginnings of a high-technology defense capacity in other than the nuclear sphere. It was likely that China would improve her satellite capabilities through cooperation with the United States or Japan but improbable that she would soon be able to protect her satellites against, say, Soviet attempts to blind or destroy them. She would be able to obtain a variety of technologies, including dual-use technologies, from the West. She would probably begin to field fairly advanced antitank missiles by the beginning of the 1980s, and far more advanced radars, and to achieve the transition to micro-electronics in some areas. But the infra-structure for substantial military improvements would remain slender. Even if, for example, China's steel production reached 60 million tons per annum by the mid-1980s, as her 1978 plans suggested, this would hardly be adequate for a massive armament program as well as the needs of industrial modernization. While she might build a more complicated force structure, with a stronger and more sophisticated system of logistic support, there were no signs in 1978 that would lead one to suppose that a substantial, high-technology defense capacity, based on a major domestic R and D and production effort, was likely to appear before the turn of the century.

In the meantime, some of China's major geopolitical problems might be less how to close the technology gap between herself and her competitors than how to prevent that gap from growing. The problem was the more difficult in that its resolution was certain to depend less on China's own development than on the effort put into developing new technologies by the United States, the USSR, West Germany, Japan, and others. These efforts would concern not only the development of scientific and technical capacities within these countries but involve the qualitative components in any Soviet-American arms-control agreement or other inter-national arrangements on scientific exchanges. In those areas where China was concerned to be industrially or militarily competitive, her government could hardly avoid making a major effort at least to avoid declining lead-time relativities.

What of the larger relationships between such a China and the outside world? It seemed clear during the years of the mid-1970s that the government's attention was principally concen-trated on the scale and complexity of its domestic problems. But the observation that foreign affairs were secondary, in the sense of being interesting mainly as an input for domestic concerns, might be made with some variation of emphasis for most major states. It was rather that there were some clear trends in China's desire to expand her influence in the world, and many of them had to do with Peking's concepts of national security and national development. The principal threat was perceived as coming from the Soviet Union. Partly to counter it and partly as a tool for rapid modernization, China expanded and strengthened her relations with the advanced industrial democracies. During 1977/78, she achieved some remarkable diplomatic successes. The recognition agreement with the United States in December 1978 and the trade and friendship agreements with Japan earlier in the year forged, largely on China's terms, a triangular relationship of considerable potential. It would give China fuller access to American and Japanese technology, even aid. It would greatly strengthen China's international position and the constraints on the Soviet Union in its confrontation with China. It would permit considerable flexibility, which might lead to tacit U.S. acceptance of Chinese aims in Southeast Asia, or which might be used to strengthen China's economic relations with Western Europe and her ability to use Europe to constrain Soviet ambitions. The removal of American recognition from Taiwan opened up a variety of possibilities, from absorption of Taiwan into the Chinese polity or the bland acceptance of Taiwan as a larger and more potent Hong Kong and, hence, a major economic and technical asset and input for China, to the role which a Taiwan politically linked with the mainland could eventually play in the naval, air, and general strategic balance of the western Pacific. A number of Taiwan's agreements with the outside world, if maintained, could become assets for China as a whole. Among these might be the island's enriched nuclear-fuel agreement with the United States or uranium supply contracts with other nations.

The most pregnant possibilities were undoubtedly those relating to Japan. By the end of 1978, Japan had become a key factor in Chinese development planning. Their economic complementarity was likely to drive the relationship further. Their cultural and emotional links were likely to strengthen their entente. Common strategic interests vis-à-vis the Soviet Union might even, in time, develop that entente into an alliance. The relationship was being forged with the goodwill, to some extent under the auspices, of the United States. Yet its very development could gradually diminish the need for American goodwill as Chinese markets became more fruitful for Japan, as Japanese technology became even more fully available to China, and as their combined military power diminished the need for U.S. support in some circumstances. In sum, the triangle of China, Japan, and the United States might not remain equilateral. If so, the changes in global power patterns of 1978 were merely the precursor of more fundamental changes, not necessarily to the advantage of the West but tending substantially to enlarge China's leverage on the international scene.

In the meantime, a number of internal Chinese developments could also have useful external payoffs. Even limited industrial and military developments could significantly alter the political and strategic balance of Southeast Asia. China was likely to enjoy other advantages, some having to do with foreign perceptions. Chinese officials were likely to encourage the foreign sense of awe in contemplating this great civilization, comprising a quarter of the human race, its cultural magnetism and the feeling that it had to be conciliated simply because it was there.[2] They were likely to try to manage the country's external relations so that China would remain mysterious and romantic, a society endlessly fascinating to outsiders, and both able and willing to use for its own pragmatic ends the sense in so many foreign quarters that a gesture from China was a prize worth winning.

At the same time, China's position had a number of weaknesses. Actions, such as those in Vietnam, were liable to create doubts about the quality of her risk-taking. Her policies and the personal positions of some of her leaders, especially of Teng, had become more vulnerable to shifts in American or Japanese policies. Her development program was likely to cause alarm abroad long before its fruition had led to means for the exercise of real power. More generally, while many of the issues of contemporary concern to the international community were irrelevant to Chinese policies, China was also irrelevant to some and peripheral to many of the issues of global politics. She had no especially influential voice in matters concerning the deep seabed, the politics of space, international monetary matters, or technology transfer. Partly in consequence, even on those matters with which she was directly concerned, such as energy issues or trade, she was largely compelled to accommodate to world conditions in whose creation or setting she had had only a minimal part.

China tended, in other words, to be a price and technology taker rather than a setter. Her policymakers labored under further difficulties. China was compelled to operate in an increasingly complex international environment but also one in which the passage of time and the obligations and precedents created by her own activities were bound to diminish her freedom of maneuver. This meant, equally, a diminution of her ability to give free rein in her foreign policies to her ideological preferences, a fact that could create problems; for example, in adjusting those policies to any shifts in the domestic political situation.

In considering the future, one should always bear in mind the power of the unexpected. China may well once more astonish the world. Political circumstances within the country might change, even dramatically. She might again react in unexpected ways to external upheavals, whether a change of regime in Japan or a war in the Middle East or Southeast Asia. In her relations with the Soviet Union, neither the extreme of war nor that of accommodation can be wholly discounted, though neither seemed imminent in 1978. A war might occur because of escalation from border clashes, or by overspill from wars elsewhere, or even through deliberate attack by one side against the other. An accommodation could spring, on China's side, from a sense of acute military danger which had to be averted even at very large political cost, or else from a need to assure peace for some period ahead so as to permit a yet greater diversion of resources away from immediate military needs. But assuming that such major upheavals do not occur, that the new relationships with Japan and the United States continue to be the main frame of China's foreign relations, it seems likely that her relative industrial, technical, and military weaknesses will not be substantially eliminated before the end of the century. In the meantime, China will continue to play from weakness, albeit sometimes brilliantly, in an arena of global great power adjustments. For all the new elements of technology, energy, and resource politics, it will be a familiar and classic game, a balance of power in which there are no permanent friends or permanent enemies.

Notes

Chapter 1

1. Not, of course, that all the men of the Long March disappeared with the old leaders. Quite a number continued in office, not least in the People's Liberation Army (PLA).

2. E. Balasz, *Chinese Civilization and Bureaucracy* (New Haven: Yale University Press, 1964).

3. Toward the end of 1978, the President of China's Supreme Court, Chiang Hua, asked delicately, "with regard to forced confessions and physical torture, can we say they are a thing of the past?" (quoted in *The Economist*, 4 November 1978, p. 61).

4. On the Chinese legal and prison system, see "Political Imprisonment in the People's Republic of China," London, Amnesty International, 1978. There have also been suggestions in the West, quoting unnamed Chinese officials that the labor camps contained 5-6 percent of the population. William Safire, *New York Times* (hereafter cited as *NYT*), 25 March 1977, p. A9. Assuming a population of 900 million that would mean some 45-50 million prisoners. When the Central Committee of the Party ordered in 1978 the release of all the people held as "rightists" since 1957, the number of people involved was given as 110,000 (see *NYT*, 3 December 1978, p. E1).

5. As late as 1978, there were cases such as the one mentioned by Amnesty International of a man executed for political offenses, namely printing and distributing a "counterrevolutionary" leaflet.

6. Jacques Guillermaz suggests that during the campaigns of 1949-52 there were five million executions (see Guillermaz, *The Chinese Communist Party in Power 1949-1976* [Folkestone: Dawson, 1976], p. 24, fn. 8). Mao Tse-tung told Edgar Snow that even the most sensational foreign reports had seriously underestimated the violence

and killing during the Cultural Revolution. U.S. estimates of the number of dead between the installation of the regime in 1949 and the fading out of the Cultural Revolution in 1969 range up to 25 or even 60 million (see Committee on the Judiciary, subcommittee to investigate the administration of the Internal Security Act and other Internal Security Laws, *The Human Cost of Communism in China* [Washington, D.C.: Government Printing Office, 1971], pp. 16-17).

7. If they were not, as in the case of the Tien Anmen Square riots of 5 April 1976, they were promptly suppressed.

8. I am indebted for this point to Professor H. F. Simon.

9. See Stuart Schram, "Introduction," in S. Schram, ed., *Authority, Participation, and Cultural Change in China* (Cambridge: Cambridge University Press, 1973), pp. 1-108.

10. At the Ninth Party Congress in 1969, three-quarters of the delegates wore PLA uniform (Juergen Domes, *China after the Cultural Revolution: Politics between Two Party Congresses* [London: C. Hurst, 1977], p. 16).

11. *Peking Review*, 24 January 1975, pp. 21-25.

12. *People's Daily*, 9 February 1975; *Peking Review*, 28 February 1975, p. 5.

13. Chang Chun-chiao, "On Exercising All-round Dictatorship over the Bourgeoisie," *Peking Review*, 4 April 1975, p. 7.

14. Yao Wen-yuan, "On the Social Basis of the Lin Piao Anti-Party Clique," *Peking Review*, 7 March 1975, p. 9.

15. Reviving an argument put by Hung Hsueh-ping, the essence of "theory of productive forces" is to oppose proletarian revolution (*Peking Review*, 19 September 1969, p. 7).

16. Quoted in Tang Tsou, "Mao Tse-tung Thought, the Last Struggle for Succession, and the Post-Mao Era," *China Quarterly* (September 1977):513.

17. The documents, in translation, can be found in Chi Hsin, *The Case of the Gang of Four* (Hong Kong: Cosmos Books, 1977), pp. 203-95.

18. Teng did not confine himself to occasional documents. In September 1975, he is reported to have said that "white and expert" was, so long as people could help China, much better than those who babbled but did not assist production (see "Teng Hsiao-ping's Comments Interposed upon Listening to Hu Yao-peng's Briefing [26 September 1975]," reported in *Issues and Studies* [September 1977]:75).

19. Tang Tsou, "Mao Tse-tung Thought," pp. 513-16.

20. Issue of December 1975.

21. *Peking Review*, 2 January 1976, p. 9.

22. It has been suggested that since Chou's and Teng's supporters controlled most of the normal party communications channels, the Shanghai group's supporters set up their own illegal document reproduction and distribution centers (see Kenneth Lieberthal, "The Politics of Modernization in the PRC," *Problems of Communism* [May/June 1978]:4).

23. As CCP chairman, Mao had the power to make temporary appointments without securing a formal vote.

24. *Peking Review*, 9 April 1976, p. 3.

25. Ibid.

26. Ibid., 14 May 1976, p. 14.

27. Ibid., 24 December 1976, p. 8.

28. The Foreign Ministry announced on June 15 to foreigners in Peking that Chairman Mao would no longer receive foreign visitors.

29. *Ming Pao*, 26 October 1976.

30. New China News Agency (hereafter cited as NCNA), 21 October 1976.

31. One version of the document was circulated internally in 1969. In it, the need for formal training is played down (see *Issues and Studies* [April 1977]). The 1976/77 version emphasizes the anti-Soviet elements, the rehabilitation of cadres who have made errors, and the need to learn from abroad as well as the needs of industrial development (see NCNA, 25 and 26 December 1976, and Mao Tse-tung, *Selected Works*, Vol. 5 [Peking: Foreign Language Press, 1977]).

32. Agence France Press (AFP), Hong Kong, 16 January 1977.

33. Kyodo, 27 March 1977.

34. See *Ming Pao*, 26 May 1977, and *Peking Review*, 29 July 1977, p. 5.

35. This would, of course, safeguard Teng's critics from any subsequent charges that they had been guilty of an error of line.

36. NCNA, 22 July 1977, and *Peking Review*, 29 July 1977, p. 5.

37. For the major documents of the congress, held from 12 to 18 August 1977, see *Peking Review*, 26 August and 2 September 1977.

38. It may also be interesting to note that the 1,510 delegates at the Eleventh Congress represented 35 million CCP members as compared with memberships of 17 million in 1961 and 28 million in 1973. Whether this expansion will dilute discipline and morale remains to be seen.

39. The taxonomy is Emily McFarquhar's; *The Economist*, 31 December 1977, p. 24.

40. It was the elite guards of Unit 8341, under Mao's Chief of

Security Wang Tung-hsing, who carried out the arrests. Wang became one of the four vice-chairmen of the CCP at the Eleventh CCP Congress in September 1977 and a member of the five-man Standing Committee of the Politburo.

41. See, for example, the editorials and reports in *Liberation Army Daily*, 8 November 1976, Foreign Broadcast Information Service, Daily Report: People's Republic of China (hereafter cited as FBIS-CHI), 9 November 1976, p. E1; ibid., p. E3; NCNA, 30 October 1976, FBIS-CHI, 1 November 1976, pp. E11-13; *People's Daily*, 31 October 1976.

42. See, for example, NCNA, 5 June 1977, FBIS-CHI, 6 June 1977, p. E4.

43. On the fears of a fresh change of line, and reluctance to take responsibility, see, for example, *People's Daily*, 9 July 1978, FBIS-CHI, 14 July 1978, p. E18. And in Hong Kong, many people in the new wave of refugees who left the PRC in the second half of 1978 said they wanted to go while the going was good; what would happen if Teng died or his policies were changed? (see *Australian Financial Review*, 14 November 1978, p. 12).

44. See his remarks of 2 June 1978, *Peking Review*, 23 June 1978, p. 20.

45. See *Kwangming Daily*, 15 November 1978.

46. At the end of 1978, the Tien Anmen riots of April 1976, for which Teng had been condemned, were declared to have been "entirely revolutionary actions," and the "Wuhan incident" of 1967, which amounted to an armed uprising against the Cultural Revolution, was exonerated. For the first, see NCNA, 15 November 1978, and the communiqué of the Third Plenary Session of the Eleventh Central Committee on 22 December 1978, text in *Newsbulletin* of the PRC embassy, Canberra, 4 January 1979. For the second, see Kyodo, 3 January 1979. During the latter part of 1978, a large number of people were rehabilitated and returned to active politics. Even Peng Teh-huai, in disgrace since 1959, was exonerated.

47. According to the *Kwangming Daily*, 29 October 1976, Mao "was a man, not a God." See also *People's Daily*, 5 November 1977, and *Li-shih yen-chiu* No. 1 (1978), FBIS-CHI, 14 November 1977, p. E14, and 24 March 1978, pp. E1-9, respectively, in which points about Mao are made in thinly disguised form by references to the former Emperor Chin Shih Huang-ti.

48. For example, *People's Daily*, 1 July 1978, published some remarks dating from January 1962 in which Mao confessed to having made erroneous decisions during the Great Leap Forward and to

being responsible for a good part of the economic disasters of the early 1960s.

49. *People's Daily*, 27 October 1978.

50. Communiqué of the Third Plenary Session of the Eleventh Central Committee, *Newsbulletin*, p. 7.

51. *People's Daily*, 21 November 1978.

52. FBIS-CHI, 15 March 1978, p. E5.

53. Compare, for example, Hua's addresses to the Fifth National People's Congress and to the National Science Conference (FBIS-CHI, 16 March 1978, Supplement pp. 3-39, and NCNA, 25 March 1978, FBIS-CHI, 27 March 1978, pp. E1-8) with Teng's address to the latter meeting (NCNA, 21 March 1978, FBIS-CHI, 21 March 1978, pp. E4-15, and *Peking Review*, 24 March 1978, pp. 9-18).

54. Address of 4 May 1977 to the National Conference on "Learning from Tachai"; *Ta-kung-pao*, 9 May 1977, p. 4.

55. Chairman Hua told the Fifth NPC that the campaign against the radicals would continue "for some time to come" (for his address, see FBIS-CHI, 16 March 1978, Supplement pp. 3-39; for a summary, see NCNA, 26 February 1978). A few months later, on 7 July, he told the National Finance and Trade Conference that in most of the country the battle against the Gang of Four had been won (*Peking Review*, 28 July 1978, pp. 6-7). Teng confirmed that the campaign was not complete (see his remarks of 2 June 1978 in *Peking Review*, 28 July 1978, p. 19). The brief announcement that the campaign would be wound up came in the communiqué of the Third Plenary Session of the Eleventh Central Committee, *Newsbulletin*.

56. See, for example, articles of 2 November 1977 and 5 November 1977 in *People's Daily* criticizing Mao and Hua; FBIS-CHI, 7 November 1977, pp. E9-13, and 14 November 1977, p. E14, respectively.

57. For the major documents of the Fifth NPC, see FBIS-CHI, 16 March 1978, Supplement.

58. Reports of his dismissal reached the West in October (see *The Economist*, 14 October 1978, p. 52).

59. *The Economist*, 9 December 1978, p. 61.

60. The *Times*, 28 November 1978, p. 1; *Washington Post*, 28 and 29 November 1978; *Australian Financial Review*, 29 November 1978, pp. 2-3; also the *Times*, 27 November 1978, p. 1.

61. Communiqué of the Third Plenary Session of the Eleventh Central Committee, *Newsbulletin*.

62. *Peking Review*, 30 April 1969, pp. 16-35.

63. *Peking Review*, 7 September 1973, pp. 17-25.

64. For Teng's address, see *Peking Review*, 12 April 1974, Supple-

ment pp. 1-5. For Chou's, see *Peking Review*, 24 January 1975, pp. 21-23.

65. At this point, I have relied partly on Kenneth Lieberthal, "The Foreign Policy Debate in Peking as Seen through Allegorical Articles 1973-76," *China Quarterly* (September 1977):528-54.

66. *Peking Review*, 26 August 1978, pp. 23-57; also *People's Daily*, 1 November 1977, on the importance of Chairman Mao's three worlds theory.

67. Communiqué of the Third Plenary Session of the Eleventh Central Committee, *Newsbulletin*.

68. See Teng's remarks to Western journalists on 7 January 1978; *The Age* (Melbourne), 8 January 1978, p. 8.

69. *Peking Review*, 2 January 1976, p. 7.

70. See, for example, an article in *Liberation Army Daily* praising Lenin for exposing "sham leftists" who in 1917 opposed signing a peace treaty with Germany (quoted in *Washington Post*, 9 February 1978, p. A17).

71. For example, *Kwangming Daily*, 10 November 1977.

72. Worse still, appeasement could become collusion, as in the case of the Soviet-American Strategic Arms Limitation Talks.

73. According to some U.S. senators who visited China in December 1978, senior Chinese military officers had dropped hints about the possibility of a U.S. naval visit to a Chinese port (see *Washington Post*, 11 January 1979).

74. The communiqué, and related documents, can be found in "America's Diplomatic Ties with the People's Republic of China," United States Policy Statement Series, 1978 (Washington, International Communication Agency, 1978); see also Chairman Hua's press conference of 16 December, in *Survival* (March/April 1979):79-80.

75. *Washington Post*, 11 January 1979.

76. See *NYT*, 17 December 1978, p. E1, for some reports of Chinese soundings for business cooperation and technical aid.

77. NCNA, 19 December 1978.

78. As Teng put it, Secretary of State Vance had told Chinese leaders in Peking that U.S. military power was greater than that of the Soviet Union, "but we don't believe him."

79. See, for example, the criticisms of Western weakness by "Commentator" in the *People's Daily*, 21 February 1978; also Huang Hua's address of 30 July 1977 to senior cadres in Peking, text published in *Background on China* (New York: Chinese Information Service, 26 December 1977), esp. pp. 28-31. Though there is some question of the authenticity of this document, its contents seem to

accord well with what is known of Huang Hua's views.

80. See, for instance, the instructions about the new U.S. relationship issued in 1973 by the Political Department of the Kunming military region for army education purposes (in *Issues and Studies* [June 1974]). They argued that President Nixon's visit to China would serve to promote Chinese views in the United States and help to exacerbate Soviet-American tensions as well as distrust between the United States and her allies. For China, the whole thing was a tactical alliance with a basically hostile regime.

81. Text in *Jetro China Newsletter* No. 18 (June 1978):25-26.

82. Kyodo news agency reported on 6 January 1979 that Chinese orders concluded or under negotiation with Japanese industry amounted to $79 billion.

83. *Australian Financial Review*, 8 January 1979.

84. Remarks at a Tokyo news conference, *Peking Review*, 3 November 1978, pp. 14-17.

85. For the text of the treaty, see NCNA Peking (English), 12 August 1978; *Peking Review*, 18 August 1978, pp. 7-8.

86. As long ago as September 1977, Teng had told Japanese visitors to Peking that Japan could not hope to avoid Soviet encroachments on Japanese sovereignty in the longer term and should consider a Sino-Japanese military alliance. The stream of Japanese visitors to Peking during the mid-1970s included a number of military men.

87. Speaking in Tokyo, Teng made it plain that he thought Korea would be unified again—someday (*Peking Review*, 3 November 1978, p. 16). See also the call for unification in the *People's Daily* editorial of 6 February 1978. This is not to say that Peking may not have found the status quo convenient for the time being.

88. In connection with the ratification of the Sino-Japanese Treaty, the Chinese side was understood to have given assurances that there would be no more Chinese-inspired incidents directed at the Japanese-administered Senkaku Islands, at the center of an oil-bearing area. Similar lessons were implied by Teng Hsiao-ping's visits to Thailand and Malaysia and Li Hsien-nien's to the Philippines in the same year.

89. For the text of the treaty, see *Soviet News*, 14 November 1978, p. 375; also *The Economist*, 11 November 1978, p. 75, and *The Age* (Melbourne), 6 November 1978, p. 8. For Teng's comment, see *Peking Review*, 17 November 1978, pp. 24-26.

90. Cf. Mark Frankland in the *Observer* (London), 14 January 1979, p. 10. For the background to the dispute, see Sheldon W.

Simon, "New Conflict in Indo-China," *Problems of Communism* (September/October 1978):20-36.

91. For Chinese support for Kampuchean guerillas, see the *Observer*, 14 January 1979, passim; the *Canberra Times*, 9 January 1979, p. 1, and 10 January 1979, pp. 1, 6. For the Chinese invasion of Vietnam, see Xinhua statement, 17 February 1979, text in *Newsbulletin* No. 7906, of 18 February 1979, PRC embassy, Canberra, pp. 1-3; *NYT*, 18 February 1979, p. 1; and for comments on the danger of a Soviet response see *NYT*, 19 February 1979, pp. A1, 10-11, and 20 February 1979, p. A6.

92. For his news conference of 8 November 1978 in Bangkok, see *Peking Review*, 17 November 1978, pp. 24-26.

93. *Peking Review*, 17 November 1978, passim.

94. Communiqué of the Third Plenary Session of the Eleventh Central Committee, *Newsbulletin*.

95. These were profound and of long standing, for example in Malaysia and Indonesia.

Chapter 2

1. *Red Flag* (August 1978); *Peking Review*, 11 August 1978, pp. 5-11.

2. For example, Chairman Hua's address of 29 May 1978 to the All-Army Work Conference (*Peking Review*, 16 June 1978, p. 9). Foreign Minister Huang Hua told the United Nations, "The continuation of fierce contention between the superpowers is bound to lead to world war some day. This is independent of man's will" (address of 29 September 1977 to the UN General Assembly, text issued by the PRC Mission to the UN; also *Liberation Army Daily*, editorial of 26 January 1978, Peking Domestic Service, 10 April 1977, Foreign Broadcast Information Service, Daily Report: People's Republic of China [hereafter cited as FBIS-CHI], 14 April 1977, p. H2). For similar remarks by Teng to the French prime minister, M. Raymond Barre, see *Le Monde*, 21 January 1978, pp. 1, 5.

3. Communiqué of the Third Plenary Session of the Eleventh Central Committee; text in *Newsbulletin* of the PRC embassy, Canberra, 4 January 1979.

4. Huang Hua, statement of 29 September 1977, p. 18. Or, as Chairman Hua put it succinctly, quoting Mao, China's attitude to world war is "First, we are against it; second, we are not afraid of it" (see his political report to the Eleventh CCP Congress on 12 August 1977, *Peking Review*, 26 August 1977, p. 41).

5. Huang Hua, statement of 30 July 1977, in *Background on China* (New York: Chinese Information Service, 26 December 1977), p. 25.

6. *The Military Balance 1978/79* (London: International Institute for Strategic Studies, 1978), p. 56.

7. *The Military Balance 1973/74* (London: International Institute for Strategic Studies, 1973), p. 46; *The Military Balance 1977/78*, pp. 52-54; *The Military Balance 1978/79*, p. 56; General George S. Brown, "United States Military Posture for FY 1979," Washington, 20 January 1978, pp. 41-42.

8. See General Brown, "United States Military Posture for FY 1979," p. 70, chart 32, for a comparison of the numbers of major U.S., USSR, and PRC ground-force weapons.

9. And not merely by purchase; in 1977, Egypt is believed to have "lent" a specimen of the Soviet Sagger wire-guided ATGM to the PRC after China had provided Egypt with MiG-21 engine replacements.

10. B. O. Suprowicz, "Electronics in China," *US-China Business Review* (May/June 1976):22.

11. Data taken from *The Military Balance 1977/78* and *1978/79*, passim; Janes Weapons Systems 1976, London; *Far Eastern Economic Review*, 9 December 1977, p. 28.

12. *Far Eastern Economic Review, Asia 1978 Yearbook* (Hong Kong: 1978), p. 36.

13. There were some differences in the details of Western estimates. General Brown listed China as having nineteen principal surface-combat vessels (cf. "United States Military Posture," p. 77).

14. Data taken from "China: Economic Indicators" (Washington, D.C.: Central Intelligence Agency Paper ER 77-10508, October 1977), Table 11B, p. 19, and Table 19, p. 35.

15. *New York Times* (hereafter cited as *NYT*), 24 June 1977, p. A3.

16. See the comments of a senior Defense Intelligence Agency official, Mr. Francis J. Romance, before a congressional committee in Washington on 30 June 1977 (*Washington Post*, 24 August 1977).

17. For most of these, see Stockholm International Peace Research Institute, *SIPRI Yearbook 1977* (Stockholm: SIPRI, 1977), pp. 401-6.

18. Circular error probable: the radius of a circle around the target within which 50 percent of the arriving warheads can be expected to fall. It is the conventional measurement of accuracy.

19. *The Military Balance 1978/79*, p. 55; General Brown, "United States Military Posture for FY 1979," pp. 41-42; *NYT*, 21 November 1977.

20. It appears to have used nonstorable liquid-oxygen fuel.

21. *The Military Balance 1978/79*, passim; also, Agence France Presse, Hong Kong, 19 July 1978, FBIS-CHI, 20 July 1978, p. E5.

22. General Brown, "United States Military Posture for FY 1979," p. 42; Secretary of Defense Harold Brown, "Department of Defense, Annual Report, FY 1979," Washington, 2 February 1978, p. 52.

23. Several kinds of difficulty might have arisen, ranging from fueling and guidance difficulties to general resource allocation problems or the political and diplomatic problems likely to be caused by deploying a weapon, one of whose principal apparent targets would be the United States.

24. There were reports that the CSS-2, for example, needed forty-eight hours to prepare for firing (*Far Eastern Economic Review, Asia 1978 Yearbook*, p. 33).

25. Some holes were kept empty, to make it difficult for an attacker to be sure just where the weapons were.

26. Janes Weapons Systems 1976, London, p. 233.

27. By 1978, Western estimates suggested that China was capable of placing four hundred kilograms into geostationary orbit, by the use of her basic launcher with suitable upper stages, including a re-startable motor for optimizing of orbit.

28. The 1976 satellites, for example, either ejected data capsules or returned to earth. The angle of orbit was such that the perigee was over the Soviet Union.

29. The *People's Daily* duly noted the military implications of this development on 8 November 1977.

30. Details of the first seven are from *Space Flight*, Vol. 19, No. 10 (October 1977).

31. *NYT*, 29 October 1977, p. 11.

32. So at least the deputy chief of the General Staff, Wu Shiu-chan, maintained to Lord Chalfont (*Times*, 10 July 1978, p. 12).

33. Carl von Clausewitz, *On War* (ed. and trans. Michael Howard and Peter Paret [Princeton, N.J.: Princeton University Press, 1976]).

34. Mao Tse-tung, *Selected Works*, Vol. 2 (New York: International Publishers, 1954), p. 192.

35. J. R. Green, *A Short History of the English People*, Everyman Series (London: J. M. Dent, 1915), p. 519.

36. Some of these views are further elaborated in my *Nuclear Weapons and Chinese Policy*, Adelphi Paper, No. 99 (London: International Institute for Strategic Studies, 1973).

37. According to the International Institute for Strategic Studies, Soviet forces in the Far East amounted to forty-five divs. (incl. eight

tank) in 1973/74, forty-five divs. (incl. seven tank) in 1976/77, and forty-four divs. (incl. seven tank) in 1978/79. The combat readiness of the force seems to have risen during this period: by 1978/79, half the divisions were classified as Category I or II, the latter meaning between half and three-quarter strength, complete with fighting vehicles (*The Military Balance 1973/74*, p. 6; *1976/77*, pp. 8-9; *1978/79*, p. 9). In October 1978, a Japanese parliamentary report suggested that the Russians had forty-three divisions (with some four hundred thousand men) on the border. Earlier in the year, John Erickson suggested that in the four Soviet military districts covering the Chinese border, the Red Army had thirty-nine motorized rifle divisions, six tank divisions, and one airborne division. Of these, the Far East had nineteen motorized rifle divisions, as well as two tank and one airborne division (see his "China Prepares for War," *The Spectator*, 27 May 1978, pp. 13, 14).

38. *The Military Balance 1978/79*, p. 10.

39. The dock had been supplied by Ishikawajima-Harima dockyard.

40. *Far Eastern Economic Review, Asia 1978 Handbook*, p. 35.

41. Harold Brown, "Department of Defense, Annual Report FY 1979," p. 3.

42. See, for example, an Agence France Presse report of 7 July 1978 from Hong Kong, FBIS-CHI, 10 July 1978, pp. A18-19. But the 1978 Chinese reports of such facilities were clearly exaggerated.

43. Chinese leaders on several occasions offered unfavorable comments on these constraints. Just after the visit to Peking by the U.S. Secretary of State Cyrus Vance, in August 1977, Teng Hsiao-ping remarked with surprising bluntness to a Japanese delegation that "the United States has the means but not the courage to start a war" (Kyodo news agency, 10 September 1977).

44. By 1977/78, Taiwan had six light-water reactors built or under construction: two of 600 Megawatt apiece from General Electric, two of 950 MW each from the same supplier, and two of 900 MW each from Westinghouse. The first GE 600 MW reactor became critical in November 1977 (see, for example, *Washington Post*, 16 November 1977, p. 20).

45. In 1977/78, the United States persuaded Taiwan to dismantle an already-assembled nuclear reprocessing plant.

46. See *NYT*, 24 June 1977.

47. Sydney H. Jammes, "The Chinese Defense Burden 1965-1974," in U.S. Congress, Joint Economic Committee, *China: A Reassessment of the Economy* (Washington, D.C.: Government Printing

Office, 10 July 1975), pp. 462-63.

48. As was once said of the Austro-Hungarian monarchy (albeit referring to princes, not peoples), *bella gerunt alii, tu felix Austria nube* ("others wage war while you, happy Austria, marry"; i.e., extend the empire by marriage, not war).

49. Peking Domestic Service, 5 February 1977, FBIS-CHI, 7 February 1977, p. E6.

50. Peking Domestic Service, 10 April 1977, FBIS-CHI, 13 April 1977, p. E5. Similar views were expressed by the theoretical group of the training department of the PLA General Staff (New China News Agency [hereafter cited as NCNA], 7 December 1976, FBIS-CHI, 8 December 1976, pp. E4-9) and a report by the PLA Academy of Military Sciences (NCNA, 4 February 1977, FBIS-CHI, 8 February 1977, pp. E4-6).

51. For example, the broadcast at the end of January 1978, attributed to the theoretical group of the National Defense, Scientific, and Technological Commission, criticized those who still thought that one could fight missiles with broadswords (Peking Home Service, 20 January 1978, in BBC Summary of World Broadcasts, FE/5721/BII/4, p. 3).

52. See his remarks of 2 June 1978, *Peking Review*, 23 June 1978, p. 21; also Peking Domestic Service, 28 June 1977, FBIS-CHI, 1 July 1977, pp. E1-6.

53. Issue of 30 January 1978.

54. NCNA, 25 September 1977, FBIS-CHI, 26 September 1977, p. E12; *Liberation Army Daily*, Peking Domestic Service, 25 June 1977, FBIS-CHI, 29 June 1977, p. E15; NCNA, 25 January 1978.

55. See the joint New Year's editorial in *People's Daily, Liberation Army Daily*, and *Red Flag*, in *Peking Review*, 6 January 1978, p. 7.

56. Address to the All-Army Work Conference on 29 May 1978, *Peking Review*, 16 June 1978, p. 10.

57. Address to the All-Army Work Conference on 29 May 1978, *Peking Review*, 23 June 1978, p. 12; also Teng at the 31 July 1978 Army Day reception, *Peking Review*, 4 August 1978, p. 3; and *People's Daily*, 3 July 1978, FBIS-CHI, 13 July 1978, pp. E3-4.

58. Chairman Hua, address of 29 May 1978, p. 10.

59. August 1978.

60. Peking Home Service, 20 January 1978.

61. For example, *Liberation Army Daily*, 9 July 1978, FBIS-CHI, 17 July 1978, pp. E19-20.

62. Issue of August 1978.

63. I have tried to classify these changes in "SALT and the

Strategic Future," *Orbis* (Summer 1978).

64. *Washington Post*, 11 January 1979.

65. Ibid.

66. NCNA (English), 7 December 1976.

67. Contained in the National Security Council's "Policy Review Memorandum," No. 24 (see *NYT*, 24 June 1977, pp. A1, A3).

68. *NYT*, 11 September 1977, pp. 1, 9; also *US-China Business Review* (September/October 1977):40.

69. *China Trade Report* (June 1978).

70. *People's Daily*, 25 September 1977, p. 5.

71. Ibid., 26 September 1977, p. 1; 27 September 1977, p. 1.

72. Ibid., 16 October 1977.

73. *Le Monde*, 22-23 January 1978, p. 5.

74. *The Economist*, 11 November 1978, p. 66.

75. For example, a report on a Chinese buying delegation to Britain in July 1978 (*Daily Telegraph*, 11 July 1978).

76. *China Trade Report* (June 1978).

77. Ibid., p. 3. The HOT had a range of up to four kilometers, longer than the range of much tank artillery.

78. Cf. *The Economist*, 11 November 1978, p. 66; also Kyodo, 10 December 1977. The MILAN has a range of up to 2,000 meters, the CROTALE of up to 8.5 kilometers, and there was also talk of a possible Chinese purchase of shorter-range missiles.

79. Cf. Kyodo from Peking, 31 January 1978, FBIS-CHI, 1 February 1978.

80. Ibid.

81. At the beginning of 1978, China purchased three large Hitachi computers, one M-170 and two M-160IIs, with COCOM approval (cf. Kyodo, 1 February 1978).

82. *The Economist*, 11 November 1978, p. 66. In January 1979, Prime Minister Callaghan told the French, West German, and U.S. leaders at a meeting in Guadeloupe that the sale would go through. It was presumably not irrelevant that the Harrier, limited to an operational range of some fifty miles, could hardly be used for extensive offensive operations in China's circumstances.

83. *Far Eastern Economic Review*, 3 February 1978, p. 26.

84. *China Trade Report* (June 1978):6.

85. *Washington Post*, 5 October 1978; also *Canberra Times*, 15 September 1978, p. 5.

86. Early in 1978, the going rate for an F5E fighter aircraft seemed to be $2 million and for a destroyer $5.5 million (see *Washington Post*, 24 February 1978, p. A23).

87. Kyodo news agency, 19 January 1978.

88. I have examined this problem in principle in "Technological Innovation and Arms Control," *World Politics* (July 1974):509-41.

89. For example, *The Military Balance 1978/79*, p. 57.

90. U.S. estimates for the 1975 GNP seem to have varied from $299 to $323 billion. Central Intelligence Agency estimates were $323-324 billion for 1975 and 1976 (see "China: Economic Indicators," Table 2A, p. 3, and "China's Economy," paper ER 77-10738, November 1977, p. 2). An estimate of $373 billion for 1977 is that of Arthur G. Ashbrook, Jr. ("China: Shift of Economic Gears in Mid-70s," in *China's Economy Post-Mao*, Vol. 1, *Policy and Performance* [Washington, D.C.: Government Printing Office, 9 November 1978], p. 231, Table 3). See also Jan S. Prybyla, "Some Economic Strengths and Weaknesses of the People's Republic of China," *Asian Survey* (December 1977):1119-1142.

91. The point has been suggested by Michael Eiland ("Military Modernization and China's Economy," *Asian Survey* [December 1977]:1152-53).

92. Jammes, "The Chinese Defense Burden 1965-1974," p. 460.

93. Ralph Powell, "The Role of the Military in China's Transportation and Communications Systems," *Current Scene* (7 February 1972):5-12.

94. Address of 2 June 1978; *Peking Review*, 23 June 1978, p. 18.

95. One might speculate whether the PLA may not on occasion oppose wage rises as likely to diminish such resources.

96. After the fall of Lin, for example, procurement dropped by some 25 percent (Jammes, "The Chinese Defense Burden 1965-1974," passim) but appeared to go up again during 1978.

97. In 1972, China purchased ten Boeing 707s with inertial guidance systems from the United States. They could be used as military transports. In 1973, thirteen Super-Frelon helicopters were bought from France. They carried surveillance radar equipment suitable for border control and antisubmarine operations. In 1975, China bought two advanced Cyber-172 computers from the Control Data Corporation, and in the following year came the Spey engine deal with Britain.

98. Peking NCNA (English), 5 February 1977, FBIS-CHI, 7 February 1977, p. E4.

99. Peking Domestic Service, 5 February 1977, FBIS-CHI, 7 February 1977, pp. E6-7.

100. *Peking Review*, 10 March 1978, p. 22.

Chapter 3

1. For some comments on this point, see Werner Klatt, "China's Food and Fuel under New Management," *International Affairs* (January 1978): especially pp. 68-71.

2. Kyodo, 23 August 1972; also Mahud Rida, "Days in China— An Interview with the No. 3 Man in China," *Al Gumhuriyah* (Cairo), 18 November 1971, Foreign Broadcast Information Service, Daily Report: People's Republic of China (hereafter cited as FBIS), 30 November 1971, p. A8.

3. P. E. C. Chen, seminar of 29 September 1972; quoted in John S. Aird, "Recent Provincial Population Figures," *China Quarterly* (March 1978):15 n. 17 and 41 n. 64.

4. *New York Times* (hereafter cited as *NYT*), 5 November 1977.

5. *Peking Review*, 17 February 1978, pp. 9-10; 28 July 1978, p. 15; and 11 August 1978, p. 11, respectively.

6. "World Development 1978," Washington 1978. The Bank expected China to reach one billion before the turn of the century.

7. *NYT*, 26 November 1978, p. E4; *China Trade Report* (August 1978):9.

8. By 1976, both Peking and Shanghai were reporting rates of increase of less than 0.6 percent (New China News Agency [hereafter cited as NCNA], 27 February 1977).

9. Aird, "Recent Provincial Population Figures," p. 40, Table 4.

10. Arthur G. Ashbrook, Jr., "China: Shift of Economic Gears in Mid-70s," in *China's Economy Post-Mao*, Vol. 1, *Policy and Performance* (Washington, D.C.: Government Printing Office, 1978), section 9.

11. NCNA Peking, 6 March 1978, FBIS-CHI, 16 March 1978, Supplement p. 27.

12. For a good brief discussion, see Leo A. Orleans, *China's Birth Rate, Death Rate, and Population Growth: Another Perspective*, report prepared for the Committee on International Relations, U.S. House of Representatives (Washington, D.C.: Government Printing Office, 1977).

13. The gross value of agricultural output declined by 20-21 percent in 1959, by 9 percent in 1960, and by 2 percent in 1961.

14. Alexander Eckstein, *China's Economic Revolution* (Cambridge: Cambridge University Press, 1977), p. 211; Ashbrook, "China: Shift of Economic Gears in Mid-1970s," section 10; Dwight H. Perkins, "Growth and Changing Structure of China's Twentieth

Century Economy," in Dwight H. Perkins, ed., *China's Modern Economy in Historical Perspective* (Stanford: Stanford University Press, 1975), pp. 140-42.

15. It has been suggested that some local investment projects are done at extremely low real cost by using otherwise unemployed or underemployed resources (see Norman Macrae, *The Economist*, 31 December 1977, p. 16).

16. See Audrey Donnithorne, "The Control of Inflation in China," *Current Scene* (April/May 1978):1-12.

17. Per-capita production of cotton cloth, for example, dropped from 8.9 meters in 1970 to 8.1 meters in 1975. A decision to raise it to 10 meters for the purpose of increasing the general cloth ration would require something like a 25 percent increase in China's cotton-cloth output (which ran at an annual 7.6 billion linear meters from 1973 to 1975) or some combination of imports and reduction of exports of cotton materials (see "China: Economic Indicators" [Washington, D.C.: Central Intelligence Agency Paper ER 77-10508, October 1977], p. 1, Table 1, and p. 43).

18. According to the chairman of the Academy of Social Sciences, Hu Chiao-mu, the grain ration in 1977 was no higher than it had been in 1955 (article in *People's Daily*, 6 October 1978, FBIS-CHI, 11 October 1978, p. E17).

19. The assertion was made after her disgrace by Chi Wei, "How the Gang of Four Opposed Socialist Modernisation," *Peking Review*, 11 March 1977, p. 8.

20. See the attack on Teng for trying to exert direct control of enterprises and wanting to enforce central control (*Red Flag* [September 1976]:25-28).

21. See, for example, the *People's Daily* editorial of 10 July 1978, FBIS-CHI, 14 July 1978, p. E3.

22. Chairman Hua's observations of 7 July 1978; *Peking Review*, 28 July 1978, pp. 7-12.

23. Communiqué of the Third Plenary Session of the Eleventh Central Committee, *Newsbulletin* of the PRC embassy, Canberra, 4 January 1979, p. 4.

24. Hu Chiao-mu, "Act in Accordance with Economic Laws, Step Up the Four Modernizations," *People's Daily*, 6 October 1978, FBIS-CHI, 11 October 1978, pp. E1-22. For Chairman Hua's views on the supervisory role of banks, see his remarks of 7 July 1978, pp. 7-12.

25. *Kwangming Daily*, 11 July 1978, FBIS-CHI, 20 July 1978, p. E10; also *Peking Review*, 24 February 1978, pp. 8-9.

26. *Kwangming Daily*, 11 July 1978, FBIS-CHI, 20 July 1978, p. E11.

27. NCNA Peking, 5 July 1978, FBIS-CHI, 12 July 1978, pp. E13-14.

28. In 1978, it was suggested that labor productivity in China's iron and steel industry was only 1 percent of that in advanced foreign countries and labor productivity in grain production was 2 percent. (*Kwangming Daily*, 4 July 1978, FBIS-CHI, 18 July 1978, p. E15).

29. Vice-Premier Yu Chiu-li; NCNA, 25 October 1977.

30. *Peking Review*, 6 January 1978, p. 8.

31. Communiqué of the Third Plenary Session of the Eleventh Central Committee, *Newsbulletin*, p. 4.

32. There was a campaign to present "to each according to his work" as a valid socialist distribution policy (see *Peking Review*, 10 February 1978, pp. 11-14; 17 February 1978, pp. 6-8; also *People's Daily*, 11 March 1977; "People's Daily Special Commentator" in *Peking Review*, 4 August 1978, pp. 6-15).

33. For a Western discussion of this interest, see the *Times*, 26 August 1978, p. 13.

34. Communiqué of the Third Plenary Session of the Eleventh Central Committee, *Newsbulletin*, p. 4.

35. *People's Daily*, 17 March 1977; also a report by Ross Munro in *Christian Science Monitor* (Boston), 7 June 1977, p. 34.

36. S. Andors, *China's Industrial Revolution* (New York: Pantheon, 1977), pp. 218-21.

37. During the same period, the government of Vietnam was suppressing the merchant classes, and especially families of Chinese origin. A grim jest made the rounds of Southeast Asia: "Both our Communist neighbours are trying to dash dynamically to freer enterprise, the Chinese by shooting workers and the Vietnamese less successfully by shooting merchants" (see *The Economist*, 18 November 1978, p. 13).

38. Chao Tsu-yang on Chengtu Radio, 9 December 1976; BBC Summary of World Broadcasts FE/5387/BII/8, 11 December 1976.

39. Peking Radio for Southeast Asia, 26 August 1976; BBC Summary of World Broadcasts FE/893/A/11, 1 September 1976; quoted in A. G. Donnithorne, "China's Economic Policy and Its Implementation by the Post-Mao Leadership" (seminar paper, Australian National University, Canberra, 14 March 1978), p. 3.

40. See, for example, the evidence of much greater effort on private plots and the evidence of barter and black-market activities, p. 103.

41. See *NYT*, 11 December 1977, pp. 1, 14; 19 December 1977.

42. For instance, *The Economist*, 15 August 1978, p. 82.

43. Donnithorne, "China's Economic Policy," pp. 11-12.

44. "Report of the Australian Iron and Steel Mission to the People's Republic of China, 18 June to 9 July 1978" (Canberra: Department of Trade and Resources, December 1978), p. 49.

45. Chairman Hua's remarks of 7 July 1978, p. 7.

46. *Red Flag* (May 1978).

47. For a brief but comprehensive account, see Henry J. Groen and James A. Kilpatrick, "China's Agricultural Production," in *China's Economy Post-Mao*, pp. 607-52.

48. Cf. Alexander Eckstein, *China's Economic Development: The Interplay of Scarcity and Ideology* (Ann Arbor: University of Michigan Press, 1975), p. 45.

49. Dwight H. Perkins, *Agricultural Development in China 1368-1968* (Chicago: Aldine, 1969).

50. Compared with twice the area of cultivable land in the United States (cf. Groen and Kilpatrick, "China's Agricultural Production," p. 609).

51. Ibid., passim.

52. Eckstein, *China's Economic Revolution*, pp. 206-13; Robert F. Dernberger, "China's Economic Future," in Allen S. Whiting and Robert F. Dernberger, *China's Future* (New York: McGraw-Hill, 1977), Chapter 3; also Lloyd Evans, "Learning from Tachai: Agricultural Research in China," *Search* (Sydney) (January/February 1978):27.

53. For example, Dwight H. Perkins, "A Conference on Agriculture," *China Quarterly* (September 1976):598.

54. Groen and Kilpatrick, "China's Agricultural Production," p. 630.

55. Ibid., p. 619.

56. Colin Clark, "Economic Development in Communist China," *Journal of Political Economy* (April 1976):239-46; Klatt, "China's Food and Fuel under New Management," pp. 69-70; Eckstein, *China's Economic Revolution*, passim; Dernberger, "China's Economic Future," passim.

57. There were a number of hints of such difficulties in domestic broadcasts during the first half of 1977. For some Western reports, see *NYT*, 20 March 1977; *Washington Post*, 25 March 1977; also *NYT*, 15 November 1977, and *Washington Post*, 28 December 1977, and 29 December 1977, p. A14.

58. For some general comments on black marketeering and "bourgeois trends," see *Red Flag* (April 1975):33-34, 41; (May 1975): 37; (June 1975):5.

59. Klatt, "China's Food and Fuel under New Management," p. 69.

60. Eckstein, *China's Economic Revolution*, pp. 306-7, Table 8-3, p. 309.

61. Ramon H. Myers, "Scarcity and Ideology in Chinese Economic Development," *Problems of Communism* (March/April 1978):86-96.

62. *People's Daily*, 16 November 1977, FBIS-CHI, 22 November 1977, p. E2; also *People's Daily*, 26 January 1978, FBIS-CHI, 30 January 1978, pp. E6-9.

63. See Alva Lewis Erisman, "PRC: 1977 Crop Output and Its Impact on China's Agricultural Trade," *Current Scene* (June/July 1978):20-28.

64. Agriculture was the first priority among the eight areas listed for modernization by 1985 by Vice-Premier Fang Yi in his address to the 1978 National Science Conference (*Peking Review*, 7 April 1978, pp. 6-14, 17).

65. Chairman Hua's address to the Fifth NPC on 26 February 1978, FBIS-CHI, 16 march 1978, Supplement pp. 3-39; for a summary, see NCNA, 26 February 1978.

66. See p. 101.

67. *Kwangming Daily*, 4 July 1978, FBIS-CHI, 18 July 1978, p. E15.

68. See Martin Karcher, "Unemployment and Underemployment in the People's Republic of China," *China Report* (September/December 1975):22-49.

69. For Yu Chiu-li's report, see FBIS-CHI, 31 January 1978, p. E6; also *Peking Review*, 17 February 1978, pp. 9-10, and 24 February 1978, pp. 10-14.

70. The official aim would bring China to the point where there was, on average, one standard tractor for every fifty hectares of farmland. The comparable Japanese or U.S. figure was probably 2:1 or even 1:1. It seemed clear that the degree of mechanization envisaged would not, by 1980 or even 1985, seriously displace rural labor.

71. See Li Hsien-nien's address to the National Conference on Capital Construction in Agriculture on 12 July 1978; NCNA, 23 July 1978, FBIS-CHI, 25 July 1978, pp. E1-4.

72. For example, to see who might be interested in Chinese technical assistance programs.

73. Li Hsien-nien's address of 12 July 1978, passim.

74. Communiqué of the Third Plenary Session of the Eleventh

Central Committee, *Newsbulletin; NYT*, 19 November 1978, p. E2.

75. Groen and Kilpatrick, "China's Agricultural Production," p. 617.

76. The price of grain under the compulsory purchase scheme was to rise by 20 percent and grain bought above the quota by 50 percent.

77. Communiqué of the Third Plenary Session of the Eleventh Central Committee, *Newsbulletin*, passim.

78. Cf. G. William Skinner, "Marketing and Social Structure in Rural China," *Journal of Asian Studies* (May 1965):363-99.

79. *China Trade Report* (April 1978):8. It was perhaps not irrelevant that the cash savings which peasants could be expected to make would flow to the banks and hence to state resources for a variety of purposes, including investment.

80. Communiqué of the Third Plenary Session of the Eleventh Central Committee, *Newsbulletin*, passim.

81. Hua's address of 7 July 1978, p. 12.

82. Cf. Groen and Kilpatrick, "China's Agricultural Production," pp. 645-46.

83. For some comparative yields, see ibid., pp. 646 and 647, Fig. 4. For a discussion of agricultural technology, see Thomas B. Wiens, "The Evolution of Policy and Capabilities in China's Agricultural Technology," in *China's Economy Post-Mao*, pp. 671-703.

84. For an assessment of the costs and benefits, see Jan S. Prybyla, "Some Economic Strengths and Weaknesses of the People's Republic of China," *Asian Survey* (December 1977):1135.

85. Cf. *Red Flag* (October 1978). For a dissenting view, which put Chinese 1978 steel production as high as 34 million tons, see "Report of the Australian Iron and Steel Mission," pp. 57-58.

86. "China: Economic Indicators," p. 35, Table 20; General George S. Brown, "United States Military Posture for FY 1979," Washington, 20 January 1978, p. 94.

87. *China Trade Report* (July 1978):6-8; also *NYT*, 16 October 1977.

88. Vaclav Smil, "China's Energetics: A System Analysis," in *China's Economy Post-Mao*, pp. 344-45; "Report of the Australian Iron and Steel Mission," p. 12.

89. In terms of heating power, the CIA assessment was that China's coal production rose from 231 million tons in 1970 to 330 million tons in 1976 (see "China: Economic Indicators," p. 26, Table 14).

90. Ibid., Table 12A, p. 20; "China Oil Production Prospects" (Washington, D.C.: Central Intelligence Agency Paper ER 77-

10030U, June 1977), p. 9, Figure 7. For the 1977 figure, see official Chinese claims of an 8 percent increase that year (NCNA, 26 December 1977). But Japanese estimates for China's 1977 production were higher: around 10 percent (see *Mainichi Shimbun*, 19 January 1978, quoted in "The Long-Term Trade Agreement and the Future of Japan-China Trade," *Jetro China Newsletter* [June 1978]: Table 9, p. 14).

91. Smil, "China's Energetics," p. 347.

92. Chairman Hua's report to the Fifth NPC, 26 February 1978.

93. Ibid., pp. 19, 23.

94. *People's Daily* editorial, 6 July 1978; NCNA (Peking), FBIS-CHI, 12 July 1978, pp. E14-17.

95. See Jack Craig, Jim Lewek, and Gordon Cole, "A Survey of China's Machine-Building Industry," in *China's Economy Post-Mao*, pp. 284-322.

96. "Report of the Australian Iron and Steel Mission," p. 12

97. Ibid., p. 27.

98. K. P. Wang, "China's Mineral Economy," in *China's Economy Post-Mao*, pp. 370-402. For a comparison of the production of some of the world's major mineral producers, see p. 374, Table 1.

99. Yu Chiu-li told a geological conference in Peking in mid-1977 that China needed a major new survey of the nation's resources.

100. Western commercial sources reported that, between May and September 1977 alone, China bought thirty-three ships in the West; perhaps sixty by the end of the year. And in February 1978, for example, it was reported that China had bought for $5.9 million a 31,000-ton bulk carrier which had cost $14 million to build (*The Economist*, 4 March 1978, p. 73; for a general view, see also *Peking Review*, 13 January 1978, p. 78).

101. Smil, "China's Energetics," pp. 342-43.

102. "Report of the Australian Iron and Steel Mission," p. 52.

103. Smil, "China's Energetics," pp. 351-53.

104. Ibid., pp. 360-64.

105. According to CIA calculations, Chinese production of electric power rose between 1970 and 1975 from 72,000 to 120,000 million kwh. For official concern at the end of 1977, see NCNA, 26 December 1977. For a general Western comment, see Vaclav Smil, *China's Energy: Achievements, Problems, Prospects* (New York: Praeger, 1976). See also William Clarke, "China's Electric Power Industry," in *China's Economy Post-Mao*, pp. 403-35.

106. See, for instance, *Red Flag* (December 1977); the joint New Year's editorial in *People's Daily, Red Flag*, and *Liberation Army*

Daily, *Peking Review*, 6 January 1978; also ibid., 20 January 1978, pp. 16-20.

107. Clarke, "China's Electric Power Industry," pp. 424-25.

108. The responsible minister, Hsiao Han, blamed lack of mechanization for the lag (*Peking Review*, 24 February 1978, pp. 5-7).

109. NCNA, 26 December 1977.

110. *The Economist*, 30 September 1978, p. 86.

111. *People's Daily* editorial, 6 July 1978; also Smil, "China's Energetics," pp. 342-44.

112. It appears that in 1964 China obtained from Cuba plans of a Shell refinery there and has, ever since, had the capability to build similar plants.

113. Western estimates suggested that China's 1977/78 refining capacity was approximately 50-55 million tons. This was well short of estimated Chinese crude-oil production levels (also Smil, "China's Energetics," p. 343).

114. Werner Klatt has suggested that even a modest expansion of energy and chemicals might require capital investment on the order of $5 billion during 1978-80 (see his review article, "Learning from Ta-Ching: China's Oil Prospects," *Pacific Affairs* [Fall 1977]:445-59).

115. Chairman Hua's report on the work of the government to the Fifth NPC; *Peking Review*, 10 March 1978, p. 24.

116. E.g., *People's Daily* editorial of 6 July 1978, FBIS-CHI, 12 July 1978, p. E17.

117. *Peking Review*, 28 July 1978, p. 3.

118. See his remarks of 20 June 1978; *Peking Review*, 28 July 1978, pp. 16-17.

119. Robert Dernberger has estimated that during the eleven years from 1950 to 1960 the PRC imported over $5 billion worth of machinery and equipment, over 90 percent of it from the socialist countries and about half coming in the form of complete plant projects. Richard Batsavage and John Davie speak of Soviet 1950-59 deliveries of equipment worth $1.3 billion and 130 complete plant projects (Dernberger, "Economic Development and Modernization in Contemporary China," in Frederic J. Fleron, Jr., ed., *Technology and Communist Culture: The Socio-Cultural Impact of Technology under Socialism* [New York: Praeger, 1977], pp. 240-41; Batsavage and Davie, "China's International Trade and Finance," in *China's Economy Post-Mao*, p. 710).

120. Dernberger, "Economic Development and Modernization," passim.

121. Kyodo, 15 March 1978.

122. Ibid.

123. For China's foreign trade, see NCNA Peking, 15 January 1978, FBIS-CHI, 16 January 1978, p. E-19.

124. See p. 41.

125. Kyodo, 6 January 1979.

126. *China Trade Report* (May 1978):6-7.

127. For figures for the 1970s, see "China: International Trade, 1976-77," (Washington, Central Intelligence Agency Paper ER 77-10674, November 1977), p. 12.

128. September 1978 was declared "quality month," and the need to improve production quality became something of a campaign, affecting not just exports but domestic deliveries (see NCNA Peking, 5 July 1978, and *People's Daily* and NCNA commentary, 8 July 1978, FBIS-CHI, 12 July 1978, pp. E7-10, E13-14; also *The Economist*, 9 September 1978, p. 60; *China Trade Report* [July 1978]:2).

129. *China Trade Report* (May 1978):3.

130. Li Chiang, "Let Us Clearly Set Forth the Good and Evil in the Policy Line and Actively Develop Socialist Foreign Trade," *Red Flag* (October 1977):34-37; Yuan Tu-hsin, "Current Changes in Communist China's Foreign Trade Policy and Their Impacts," *Chinese Communist Affairs Monthly* No. 7 (1978):64-69.

131. *Nihon keizai shimbun* (Tokyo), 17 April 1977, p. 4; *China Trade Report* (July 1978):2.

132. *The Economist*, 15 July 1978, p. 74; *Financial Times*, 10 July 1978.

133. *Peking Review*, 17 February 1978, p. 4; *People's Daily*, 4 February 1978, FBIS-CHI, 4 February 1978, p. E1; *China Trade Report* (May 1978):6; *People's Daily*, 4 January 1978. For some Western reports and comments, see *Washington Post*, 20 October 1977, and 5 January 1978, pp. A1, 29; *Frankfurter Allgemeine Zeitung*, 9 January 1978, p. 2.

134. *People's Daily*, 4 January 1978.

135. See Chairman Hua, *Peking Review*, 28 July 1978, p. 12; also *People's Daily* and NCNA commentary of 8 July 1978, FBIS-CHI, (12 July 1978), p. E8. There were also suggestions that the foreign exchange allocations to provinces would be gradually increased to allow them to make their own purchases.

136. In spite of her very large resources of many nonferrous metals, China, by the 1970s, had been compelled, largely because of lack of development and investment, to import quantities of them (see "China: The Non-Ferrous Metals Industry in the 1970s" [Washington, D.C.: Central Intelligence Agency Paper ER 78-10104U, May 1978]).

137. By the end of 1978, Japanese firms had major interests in Chinese offshore oil exploration and exploitation projects. In late July, for example, Peking concluded an agreement with the Japan National Oil Company for joint exploration of the Po Hai Gulf, and in December there were reports of agreements signed by Peking with Japanese groups covering $2.5 billion worth of petrochemical developments. For a general comment, see Hans Heymann, Jr., "Self-Reliance Revisited: China's Technology Dilemma," in Bryant Garth, ed., *China's Changing Role in the World Economy* (New York: Praeger, 1975).

138. Even before normalization, a number of U.S. companies were invited to discuss offshore oil developments (for example, *Time* magazine, 4 December 1978, p. 57; *Australian Financial Review*, 15 August 1978, p. 43).

139. Article 2 of the agreement; "The Long-Term Trade Agreement and the Future of Japan-China Trade," p. 25.

140. In 1977/78, China imported some 600,000 tons per annum from Algeria.

141. For example, *Australian Financial Review*, 14 November 1978, p. 2.

142. *The Economist*, 23 September 1978, pp. 96-97.

143. *Jetro China Newsletter* (June 1978):14.

144. Wang, "China's Mineral Economy," p. 391.

145. *China Trade Report* (April 1976):6.

146. Ibid., (May 1978):10.

147. The Japan-China Trade Agreement provided for Japanese imports of 15 million tons of Chinese oil by 1982, not the 50 million tons which the Chinese had originally suggested (see also *Japan Economic Journal* [14 March 1978]:7).

148. By early 1978, the Chinese were suggesting an easing of Japanese payment terms to offset these price movements (see *Mainichi Shimbun*, 1 April 1978, p. 7).

149. These crude calculations suggest that the proportion of import-related investment to total domestic investment might range from 19 to 32 percent.

150. Li Chiang, "Let Us Clearly Set Forth the Good and Evil in the Policy Line and Actively Develop Socialist Foreign Trade," pp. 34-37.

151. NCNA, 4 April 1978, FBIS-CHI, 4 April 1978, pp. A9-10; also *The Economist*, 14 October 1978, p. 44.

152. NCNA, 3 December 1978.

153. Text in *Jetro China Newsletter* No. 18 (June 1978):25-26. For general discussions of Sino-Japanese trade, see also *Jetro China*

Newsletter No. 15 (December 1977):20; No. 16 (January 1978):1-8; and No. 18, passim.

154. *The Economist*, 28 October 1978, p. 76.

155. Kyodo, 6 January 1979.

156. *The Economist*, 2 December 1978, p. 86.

157. Preliminary discussions were held with Energy Secretary James Schlesinger and Agriculture Secretary Berglund in Peking. There were certain obstacles to trade, quite apart from questions of diplomatic normalization. These included the 1974 Jackson-Vanik amendment, prohibiting MFN treatment for any Communist nation that did not lift barriers to free emigration, and the problem of U.S. assets in China that had been seized after 1949. Resolutions to these problems were to be found in 1979.

158. For the years 1970-76, see "China: International Trade, 1976-77," p. 9. For 1977, see *Jetro China Newsletter* No. 17 (April 1978):1-3. The Jetro figures differ somewhat from Washington estimates for 1977. Jetro puts Chinese 1977 imports at $6.4 billion and exports at $7.8 billion, yielding a total trade figure of $14.3 billion and a trade surplus of around $1.4 billion. U.S. figures suggest imports of $6.9 billion and exports of $7.9 billion, yielding total figures of $14.9 billion and a $1 billion surplus.

159. Dernberger, "Economic Development and Modernization in Contemporary China," p. 236.

160. *Jetro China Newsletter* (October 1977):18.

161. Figures from "China: International Trade, 1976-77," p. 1, and Batsavage and Davie, "China's International Trade and Finance," p. 733, Table A1.

162. The lower figure in Kyodo, 6 January 1979, the higher one in *Yomiuri* (Tokyo); quoted in *Australian Financial Review*, 8 January 1979.

163. See, for instance, *The Economist* survey, "Must Lend, Will Travel," 4 March 1977.

164. Christopher Howe, *China's Economy* (London: Paul Elek, 1977).

165. According to Li Hsien-nien, in mid-1978, China had foreign currency reserves of "well over 2 billion dollars" (Kyodo [Peking], 13 July 1978; also *China Trade Report* [August 1978]:4). The net PRC reserves with Western banks who were members of the Bank of International Settlements were estimated to have risen from $270 million in the third quarter of 1976 (when some of the trading and payments difficulties were at their height) to $2.1 billion in the fourth quarter of 1977 (cf. Cary Reich, "China: The Bankers' Grand

Illusion?" *Institutional Investor*, International Edition [January 1979]:39).

166. The *Times*, 25 August 1978, p. 13.

167. *China Trade Report* (August 1978):2.

168. *The Economist*, 18 November 1978, p. 119.

169. In 1978, there were reports of substantial buying on Chinese account on the Tokyo stock exchange. The buying seemed to be concentrated on stocks that stood to gain from the Japan-China Treaty of Peace and Friendship and from their trade agreements.

170. Kyodo (Peking), 13 July 1978, FBIS-CHI, 13 July 1978, p. A2; also Reich, "China: The Bankers' Grand Illusion?" p. 39.

171. AFP (Peking), 26 October 1977, FBIS-CHI, 6 October 1977, p. A14.

172. *Jetro China Newsletter* (October 1977):18; also Kyodo, 24 August 1978, and *Kwangming Daily*, 18 August 1978, FBIS-CHI, pp. A1-2 and E1-2, respectively.

173. *China Trade Report* (August 1978):6.

174. Kyodo (Peking), 13 July 1978, FBIS-CHI, 13 July 1978, p. A2.

175. *Far Eastern Economic Review*, 8 April 1977, p. 81.

176. Kyodo (Tokyo), 16 February 1978.

177. Li Chiang; NCNA Peking, 19 December 1978, reporting his news conference of the previous day in Hong Kong; also *The Economist*, 21 October 1978, p. 76.

178. Li Chiang; NCNA Peking, 19 December 1978.

179. For a general discussion, see *The Economist*, 9 December 1978, p. 119.

180. Reich, "China: The Bankers' Grand Illusion?" p. 41.

181. For the higher figure see ibid., p. 38. For the lower, see Batsavage and Davie, "China's International Trade and Finance," p. 720.

182. Batsavage and Davie, "China's International Trade and Finance," p. 732.

183. Apart from the general reasons for such a policy, it may be significant that the international banking guidelines prevailing in 1978 precluded the use of supplier credits where the debt-service ratio was higher than 20 percent.

Chapter 4

1. Issue of October 1962, p. 4.

2. Richard Baum, "Diabolus ex Machina: Technological Development and Social Change in Chinese Industry," in Frederic J.

Fleron, Jr., ed., *Technology and Communist Culture: The Socio-Cultural Impact of Technology under Socialism* (New York: Praeger, 1977), p. 324.

3. According to one OECD estimate, in a typical industrial country the cost of one researcher, allowing for his training and equipment, absorbs the "economic surplus" of 10-100 industrial workers. In a typical LDC, he absorbs the surplus of 1,000-50,000 farmers (cf. Nicolas Jéquier, ed., *Appropriate Technology: Problems and Promises* [Paris: OECD, 1976], p. 100).

4. A. Fitzgerald and C. P. Slichter, eds., *Solid State Physics in the People's Republic of China*, CSCPRC Report, No. 1 (Washington, D.C.: National Academy of Sciences, 1976), p. 10.

5. See *Red Flag* (June 1972):30.

6. G. C. Dean and F. Chernow, *The Choice of Technology in the Electronics Industry of the People's Republic of China: The Fabrication of Semiconductors*, United States–China Relations Program, Report No. 5 (Stanford: Stanford University, 1978), p. 18.

7. *China Reconstructs* (February 1974):6.

8. B. O. Suprowicz, "Electronics in China," *US-China Business Review* (May/June 1976):22; quoted in Dean and Chernow, *The Choice of Technology in the Electronics Industry*, p. 19.

9. These controls are, of course, much more rigid than in the West, given the inability of the Chinese worker to change his place of work, residence, or rate of pay.

10. The classification is Baum's, using the official Soviet typology of stage 1, mechanized manual production; stage 2, mechanized production; stage 3, integrated mechanized production; stage 4, automated production; and stage 5, integrated automated production (Baum, "Diabolus ex Machina," pp. 319, 326).

11. This might have had feedback results in further diminishing the role of industrial demand as a stimulant to R and D.

12. For some comments on Chinese capacities in this area, see Hans Heymann, Jr., *China's Approach to Technology Acquisition* (Santa Monica: RAND Corporation, 1975), Pt. 1, esp. pp. 51-53.

13. Jack Craig, Jim Lewek, and Gordon Cole, "A Survey of China's Machine-Building Industry," in *China's Economy Post-Mao*, Vol. 1, *Policy and Performance* (Washington, D.C.: Government Printing Office, 9 November 1978), pp. 294-95, 300.

14. Dean and Chernow, *The Choice of Technology in the Electronics Industry*, p. 16.

15. Fitzgerald and Slichter, *Solid State Physics in the People's Republic of China*, pp. 67, 134-35.

16. Ibid., p. 9. Each research institute under the Academy of Sciences had a Planning Bureau to coordinate research proposals. Several of the members of these bureaus were lay persons, without professional training in the science concerned.

17. Jon Sigurdson has suggested that in 1973 China spent approximately 1 percent of her GNP, or a little less, on R and D and, of that, 2.4 percent or some $55 million, went to basic research (see his "Technology and Science—Some Issues in Chinese Modernization," in *China's Economy Post-Mao*, p. 494).

18. Benjamin Schwartz, "Thoughts of Mao Tse-tung," *New York Review of Books*, 8 February 1973.

19. C. H. G. Oldham has suggested that in 1967 a majority of China's 2.4 million scientists and engineers had either been trained abroad before 1949 or promoted to technical positions without the benefit of full-time technical training (cf. M. Oksenberg, ed., *China's Developmental Experience* [New York: Proceedings of the Academy of Political Science, Columbia University, March 1973]; also Fitzgerald and Slichter, *Solid State Physics in the People's Republic of China*, p. 59).

20. Fitzgerald and Slichter, p. 83.

21. *Peking Review*, 3 February 1978, p. 17.

22. These criteria for admission were introduced during the Great Leap Forward of 1958 and then retained.

23. Cf. *People's Daily* editorial, 31 March 1966.

24. Suzanne Pepper, "Education and Revolution: The Chinese Model Revised," *Asian Survey* (September 1978):850, 858.

25. See the article by the vice-chairman of the Peking University Revolutionary Committee, Chou Pei-yuan, in *Kwangming Daily*, 6 October 1972.

26. See the well-known letter by the student, Chang Tieh-sheng, in the *People's Daily*, 10 August 1973. Later he became an equally well-known subject for criticism (cf. *Peking Review*, 28 July 1978, pp. 18-19, 22).

27. For example, "New High Tide in Nation-Wide Learn-From-Lei-Feng Movement Shaping Up," New China News Agency (hereafter cited as NCNA) Peking (English), 6 March 1977.

28. Pepper, "Education and Revolution," p. 872.

29. For a contrary view, see Sigurdson ("Technology and Science," pp. 509-11) who attempts to argue that in 1966 the PRC had an excess of graduates and could therefore afford a temporary closure of its universities. In my view, the argument is not substantial.

30. Baum, "Diabolus ex Machina," p. 341.

31. The Central Committee itself admitted later that "the number of scientists and experts in technology is insufficient and their standard is not high" (*People's Daily*, 23 September 1977).

32. Fang Yi, *Peking Review*, 13 January 1978; also *Washington Post*, 20 March 1977; *New York Times* (hereafter cited as *NYT*), 22 October 1977.

33. *People's Daily*, 23 October 1977.

34. In 1975, a U.S. delegation remarked on the close resemblance between Chinese engineering curricula and U.S. engineering curricula of the pre-1941 period (Fitzgerald and Slichter, *Solid State Physics in the People's Republic of China*, p. 87).

35. See the address of 27 December 1977 by Fang Yi; *People's Daily*, 30 December 1977, and *Peking Review*, 13 January 1978, pp. 15-19. It was not the first time gloomy views had been expressed about the relative status of Chinese science (see Chien Hsueh-sen, "Science and Technology Must Catch Up with and Surpass Advanced World Levels before the End of the Century," *Red Flag* [July 1977]; BBC Summary of World Broadcasts, FE/5563/BII/6; also *People's Daily*, 23 September 1977; *Peking Review*, 3 February 1978, pp. 16-21).

36. See Teng's address to the National Science Conference, NCNA, 21 March 1978; also *Peking Review*, 28 July 1978, pp. 18-19, 22.

37. It is not without irony that during the later 1970s, while China was trying with some energy to revive work in theoretical and abstract areas, the populist antiscience movement in the West was vehemently criticizing big science on the grounds that it was not "useful."

38. See *Kwangming Daily*, 16 December 1977; and Teng's report to the National Science Conference, NCNA, 21 March 1978, and *Peking Review*, 24 March 1978, pp. 9-18. It was, perhaps, not surprising that *Red Flag* should take care to argue that theoretical studies should nevertheless serve practical needs (issue of August 1977, p. 49).

39. NCNA Peking, 10 July 1978, FBIS-CHI, 17 July 1978, pp. E8-10; NCNA (English), 13 July 1978, FBIS-CHI, 14 July 1978, pp. E10-13; *Kwangming Daily*, 7 July 1978, FBIS-CHI, 18 July 1978, pp. E12-13; Communiqué of the Third Plenary Session of the Eleventh Central Committee, text in *Newsbulletin* of the PRC embassy, Canberra, 4 January 1979.

40. One might even interpret the principle as "By their fruits ye shall know them."

41. T. B. Tang, "Two Major Controversies," *Nature* (8 December 1977):265-66.

42. *Peking Review*, 28 October 1977, p. 9.

43. NCNA, 22 September 1977; *Peking Review*, 17 February 1978, p. 31; also *NYT*, 4 February 1978.

44. NCNA, 22 September 1977; also *People's Daily*, 1 October 1977.

45. Hua's address to the conference can be found in NCNA, 25 March 1978, and Teng's in NCNA, 21 March 1978. For Fang Yi's "Outline National Plan for the Development of Science 1978-85 (Draft)," see *Peking Review*, 7 April 1978, pp. 6-14, 17.

46. See, for example, Chien San-chiang's remark that China's scientific studies were, on average, ten to twenty years behind those of the advanced countries (interview with the Yugoslav news agency Tanjug; reported in *Ta-kung-pao*, 27 January 1978).

47. *People's Daily*, 23 September 1977, p. 1; *China News Analysis*, 4 November 1977, p. 5.

48. See, for example, *Washington Post*, 27 January 1978, p. 27.

49. *Le Monde*, 22-23 January 1978, p. 5.

50. There were reports of Chinese visitors ripping pipes off the walls of Japanese factories in their anxiety to get samples.

51. Some Chinese observers in Peking claimed they regarded Dr. Press's as the most important American visit since that of President Nixon. For Dr. Press's comments at a banquet given for him by Fang Yi on 7 July 1978 and at another two days later, see NCNA Peking (English), 7 July 1978, FBIS-CHI, 10 July 1978, pp. A4-A6; and NCNA Peking (English), 9 July 1978, FBIS-CHI, 10 July 1978, pp. A6-A7.

52. See a Ministry of Education article in *Red Flag* (November 1977).

53. For example, NCNA, 30 December 1976, FBIS-CHI, 3 January 1977; and Peking Radio, 22 February 1977, FBIS-CHI, 28 February 1977.

54. Fang Yi, 27 December 1977; *People's Daily*, 30 December 1977.

55. See article by the Mass Criticism Group of the Education Ministry, *Red Flag* (March 1977):53.

56. Theoretical Group of the Education Ministry, *Kwangming Daily*, 14 September 1977.

57. Fang Yi, 27 December 1977; *People's Daily*, 7 December 1977; *Kwangming Daily*, 25 January 1978; and *Peking Review*, 24 January 1978, pp. 14-16.

58. *People's Daily*, 23 April 1978.

59. *Kwangming Daily*, 23 January 1978.

60. For a summary of the academy and its functions, see Washington, National Academy of Sciences, *China Exchange Newsletter* (June-August 1978):9-14.

61. *Ta-kung-pao*, 22 November 1977.

62. NCNA Peking, 19 July 1978, FBIS-CHI, 20 July 1978, p. E14.

63. NCNA Peking, 19 July 1978, FBIS-CHI, 20 July 1978, p. E13.

64. *Ta-kung-pao*, 12 February 1978.

65. The number of applicants for places in 1978 was bound to be exceptionally large, with up to twelve generations of secondary-school graduates applying (see *Peking Review*, 13 January 1978, p. 30, and 4 August 1978, pp. 4-5; also Pepper, "Education and Revolution," pp. 881-84).

66. *Peking Review*, 28 July 1978, pp. 18-19, 22.

67. *Kwangming Daily*, 20 January 1978; NCNA, 29 January 1978 and 19 February 1978.

68. *People's Daily*, 2 March 1978; NCNA, 1 March 1978.

69. *Red Flag* (December 1977):37; *Kwangming Daily*, 19 January 1978. There were reports that, for example, in the Physics Department at Chungshan University, students would have to do 360 hours of study instead of 100, as before (*China Trade Report* [May 1978]:10).

70. NCNA Peking, 15 July 1978, FBIS-CHI, 20 July 1978, p. E16.

71. *People's Daily*, 6 July 1978, in NCNA, 6 July 1978, FBIS-CHI, 12 July 1978, p. E16.

72. *Kwangming Daily*, 10 November 1978.

73. *Kwangming Daily*, 9 July 1978, FBIS-CHI, 20 July 1978, p. E17.

74. The letter, dated 30 July 1961, praised the Kiangsi Communist Labour University as embodying Maoist philosophy. It was a work-study institution embracing primary school, middle school, and college courses. Its work provided for part-time study and farming activities. Publication of the letter in 1977 may well have been a sign that some people wished to slow down the wholesale changes being introduced by the new government into the education system.

75. *People's Daily*, 3 July 1978.

76. Cf. his address to the National Science Conference; NCNA, 21 March 1978.

77. J. L. Pressman and A. Wildavsky, *Implementation* (Berkeley: University of California Press, 1973), p. 125.

78. Even so simple an institution as the barefoot doctors has been subjected to a multiplicity of administrative and political controls (see Robert C. Hsu, "The Political Economy of Rural Health Care in China," *Review of Radical Political Economics* [Spring 1977]: 134-40).

79. At the beginning of the 1970s, the OECD estimated that two-thirds to three-quarters of all innovations were produced by need-pull (OECD, *The Conditions for Success in Technological Innovation*

[Paris: OECD, 1971]).

80. Dean and Chernow, *The Choice of Technology in the Electronics Industry*, p. 58.

81. Jéquier, *Appropriate Technology*, p. 107.

82. D. A. Schon, *Technology and Change* (New York: Dell, 1967).

83. R. K. Merton, *Social Theory and Social Structure* (New York: Free Press, 1949).

84. T. S. Kuhn, *Structure of Scientific Revolutions* (Chicago: Chicago University Press, 1962).

85. T. S. Kuhn, *The History of Science*, Vol. 14, *The International Encyclopaedia of the Social Sciences* (1968), pp. 74-83.

86. M. J. Mulkay, "Sociology of the Scientific Research Community," in I. Spiegel-Roesing and D. de Solla Price, eds., *Science, Technology, and Society: A Cross-Disciplinary Perspective* (London: Sage Publications, for the International Council for Science Policy Studies, 1977), pp. 100-102.

87. Thomas J. Allen, *Managing the Flow of Technology* (Cambridge, Mass.: M.I.T. Press, 1977), pp. 38-39.

88. Central Advisory Council for Science and Technology, *Technological Innovation in Britain* (London: HMSO, 1968), p. 4.

89. Allen, *Managing the Flow of Technology*, pp. 48-49.

90. Karl R. Popper, *Conjectures and Refutations*, 4th ed., rev. (London: Routledge and Kegan Paul, 1972), p. 121.

91. Ibid., p. 129.

92. As Alfred Whitehead once remarked, the greatest invention of the nineteenth century was the invention of the method of invention (A. N. Whitehead, *Science and the Modern World* [London, 1926]).

93. Fitzgerald and Slichter, *Solid State Physics in the People's Republic of China*, pp. 153-54.

94. "Scarcity and Ideology in Chinese Economic Development," *Problems of Communism* (March/April 1978):94-95.

95. *Modern Economic Growth: Rate, Structure, and Spread* (New Haven: Yale University Press, 1966), p. 287.

96. These include the care with which copies of foreign machines have at times been distributed as "Chinese manufactured" and even foreign machines themselves passed off as Chinese.

Chapter 5

1. For alternative projections of GNP ratios among the five large powers—the United States, the USSR, Japan, China, and the European Community—see Nai-Ruenn Chen, "Economic Modernization in

Post-Mao China: Policies, Problems, and Prospects," in *China's Economy Post-Mao*, Vol. 1, *Policy and Performance* (Washington, D.C.: Government Printing Office, 9 November 1978), p. 203.

2. See the article by Australia's first ambassador to Peking, Stephen Fitzgerald; "China, A Stabilising Influence?" *Pacific Defence Reporter* (Sydney), (November 1978):6-12.

Index